CHRISTMAS AS RELIGION

Christmas as Religion

*Rethinking Santa, the Secular,
and the Sacred*

CHRISTOPHER DEACY

OXFORD
UNIVERSITY PRESS

OXFORD
UNIVERSITY PRESS

Great Clarendon Street, Oxford, OX2 6DP,
United Kingdom

Oxford University Press is a department of the University of Oxford.
It furthers the University's objective of excellence in research, scholarship,
and education by publishing worldwide. Oxford is a registered trade mark of
Oxford University Press in the UK and in certain other countries

Published in the United States of America by Oxford University Press
198 Madison Avenue, New York, NY 10016, United States of America

British Library Cataloguing in Publication Data

Data available

Library of Congress Control Number: 2015957293

ISBN 978–0–19–875456–5

Printed in Great Britain by
Clays Ltd, St Ives plc

For my four beautiful children—Estelle, Celeste, Rupert, and Theodore

Preface

This book begins with the premise that religion plays an elementary role in our understanding of the Christmas festival, but takes issue with much of the existing literature which is inclined to associate 'religion' with formal or institutional forms of Christianity or to construe Christmas as a commercial and secular holiday. In *Christmas as Religion*, I argue that such approaches fail to take adequate stock of the manifold ways in which people's beliefs and values take shape in modern society. It may be, for example, that a supernaturally-themed Christmas film about Santa Claus or a Christmas radio programme such as *Junior Choice* comprises a non-specifically Christian, but nonetheless religiously rich, repository of beliefs, values, sentiments, and aspirations. This book thus makes the case for laying to rest the secularization thesis, with its simplistic assumption that religion in Western society is undergoing a period of escalating and irrevocable erosion, and to see instead that the secular may itself be a repository of the religious. I posit that a festival of consumerism can be an unexpectedly fertile site of spirituality and transcendence and that materialism and consumption need to be understood within a context of familial, social, and interpersonal connection and, even, transformation. Rather than see Christmas as comprising an alternative or analogous form of religious expression, or dependent on any causal relationship to the Christian tradition, my premise is that it is religious per se, and, moreover, it is its very secularity that makes Christmas such a compelling, and transcendent, religious holiday.

Acknowledgements

This book was originally conceived as merely a single chapter in what was to become my 2012 monograph, *Screening the Afterlife*, where I thought that having an extended case study of Christmas movies would serve to illuminate wider arguments relating to how films about life after death might be said to comprise secular paradigms of resurrection, redemption, and the transcendent and to contribute to the theological task of exploring the meaning and function of death, judgement, heaven, and hell in the twenty-first century. As the work on that book progressed I found that there was sufficient material here for a monograph in its own right and the filmic angle ended up being relegated to a single chapter while the focus on radio took its place. My radio obsession predates my passion for the cinema as anyone who used to know me at school or university will testify and it would not exactly be wide of the mark to say that the preparation for this book has been a labour of love. From writing down the Top 40 singles chart every Sunday evening in the 1980s to studying Theology at university in the 1990s with the warm and enchanting presence of Chris Stuart, Sarah Kennedy, Steve Madden, Debbie Thrower, and Ed Stewart—now sadly vestiges of a bygone era—to keep me company while I read my books and wrote my assignments, radio has played a seminal role in my life and it feels that I have come full circle in producing this book. I have often wondered what Ed Stewart,[1] who features prominently in the pages that follow, would make of my argument that *Junior Choice* (which was, curiously, on the radio the morning that I was born) constitutes an important site of religious meaning, ritual, and agency in the world today, and if nothing else I hope that I have managed to engender a debate about the way in which the relationship between the sacred and the secular is a very porous and permeable one, and one that also straddles the artificial divide between religion and popular culture. I am most grateful to Tom Perridge, the Senior Commissioning Editor at OUP, for supporting this book on Christmas and religion from the outset,

---

[1] Following this book's completion in December 2015, Ed Stewart passed away on 9 January 2016 after suffering a stroke.

and, together with Karen Raith, the Assistant Commissioning Editor, Saraswathi Ethiraju, the Project Manager, and Michael Janes, the Copy Editor—all of whom have been incredibly efficient and a pleasure to work with—for seeing this project through to completion.

Christmas as Religion was written at a time of great personal change. My (and Caroline's) four adorable children—daughters Estelle and Celeste and twin sons Rupert and Theodore—were all born during the period that I was working on this project and my life has been enriched beyond measure since they came into the world. My daughters in particular spent many an hour sitting patiently (and not so patiently, and not always sitting) in my office while I was putting the finishing touches to this book. None of my children were even born when I first began this research back in 2011 and it is impossible for me not to chart their development in conjunction with the different stages that this project has undergone. I am closer to my family now than ever and to this end I want to thank my wonderful parents, Gerald and Jennifer Deacy, and my late grandfather, Arthur Philip Stokes, for everything they have done for me. My sister Susan and I were the first in our family to go to university and they have supported us and believed in us from the very outset. Without my family's emotional and financial support I wouldn't be in this profession today and there hasn't been a day when writing this book that I haven't been aware of just how lucky I am to be the recipient of Mum's, Dad's, and Grampy's unceasing love and support. I have the best family in the world and I am so glad that Grampy was still alive when I completed the first draft of this monograph in September 2015 and that I was able to talk to him about this project, which fascinated him, before he passed away just a few weeks later at the remarkable age of 95.

There are also a number of colleagues at the University of Kent whose friendship, wisdom, and encouragement has made me a far happier and healthier person. In particular, I want to thank Anne Alwis, Kerry Barber, Francesco Capello, Jeremy Carrette, Abby Day, Jessica Frazier, Robin Gill, Elaine Gilman, Fiona Godfrey, Jessica Hudson, Lawrence Jackson, Leonie James, Richard King, Gordon Lynch, Jacqui Martlew, Sandra Maurer, Gina May, Lorraine Millard, Coralie Norwood, Dani Shalet, Yvonne Sherwood, Richard Stack, Celia Warrick, Shane Weller, and Allia Wilson. They have all given me a much needed anchor and sense of perspective during a particularly difficult period in my personal life. I am also indebted to Rachel Briden and Becky Kennington whom I haven't seen or spoken to in nearly twenty years but who have had a formative impact on my life today. I hope that they all get the chance to read this book for they have played a crucial role in ensuring that the project was able to be completed. By the same token, I want to thank several generations of students in my eleven years at the University of Kent who have taken courses with me in 'Religion and Film' or 'Death of God?', the most recent of whom have heard me speak about the crossover between Christmas, theology, and religion and have on many occasions prompted me to rethink and revisit some of the claims that appeared in earlier drafts of this book. I am privileged to have tutored so many brilliant students and even though I cannot mention everyone by name the impact on my own personal as well as intellectual development has been substantial. A massive Thank You to all.

Chris Deacy

University of Kent, Canterbury
December 2015

Contents

Introduction

The Parameters of this Book

The rationale for writing this book is necessarily a complicated one. We all know, or think we know, what Christmas signifies emotionally, experientially, pragmatically, financially, ritualistically, and (perhaps even) theologically. Everyone has 'celebrated' Christmas in one way or another regardless of geographical location or religious or ethnographic background. As Daniel Miller attests, the modern Christmas 'has conquered not only Christian areas... but also people of a variety of other religions such as in Japan' (Miller 2001: 5), and, indeed, 'Christmas has become if anything more important to Hindu and Muslim peoples of Trinidad than to Christians' (Miller 2001: 24). On the other end of the spectrum, Tom Flynn, an American atheist philosopher, feels that Christmas is so indissolubly Christian in its frame of reference that for anyone who does not practise the Christian faith the only authentic and honourable position is to boycott Christmas outright: 'If we infidels believe that Christianity is untrue, the alleged birth of Christ is not something we ought to celebrate' (Flynn 1993: 232). Yet, while their emphases are different, underlying both Miller's and Flynn's analyses is the proposition that there is something quintessentially, even innately, religious about Christmas which, for good or ill, is the pivot around which any understanding of the festival is anchored. Accordingly, any attempt to examine Christmas without reference to religion would lack coherence.

Even when a book is published which has no interest in exploring the religious antecedents or characteristics of Christmas, the author is defensive about his or her strategy. In the case, for instance, of

William B. Waits' *The Modern Christmas in America*, while emphasis is laid from the outset on the fact that 'This book does not discuss the religious aspects of Christmas' (Waits 1993: 3), Waits' rationale is not that Christmas does not have a religious component; rather, his premise is that 'the secular aspects of the celebration, such as gift giving, the Christmas dinner, and the gathering of family members, have dwarfed its religious aspects in resources spent and in concern given' (Waits 1993: 3; see also Deacy 2013: 198). Waits is simply keen to ensure that the festival's *raison d'être*, which he identifies as being 'the celebration of the birthday of Jesus', is not confused 'with what is central to the celebration as indicated by the behavior of celebrants' (Waits 1993: 3). A similar defensive strategy can be seen with respect to Mark Connelly's examination of the social history of Christmas in the West in the period up to 1952. Connelly writes that 'This study will hardly make any mention of religion or the Church of England or any other Church', on the grounds that the festival's 'residual pagan and secular influences' were more pronounced in the first five centuries of the Church's existence and that any influence in more recent times by churches and sects have tended to be no more than 'oblique' (Connelly 2012: 7).

These are significant positions, as they draw an implicit connection between the role played by formal or institutional forms of Christianity and that of more secular and commercial forces on the way in which Christmas is prioritized and celebrated. 'Religion' is tacitly identified as having an ecclesiastical frame of reference, so that if the Church is not deemed to play a central role in the practice of Christmas for many people today then it can legitimately be sidelined and relegated to the periphery of any discussion relating to what Christmas 'means'. Yet, paradoxically, it is those traditional delineations of what Christmas signifies that are often invoked in order to supply a commentary or a critique of what the modern, secular Christmas represents. Connelly has written elsewhere, for example, that at Christmas the 'tenets of Christianity, of love and selflessness' are usurped by the 'beatific significance' of the quintessentially 'secular' (Connelly 2000b: 120; see also Deacy 2013: 196) mythological figure Santa Claus. Similarly, for Leigh Eric Schmidt, Christmas is a time of the year when 'the transcendent claims of Christian time' are disconnected, displaced, and 'dwarfed by the mundane claims of the merchant's time' (Schmidt 1995: 7; see also Deacy 2013: 196). We see a further binary at work in the case of

James G. Carrier, a social anthropologist, for whom 'the majority of Americans are practising Christians, and the materialistic, commercial air of Christmas conflicts with important religious values' (Carrier 2001: 62; see also Deacy 2013: 196). In non-academic, faith-based literature on Christmas, of which there has been a profusion in recent years, we see a similar tendency to draw a contrast between Christmas as it is and Christmas as it once was and, for the authors, should be. A case in point is Bill McKibben's Methodist church-based book from 1998, *Hundred Dollar Holiday: The Case for a More Joyful Christmas*, the premise of which is that 'the story of the birth of this small baby who would become our Savior, a story that should be full of giddy joy, could hardly break through to our hearts amid all the rush and fuss of the season' (McKibben 1998: 12). Implicit here is the idea that Christmas is at its heart a wholesome and edifying spiritual celebration which has been compromised, degraded, and usurped by its more materialistic and commercialized dimensions.

Regardless of where authors stand on the matter, the religious/ secular binary is one of the most characteristic features of the litera-ture on Christmas. Even when Flynn counsels non-Christians to eschew the festival altogether, he does so because he thinks that anything associated with Christmas, even the decision to stay at home rather than go to work, cannot escape a Christian identifica-tion. Having categorized Christmas as an inherently Christian cele-bration, Flynn cannot see anything associated with the festival, even those elements which Waits might construe as belonging to the realm of the secular such as shopping, feasting, drinking, watching televi-sion, and even spending (varying degrees of) quality time with family members, as being devoid of a religious sensibility, on the grounds that the only reason why we are enabled to partake in such activities is because a religious celebration has made them possible in the first instance. So, the ritual of opening presents or watching a Christmas film after lunch on Christmas afternoon is religious by association. Flynn's solution is to treat Christmas as an ordinary day and to carry out the same practices that we would undertake on any other 'normal' day in the calendar, including spending the day in the office should Christmas fall on a weekday. Quite how Flynn's plea to 'atheists, agnostics, free-thinkers, and secular humanists' to 'sit out the winter holidays' (Flynn 1993: 234) will result in anything functionally dif-ferent from how for many people at present it is Santa Claus rather than the baby Jesus in a manger who is the festival's chief and most universally recognized representative and exemplar is not really spelled out in Flynn's polemic, where the uncompromising line is taken that 'no holiday is viewed by non-Christians as more represen- tative of Christian culture' (Flynn 1993: 37).

The aim of my book is to agree with the aforementioned writers that religion plays an elementary role in our understanding of the Christmas festival, but I differ from them on the question of the location and parameters of where religion can be found. I will query the established wisdom that the celebration of so-called secular and consumerist values is evidence of a decline of religious significance in the modern world. Rather, I will argue that the celebration of consumerism is itself a repository of 'sacred time' and that Christmas is one of the most fertile embodiments of religious activity in the world today. I will interrogate the way in which Eliade, Tillich, and Durkheim understand the relationship between religion and culture, the sacred and the profane, to present a more subtle understanding of the interplay between material and spiritual configurations, to the point that Christmas is a religion *because of* rather than *in spite of* its material and commercialized teleology. In so doing I will posit the need to move away from conventional binary language in order to develop a more sophisticated and realistic understanding of where religion can be encountered. Accordingly, it will be possible to coun- ter the prevailing orthodoxy that the study of Christmas lacks serious scholarly ballast. As Connelly puts it, very few works on Christmas amount to 'modern, critical studies', and 'For a long time the study of something like Christmas would have been regarded as a somewhat frivolous and entirely unrevealing way of studying history' (Connelly 2012: 1). Waits similarly highlights the relative scarcity of 'Scholarly secondary literature on the American Christmas celebration' and notes, à la Connelly, that 'historians, for example, have virtually ignored the festival' (Waits 1993: xviii).

The relatively small quantity of academic literature on Christmas from within theology and religious studies suggests that similar pre- dispositions are in vogue. Although Flynn's own book is, on his own admission, 'not a scholarly work', he makes the significant point that 'Considering the scope and importance of Christmas in our culture, it is amazing to behold the broad vistas of holiday lore that have never been studied—or on which studies have never been published—whose depth of analysis would support a scholarly attempt at synthesis' (Flynn 1993: 9). Although the situation has changed in the twenty years since he was writing, as the work in particular of Schmidt and Dell deChant has illustrated, there is a certain paradox afoot in that scholars no less celebrate Christmas than anyone else. In Waits' words, 'Each winter the public energetically shops, wraps presents, prepares holiday foods, and performs the multitude of other tasks that are necessary for a proper celebration' (Waits 1993: xix), with all the financial ramifications that are entailed, an area richly highlighted in Schmidt's detailed study of the relationship between American holidays, especially Christmas, and the culture of consumption in *Consumer Rites: The Buying & Selling of American Holidays* (1995). Yet, just two decades ago Waits made the instructive observation that there had been little scholarly interest in how businessmen have used Christmas gift-giving to increase their sales (see Waits 1993: xix).

In view of the paucity of literature, it is thus ironic that where scholarly attempts have been made to explore the festival their efforts have yet to find much in the way of consensus. Richard Horsley and James Tracy's *Christmas Unwrapped*, when published in 2001, was quick to attack the extant literature, arguing that Penne Restad's *Christmas in America* (1995) was 'largely devoid of any compelling analysis' and that Schmidt's *Consumer Rites* offers a merely 'superficial analysis' (Tracy 2001a: 5). Yet, Horsley and Tracy's book is far from the definitive work in the field. At the heart of their work is the problematic assumption that their publication will 'contribute to a new appropriation of Christmas by Americans away from the commercial paradigm that now dominates toward a model that will foster more humane and humanizing values' (Tracy 2001a: 5–6). They write, for example, that 'Working longer hours with record numbers of bankruptcies, spending more time shopping and commuting and less time with their own children than ever before while their junk overflows into storage facilities, Americans . . . pay a heavy price for this secular faith in legitimating oneself by dying with the most toys' (Tracy 2001b: 15). Their didactic critique underpins their study of the festival, to the point that, rather than a dispassionate or observational account of the relationship between Christmas and Christianity, the contributors to this edited collection, who are academics working in the fields of theology, religious studies, history, and political science, share the line that, as encapsulated by Horsley, 'the world cannot sustain for very long the level of consumption driven by consumer capitalism and mystified, enhanced, and legitimated by the Christmas festival under the guise of gift-giving' (Horsley 2001b: 221).

These are worthy aspirations, but Horsley and Tracy are too beholden to the binary divisions that characterize the field in their understanding that religion and capitalism offer competing and antithetical positions and that the former is preferential to the latter. While I do not disagree with their assessment per se, what their thesis lacks is an awareness of the more complicated and fluid relationship between the religious and the secular, to the extent that, in line with Dell deChant's position, it may be that the secular, commercialized, marketplace values we associate with Christmas are themselves performing a religious function because they are 'in harmony with the sacred order and process of the economy' (deChant 2002: 40). Capitalism may well have its drawbacks, but how is it *de facto* the opposite of what we would seek to label as religious? What is it that makes religion and the secular dichotomous rather than functionally (at least potentially) one and the same thing? Might it not precisely be *because of* rather than *in spite of* its consecration of a consumerist teleology that Christmas is, as deChant puts it, 'the best example of religiosity in our culture' (deChant 2002: 3)?

In this book I will seek to address such questions. Whereas Horsley and Tracy concede that Christmas has become a new religion in America—namely, the religion of consumer capitalism—they do so with a view to offering a critical and condemnatory approach, similar in essence to the 'Christ against Culture' model put forward in 1952 by H. Richard Niebuhr, where the argument is adduced that 'Whatever may be the customs of the society in which the Christian lives, and whatever the human achievements it conserves, Christ is seen as opposed to them, so that he confronts men with the challenge of an "either-or" decision' (Niebuhr 1952: 54). Applying this position to *Christmas Unwrapped*, it is clear that for Horsley and Tracy Christmas represents and encapsulates a very different set of values to those that they see as standing at the kernel of Christianity. For Horsley, 'The capitalist commodification of culture in fact culturally impoverishes people and diminishes their social and familial life as well' (Horsley 2001b: 221). Accordingly, if someone from the nineteenth century, for example, were to travel forward in time to the present day and thereby witness first hand how Christmas has become depersonalized through the bombardment of advertising and the shopping frenzy, then, attests Tracy, this 'would lead our imaginary Victorian to get down on her knees and plead with the Spirit to assure her that this is not the inexorable shape of the Christmas of her heirs' (Tracy

2001b: 10). Their position and goal is simple: Christmas has been distorted and no longer embodies the characteristics it once did and which must be re-harnessed if the 'true meaning' of Christmas is not to be altogether, and forever, lost. Instead of such an 'either/or' position which holds that Christmas is anathema to 'spiritual' values, my goal is to examine whether, as deChant suggests, precisely in view of its commercialized and ostensibly secular teleology Christmas is the prime example of postmodern religiosity in Western culture today. Rather than claim, therefore, that the 'religious' Christmas has been 'lost' to consumerism, I want to move the debate forward into more challenging areas, by focusing on the possibility that the market-oriented Christmas is itself a pivotal site of religious activity. The aim is not to critique the commercialized Christmas or to suggest that the religion of consumer capitalism is an impoverished and defective 'type' of religious activity but to examine the extent to which Christmas is per se one of the more salient and authentic religious configurations and expressions of our time.

It could of course be objected that the kind of religion that I am here advocating (which might be characterized or dismissed as quasi-religious, proto-religious, or pseudo-religious) is not really authentically religious because it does not offer practices that set something apart as special or sacred to which a practitioner can devote themselves in a manner that is discrete from any lingering or residual allegiance to Christianity.[1] Indeed, there is no doubt for many families that Christianity remains embedded in the festival, due to its association with the birth of Jesus, even if their attachment or allegiance to the Christian faith is no more than nebulous and loose. However, whether someone subscribes to Christianity or not, my argument is that we are all inclined to hold various, often heterogeneous or at the very least overlapping, commitments at one and the same time, as the chapter on Implicit Religion will outline. It may be difficult for some people to completely extricate Christianity from the celebration of what is for all intents and purposes a 'religion of materialism', and it may matter to them that, however 'secular' it is deemed to have become, Christmas is still framed and anchored within the language and categories of the Christian tradition, not

---

[1] I am most grateful to the peer reviewer who made this particular objection to those attempts which construe consumerism as a religion since, ultimately, Christmas has not completely lost its Christian purpose or affiliation.

least through the importance that is accorded to the Nativity story which will not resonate in the same way for non-Christians.[2] This does not, though, stop them from enjoying those more 'secular' aspects of the festival, such as watching an afternoon film or gorging on roast turkey and mince pies. In terms of Implicit Religion, 'religion' and 'non-religion' are diffuse and permeable categories and it would thus be absurd to try and suggest that Christmas is *either* a religious *or* a secular festival. It would be more profitable to construe Christmas as being both—or, equally for that matter, as neither.

This book will be divided into six chapters. Chapter 1, 'What is Christmas?', examines the significance and paradoxes of the Christmas festival. Why do we celebrate Christmas? How do we explain its longevity? What sort of expectations does it meet or fail to meet? What are its core values and rituals? Can its spiritual and material dimensions be reconciled along the lines of Marling's claim that 'the most materialistic and nostalgic of all holidays is also the year's primary occasion for considering the harsh realities of the world' (Marling 2000: 159)? Might, for example, the consumerism that is integral to the Christmas season literally be a 'price worth paying' for the other less material benefits that typify the festival? Could Christmas be construed as a site of transformation and as an oasis of the transcendent within a festival that is itself characterized by a surfeit of consumption? The significance of Christmas will be introduced with reference to Mircea Eliade's understanding of 'sacred time' whereby Christmas can be understood to encompass an inversion of everyday rules, in which home and work are seen as separate spheres, and where a special economy is operative in which, though a consumer festival, it is also, paradoxically, the one day in the year when retail outlets are closed. Christmas may ostensibly take place in historical, linear time, but in a manner analogous to the biblical notion of the New Jerusalem, it also functions eschatologically, encompassing the quest for perfection and fulfilment and a refashioning of the relationship between past, present, and future, and in which the participant is, simultaneously, temporarily detached from actual time and transported to a prelapsarian state, a promised land, where he or she dwells in a form of 'holy community'. Attention will also be paid to whether there are grounds for construing Christmas in terms of

---

[2] Again, I am most grateful to the peer reviewer for making this point.

Victor Turner's understanding of *communitas*, whereby the festival amounts to a transgression or dissolving of the 'norms that govern structured and institutionalized relationships and is accompanied by experiences of unprecedented potency' (Turner 1969: 128). By indulging in a world of magic and transcendence for a brief but intense period, does it follow that we can come to understand the ordinary, mundane world better? The discussion will then lead to a consideration of the extent to which Christmas is a festival of paradox—religious holy day vs. commercial holiday—in the light of Golby and Purdue's claim that the US is 'at once the most overtly consumer society and the most Christian in terms of church attendance' (Golby and Purdue 2000: 140).

Chapter 2, 'Revisiting the Religious Origins and Essence of Christmas', explores the religious antecedents and substance of Christmas and will specifically focus on the difficulties which have beset scholarly attempts to construe Christmas as an explicitly Christian religious festival in view of its syncretic pagan ingredients (and concomitant competing this-worldly vs. other-worldly cosmologies). Such a fusion of Christianity and wider cultural and ideological values characterizes the Victorian era as when the Christmas literature of Charles Dickens has been both acclaimed and adopted, even usurped, by Christians as epitomizing the essence of the Christian story of redemption while also being seen to offer a creative reworking of that narrative in a way that accommodates peculiarly Victorian tastes and tensions. What particularly stands out, for instance, in *A Christmas Carol* is the private rather than communal dimension of the 'redemption' experienced by Scrooge and the redemption of a rich man into a philanthropic (but still rich) one. Even if we are disposed to use the language of redemption, conversion, or salvation, it would be inaccurate to characterize what happens to Scrooge as synonymous with the birth and life of Jesus Christ. If anything, Christianity's gospel of redemption is subsumed within Dickens' 'gospel' of social and humanitarian reform with the concomitant need to extend compassion and charity to the poor and disadvantaged. Ahead of the discussion in chapter 5 concerning whether Christmas films comprise secular analogues of Christian transcendental beliefs and values while nevertheless explicitly bearing witness to the supernatural in the form of other-worldly redeemer figures, chapter 2 will look at the origins and precursors to contemporary cinematic depictions of Christmas with reference to a range of historical, biblical, folklorist, mythological, and anthropological literature. The core of this chapter will consist of a detailed exposition of attempts to draw parallels between Santa and Jesus (see e.g. Russell Belk [2001]). This will be explored in the light of Dell deChant's analysis that 'If Christmas is the representative religious event of postmodern cosmological culture . . . then Santa Claus is the apotheosis of the sacred. In short . . . Santa is a god' (deChant 2002: 185). Departing from much of the extant literature, however, I will demonstrate in this chapter that attempts to draw parallels between the two remain at the superficial level in their implicitly uni-directional trajectory, suggesting as they do that Santa simply points to and fulfils Jesus. There is no doubt, for instance, that for Belk Santa's sacredness would not exist were it not for any Christological association. I will debunk this trend, showing that if there is a heroic, messianic, or supernaturally-tinged figure it is Santa who alone fulfils this role. Jesus has been removed from the equation, and indeed for many people today the iconic image of Christmas is not Jesus in the manger but Santa in the department store. My argument is that Santa and Jesus comprise separate, competing mythologies. It is not therefore sufficient to argue that Santa owes his sacredness to his association with Jesus when it is their separation from one another that paints a more accurate picture. Santa and Jesus inhabit incommensurate religious realms which for the most part have nothing to do with one another, the net result of which is that, ironically, this makes it easier for Christians to believe in the existence of both Santa and Jesus as neither impinges on the territory of the other. It is their separation which, paradoxically, makes them complementary figures who exist independently yet without conflict as no one (including Christians) has to choose between them.

Chapter 3, 'Is Christmas a "Secular" Religion?', moves the debates explored above into the territory of religious and theological definition. According to Mazur and McCarthy, 'As religious institutions have lost their monopoly on the construction and maintenance of meaning, religiosity has found expression in a wide variety of human practices' (Mazur and McCarthy 2011b: 9). Similarly, for Clark, 'whenever something religious can be said to have happened, it must be understood as doing so in relationship to other things that are not considered sacred. This insight represents a revolution in thinking about the role of religion in culture, especially in the Western world' (Clark 2012: 8). In the light of such trends, chapter 3 will look at the culturalist turn in the study of religion and ask whether

Christmas music, films, or radio might be shaping the format and content of religion in the modern world where we are witnessing not religious decline but change. If 'religion' is seen to be limited only to particular representations and manifestations of institutional religions then one may end up missing out on the larger picture of the ways in which people's beliefs and values take shape in modern society. It may be, for example, that Christmas pop songs comprise a non-specifically Christian, but nonetheless religiously rich, repository of sentiments and aspirations, which increasingly characterize and epitomize the modern Christmas landscape. My particular focus will be on the way in which the radio programme *Christmas Junior Choice*, fronted by veteran presenter Ed Stewart on BBC Radio 2 each Christmas morning, is no less fecund when it comes to exploring matters of faith, identity, beliefs, and values than programmes made within the auspices and remit of religious broadcasting. I will propose in chapter 3 that it is never possible to construe religion as some sort of pure or objective essence which exists in a vacuum, impervious to what is happening in culture at large, although there is the irony that Christmas is one festival of the year which strongly polarizes people precisely because it is either seen as inescapably secular (due, as we shall see, to its commercialized and consumerist pedigree) or as a quintessentially religious festival in view of its Christian origins. Indeed, as I will demonstrate, the way forward is thus to lay to rest the secularization thesis, with its simplistic assumption that religion in Western society is undergoing a period of escalating and irrevocable erosion, and to see instead that the secular may itself be a repository of the religious. Rather than see Christmas as comprising *alternative* or *analogous* forms of religious expression, or dependent on any causal relationship to the Christian tradition, it is religious per se, and, I will outline, it is its very secularity that makes Christmas such a compelling, and even transcendent, religious holiday.

The discussion advanced in chapter 3 that an undue emphasis on what comprises the 'sacred' and what comprises the 'profane' only serves to distort rather than inform the nature of contemporary religious debate will be developed in chapter 4, 'Christmas as a Site of Implicit Religion', where specific reference is accorded to Edward Bailey's category of Implicit Religion. Bailey's work is predicated on the notion that what we consider to be the realm of the secular and of ordinary life may contain unacknowledged and unarticulated

religious elements, to the extent that the secular has an important
contribution to contemporary religious debate in its own right and
not simply because it stands in direct contrast to the realm of the
religious. As chapter 4 will outline, although the term itself may be
new, Implicit Religion is not about identifying and labelling a new
type of religion (as if it is functionally equivalent to Christianity,
Buddhism, or Islam) but comprises a new method for examining
the interrelationship between religious and quasi-religious behaviour
in society. Where Bailey's model comes into its own is in its preparedness to look at the phenomena first and only then to ascertain
its religious provenance, and to this end I will posit that *Christmas
Junior Choice* may contain a number of implicitly religious elements
which warrant seeing it through a different lens and which can foster
questions about the various ways in which it might be possible to
practise, encounter, experience, or understand religion in the modern
world. It may even have more impact and comprise more of a
commitment on the part of the listener than allegiance or devotion
to mainstream, explicit religion, and, I will indicate, it is no less
profound or efficacious for that. Ultimately, in this chapter I will
argue that it is not the location—such as a church, synagogue, temple,
or mosque—but the force or the power of one's commitment that
characterizes and determines religion's implicit ethos, and this will be
achieved with reference to Bailey's threefold typology which specifically encompasses 'what a person is committed to; when one uncovers
the integrating foci of their individual and communal experience; and
when one reveals the ways in which commitments and integrating
foci transcend the narrow confines of specific experiences to affect the
entirety of a person's life' (Porter 2009: 277).

The particular focus of chapter 5, 'Christmas Films and the Per-
sistence of the Supernatural', will be on Christmas movies, which are
a staple of the film industry, as key sites of religious and theological
activity. Although organized religion plays almost no part in the plot
of Christmas movies, Christmas is customarily presented in movies
such as *Holiday Inn* (1942), *Die Hard* (1988), and *Home Alone* (1990)
as a 'comforting ideal' where families are brought together and problems overcome. There may be those who think that Britain is now 'a
secular culture with traces of a Christian identity, where secular means
a rational worldview without beliefs in supernatural powers' (Day
2012: 442) but it is significant that in Christmas films the supernatural
is back in vogue and there is the (at times intentional) conflation

between the Christian drama of redemption and secular narratives of conversion and renewal, where one set of supernatural redeemer figures is replaced by another, such as angels (*It's a Wonderful Life* [1946]) or Santa Claus (*The Santa Clause* [1994]), paradoxically within a distinctly secularized setting. Using Don Cupitt's interpretation of the myth of a supernatural redeemer and Rudolf Bultmann's programme of demythologization as examples, I will be asking whether Christmas movies offer challenges to the theological task of exploring the roles, rituals, mythologies, and agencies of Christmas in the twenty-first century. In short, how do we address the dichotomy between much modern theology, which is disposed to allegorize, spiritualize, or existentialize the supernatural and metaphysical, and the predilection in popular films to render literally on screen angels, elves, and Father Christmas? What are the ramifications for scholarship? It may be argued that film is an entertainment medium and less capable of articulating the religious/sacred than, say, news media or documentaries, but as Jonathan Brant notes in relation to Paul Tillich 'an art object that is not highly regarded with regard to "quality" can still have a profound, and by implication revelatory, effect at the point of "involved encounter"' (Brant 2012: 223). This will be discussed with specific reference to the genre of Christmas films which at first sight would appear to be lacking in theological depth, as betokened by Ian Nathan's review of *Trapped in Paradise* (1994) in which the film's moments of promise are identified as mere 'ripples in an ocean of overacted slapstick, put together with little attention to detail' (Nathan 1995: www.empireonline. com/reviews/reviewcomplete.asp?FID=3442). I will conclude by arguing that, rather than dismissing them for their fantastic or escapist predilections, Christmas movies offer one of the most blatant challenges to the secularization thesis in the contemporary world and amount to 'a remarkably sophisticated sub-genre that utilizes visual and musical iconography to great effect' (Agajanian 2000: 162). Indeed, in an inversion of the premise of deChant's *The Sacred Santa*, I will be asking whether, precisely in view of their transcendental (rather than as de Chant sees it their naturalistic) elements, Christmas films might not so much comprise secular paradigms of Christmas but function in their own right as new forms of religiosity and sacred activity in contemporary culture. I will explore the paradox that Christmas movies are spaces in which the transcendent appears in an otherwise secularized milieu.

Finally, in chapter 6, 'Reframing Christmas and the Religion of Materialism', I will posit that while the emphasis in Christmas films on the miraculous is a staple of the genre, there is, paradoxically, another, quite divergent, dynamic in Christmas films and in the celebration of Christmas more generally. Building on the work of Dell deChant, according to whom when we engage in the ritual of consumption many of us do so 'with a seriousness that in earlier times was restricted to religious activity' (deChant 2002: 40), my aim in this chapter is to explore the extent to which Christmas is a religious festival—but not a Christian, or indeed a pagan one, but one characterized by materialism and consumerism. Rather than claim, therefore, that the 'religious' Christmas has been 'lost' to consumerism, along the lines of Robinson and Staeheli's argument that 'Christmas is becoming ever more commercial, expensive, hectic, pressured, impersonal, and materialistic' (Robinson and Staeheli 1982: 12), this chapter will focus on the possibility that the market-oriented Christmas is itself a pivotal site of religious and even soteriological activity. It is thus ironic that Christmas films ostensibly preach values of family, peace, and love and, in Kim Newman's words regarding *Santa Claus: The Movie* (1985), will 'whine about the commercialisation of Christmas *while indulging in it on a monumental scale*' (Newman 1985: 387; my italics). This disjuncture, which is a mainstay of many of the reviews of Christmas films including *Miracle on 34th Street* (1994), *Jingle All The Way* (1996), and *How the Grinch Stole Christmas* (2000), relates to how, as debates in Implicit Religion have shown, it is customary for us to subscribe to multiple commitments concurrently, even ones which are discordant, 'unrelated or competitive' (Jespers et al. 2012: 536). Consequently, rather than concentrate, as does much of the current literature, on the disingenuousness of Christmas films for how they simultaneously celebrate consumerism while also affirming the importance of family values and antipathy towards the materialism of Christmas and the mass production of toys, chapter 5 will conclude by asking whether such films, as a microcosm of Christmas more generally, are able to teach us about generosity, wonder, miracles, joy, belief, fellowship, giving, celebration, community, love, and even redemption because of, rather than in spite of, the unalloyed consumerism on display. This will be undertaken with specific reference to Daniel Miller's ethnographic work on shopping in which the argument is adduced that, paradoxically, 'love is not only normative but easily dominant as the context and motivation for the bulk of actual shopping practice' (Miller 1998: 23) and that 'Shopping, so far from being, as it is inevitably portrayed, the essence of ungodliness, becomes as a ritual the vestigial search for a relationship with God' (Miller 1998: 150).

There is thus a closer and more complicated relationship between consumerism and religion than many of the works presently in the field, especially Horsley and Tracy's edited volume, address. Even deChant's *The Sacred Santa*, though a pivotal influence on my thesis that Christmas is a religion, is dependent on the same sort of binary division that characterizes much of the literature in the field in that for deChant there is a clear division between the spiritual and transcendental character of traditional Christianity on the one hand and the materialistic *telos* of postmodern culture on the other. He argues that 'our identification of religion with transcendental religions' (deChant 2002: x) is to blame for our failure to see how the rituals of consumption in the form of retail spending which we perform at malls and department stores (especially in the run-up to Christmas) is actually analogous to the practices that took place in temples and shrines in the ancient cosmological world. On one level, deChant is suggesting that religion has not changed over the centuries—just as in the ancient world the ground of the sacred was nature, in the respect that 'everything depended on the cycles of nature and fertility' (deChant 2002: 30; see also Deacy 2013: 201), today it is the economy that has taken on this role. But, on another level he seeks to make his argument by overplaying the contrast between the transcendental dimension of traditional religions and current trends in postmodern culture, as when he writes about the need to 'delegitimate the foundational faith claims of transcendental religions while simultaneously offering new and contrasting claims about the ultimate meanings and values of life' (deChant 2002: 4).

Such an analysis paints too simplistic a picture concerning Christianity's transcendental and Christmas's cosmological dimensions and overlooks the strong degree to which, as I showed in *Screening the Afterlife* (2012), Christianity itself has, from its very origins, often tended to use earthly realities as the point of departure and to visualize the transcendent through the lens of this-worldly phenomena. The central thrust of that book was, indeed, to demonstrate that when it comes to questions of death and eschatology, theology does not exactly comprise a settled, consistent, or coherent area of discourse as betokened by the wide differences of emphasis between present and future forms of eschatology, to the point that the same terminology is often expected to accommodate both the quest for an afterlife and the search for transcendence within present experience in this life on earth. Lucid and compelling though deChant's analysis is, it would be better to see Christianity as having historically struggled to conceptualize the relationship between the transcendent and the immanent, and it is with this tension in mind that we can come to a better understanding of how, as we shall see in chapter 5, Christmas films prove that the transcendental aspect of Christmas is as strong as ever. deChant sees a straightforward transition from the ancient to the postmodern cosmological world, where in neither case does the metaphysical or supernatural have a role to play. He may see Christianity's transcendental dimension as something of an aberration or an anomaly, but deChant's thesis does not accommodate the reality of Christmas for many people today where interspersed with the postmodern naturalistic Christmas in which the economy is supreme lies a surfeit of supernatural, transcendental, even magical, phenomena and agencies which are far from peripheral to the way in which the festival is celebrated. It is this paradox which has yet to be addressed in any of the existing literature, and which supplies the rationale, indeed the *raison d'être*, of this book.

1

What is Christmas?

WHY IS CHRISTMAS SIGNIFICANT?

In view of the relative paucity of literature on Christmas, we are faced with the first of many paradoxes. If, as Marling attests, 'Christmas is the universal memory, one of the few rituals on the calendar of life that virtually everybody has played a part in' (Marling 2000: ix; see also Deacy 2013: 195), then why is it the case that such little serious scholarship has been undertaken in this area? Perhaps that is the central problem—we all (think we) know what Christmas is, we all celebrate it, and there is not, accordingly, much that is new to discover in or about it. It is almost an aberration in that it is a time of the year when our normal rituals and schedules are disrupted, even dissolved, it is relatively fleeting (though the run-up to Christmas, not least the many weeks of gift-buying that dominate the months of November and December, is invariably protracted), and, once it is over, some semblance of routine returns. Christmas is a once-off—we do not decide when to celebrate it, in contrast to, say, a family holiday which can be taken at a time of our choosing at any point in the calendar. We are never in control of Christmas; it controls us with respect to its timing, as well as in terms of the stranglehold it has over us. We can contemplate escaping to another country, even climate, for a period, but as Daniel Miller has found, Christmas is no less celebrated in Japan or Trinidad than it is in the West, and even an environment as far removed as one can imagine from the cold, snowy vistas of Lapland—the comparatively tropical heat of Florida, for example, where many British tourists go to flee the bleak mid-winter—is not without the decorative, kitschy, reminders of home in the form of the adornment of Christmas trees, the giving of cards and presents, the singing of carols, the familiar icons everywhere of Santa and his reindeer and of snowmen, and even the serving of the traditional turkey dinner.

Regardless of geographical place, Miller is correct that 'we are faced with the extraordinary phenomenon of a global festival which seems to grow in its accumulated rituals and the extravagance of the homage paid to it, even as all other festivals and comparable events have declined' (Miller in Miller 2001: 5). Harrison is not therefore wide of the mark when he observed in the early 1950s that 'before the world was to achieve a universal currency, a universal law, a universal government, language or system of weights and measures, it was to achieve a universal Christmas' (Harrison 1951: 179). Christmas is not an optional festival to be celebrated according to the strengths or fervour of one's Christian faith. Irrespective of whether one believes in a transcendent God, the transcendence, even the transformation, afforded by the event is what makes Christmas genuinely different from any other time of the year. Indeed, as Restad puts it, 'Almost alone, the keeping of this holiday provides a communal and calendrical touchstone of the nation's faith, hope, and moral aspiration, a national moment of harmony and transcendence' (Restad 1995: 162; see also Deacy 2013: 198). Any event that can unite 'a disparate people in rites and impulses' and which 'cradles myriad sentiments concerning friends, family, age, place, heritage, and values' (Restad 1995: 162) would seem to be functionally similar to what Durkheim was proposing a century ago concerning the way in which the influence of the group over the individual comprises a shared, symbolic account of one's place in the world and whose communal dimension affords the individual within the group greater strength to endure and surmount the trials of existence (see Deacy 2013: 200).

This, then, is the irony, for one can *choose* whether or not to celebrate a religious festival or to subscribe to the tenets, doctrines, and values of a particular religious tradition. Indeed, as Sands puts it, 'to observe or not observe religious holidays—these are counted among our most basic political freedoms' (Sands 2001: 58). But, when it comes to Christmas it is difficult if not impossible to escape the festival. Back in 2004, former British Foreign Secretary Robin Cook wrote in a newspaper column that he regarded it as 'unpatriotic to go abroad for Christmas', not least because 'For one weekend in the year even strangers will say hello to you in the street' (in BBC News 2004: http://news.bbc.co.uk/1/hi/uk_politics/4104745.stm). But, even in going abroad one is not so much escaping Christmas as escaping the climate associated with the time of year. *If* one were to go further and boycott Christmas altogether—the premise of the John Grisham novella *Skipping Christmas*, which was made into a film titled *Christmas with the Kranks* in 2004 in which a middle-aged Chicago couple decide not to partake in any of the customs and rituals associated with Christmas, leading to derision and ostracism at the hands of their neighbours until they finally succumb and normality is resumed—Sands affirms that 'to refuse the Christmastime giving and receiving of gifts, the parties and songs, the decorations and shows' is to 'face penalties ranging from ridicule to social excommunication' (Sands 2001: 58).

We are thus brought to the heart of what it is that Christmas signifies and why its observance is mandatory. Sands' take on the matter is that Christmas 'deflects critique by passing itself off as morally or philosophically trivial' (Sands 2001: 58). Precisely because it is seen as an opportunity to rest, to indulge, and to take a break from the routine, Christmas is harmless and non-sectarian. It may have its roots in a Christian celebration (though as we shall see in chapter 2 the festival's antecedents are somewhat more complicated and heterogeneous than such a straightforward reading allows) but when, as Tracy discerns, 'Christmas summons images of family gathered around a decorated tree, of music and light and the comforting smell of a special dinner cooking on a snowy winter day', then Christmas overcomes any denominational or theological obstructions because these are inclusive and wholesome 'symbols of the values we hold dear and of a world for which we yearn' (Tracy 2001a: 1). The fact that Christmas is also a time of excessive consumerism, materialism, and greed somehow fails to dent this enriching and edifying image, even if the latter is the more realistic face of Christmas. After all, to give one example, Moore notes how book publishers will commonly schedule their whole year with a view to maximizing Christmas profits, with December sales comprising around twenty-five per cent of their yearly income and sales in the month up to Christmas being some fifty per cent higher than during any other month of the year (see Moore 2009: 148).

It is for this reason that Christmas is such a conundrum. It may be a festival of unalloyed, and undisciplined, materialism where twenty per cent of all retail goods sold in the United States are Christmas purchases, in which nearly sixty per cent of Americans incurred credit card debt at Christmas 2004, with some fourteen per cent still paying off debts from the previous year when Christmas 2005 came around (see Forbes 2007: 126), but such a narrative is not always the one we choose to hear. Rather, Christmas is a time associated with what Agajanian refers to as 'a focus on the children, humanitarianism toward the under-privileged and vulnerable, and a feeling of nostalgia for good times past' (Agajanian 2000: 145). We may seek to complain that Christmas has become too money-oriented and opt to 'hark back to a time when Christmas was simpler, more authentic, and less commercial than it has become' (Nissenbaum 1996: loc. no. 2722), but the consumerism that is integral to the modern Christmas is literally a price worth paying for the other less tangible benefits that characterize the season. Indeed, as Golby and Purdue see it, built into Christmas is 'a strong element of nostalgia: a feeling that somehow past Christmases were happier, more enjoyable' (Golby and Purdue 2000: 9) occasions. Even though, as they acknowledge, it is 'impossible . . . to find any period when this ideal Christmas actually existed' (Golby and Purdue 2000: 9), it is this element of nostalgia for Christmas as a past idyll which holds particular sway in the literature associated with the festival. Connelly, for example, accords much attention to this romanticized vision of Christmas as a treasure-trove of sentiment for halcyon days, which operates on the premise that 'the past was better and can never be recovered in its entirety' (Connelly 2012: xiv). We may never be able to get it back or recapture it. It may remain as distorted, idealized memories of long since past glory days, but the urge to cherish and treasure that past becomes the *modus operandi*. It becomes almost an eschatological point of reference, as evinced in terms of the following definition of nostalgia as proffered by Andrew Higson:

> Nostalgia posits two different times which are opposed to one another, one negative, the other positive: the present, marked by moral disintegration, deterioration, and degeneration, and the longed-for past, marked by purity, truth, and fullness . . . The imagined past is constructed in terms of what the present is felt to lack, it is the imaginary site of plenitude in relation to the experience of loss or lack in the present. Nostalgia thus uses an image of the past to enter into dialogue with the present (qtd in Connelly 2012: xiv–xv).

This notion of Christmas as the site of one's nostalgic longing for a prelapsarian universe, which though situated in the past is nevertheless the motivation and impetus for the present, is one of the festival's most enduring features. As Connelly sees it, Christmas is 'associated with the perceived solidity of the past and the beneficial example that is thought to set' (Connelly 2012: xv). It may ostensibly exist in linear, historical, chronological time, but this is a festival which more accurately refashions the relationship between the past, the present, and the future. As Kuper puts it, Christmas 'ignores time and breaches secular boundaries' (Kuper 2001: 169; see also Deacy 2013: 195). To this end, there is an analogous relationship with the way in which the New Jerusalem is envisaged in the Old Testament, where a physical and material place which, as McGrath construes it, supplies 'a tangible image of the presence and providence of God within its sturdy walls' exists *at the same time* as 'a pointer to the fulfillment of messianic expectations' (McGrath 2003: 6; see also Deacy 2012a: 112). The terrestrial and the celestial Jerusalem were thus intertwined. A geographical city it may have been, but it encompassed so much more, paved as it was with 'gold and decked with jewels and precious stones, dazzling its inhabitants and intensifying the sense of longing to enter through its gates on the part of those still on earth' (McGrath 2003: 11; see also Deacy 2012a: 116).

Just as the heavenly Jerusalem pre-exists and is the template for the earthly Jerusalem,[1] so in the case of Christmas the ideal that the festival encapsulates becomes a benchmark and a catalyst for the way in which Christmas is celebrated. As Marling sees it, Christmas is when 'family members come home again, gifts bring joy to both donor and recipient, and goodwill pours from every lighted window' (Marling 2000: 64). This sense of Christmas as an inclusive and utopian celebration fits in well with how the New Jerusalem has been construed by some scholars as a place of homecoming and security for everyone, even the lost and exiled (see Deacy 2012a: 112), and which has the capacity to draw 'people from afar to the safety and rest that it offers' (McGrath 2003: 9; see also Deacy 2012a: 113). Indeed, as Patrick Miller construes it, the New Jerusalem amounts to 'a feast "for all peoples"' (Miller 2000: 162; see also Deacy 2012a: 112) where all

---

[1] As discussed in *Screening the Afterlife*, though, this is a contested point as according to some scholars it was the geographical Jerusalem that preceded the heavenly Jerusalem. See e.g. Russell for whom the 'glorified earthly Jerusalem was the model for, and gradually merged with, the heavenly city of Jerusalem' (Russell 1997: 32, cited in Deacy 2012a: 170).

previous enmity between people is overcome, and, notwithstanding the theocentric emphasis in biblical literature on the New Jerusalem (see Deacy 2012a: 113), the idea of the New Jerusalem as an ideal society where, as Hick sees it, the social and interpersonal character of human existence is brought to perfection (Hick 1976: 203; see also Deacy 2012a: 113) has much in common with Christmas as 'the marker of progress and the turning point' (Parker 2005: xi) and, even, as 'a time when utter perfection seems within human reach' (Marling 2000: 64).

The New Jerusalem may ultimately be about *place* while Christmas is about *space*, but the analogy between the two works on a different level also. The failure of the New Jerusalem to materialize in this lifetime is a familiar refrain, and is perfectly encapsulated by Robert Strachan's phrase from the early twentieth century with respect to the feeling of unease on the part of the first generation of Christians that 'Believers were dying, and He [Christ] did not come' (Strachan 1920: 17; see also Deacy 2012a: 82). In short, expectations may not have been realized, but rather than invalidate biblical hopes concerning the imminent end the result has been a systematic re-evaluation of what those texts mean. For some New Testament interpreters, such as C.H. Dodd or Rudolf Bultmann, it makes sense to re-examine the future hope in terms of realized and this-worldly expectations, whereby the *eschaton* has entered history and that this is actually a more authentic way of understanding eschatology than the future-direction of the biblical language (see Dodd 1944: 76). While for others, such as Jürgen Moltmann and Wolfhart Pannenberg, the primitive witness of the first disciples is pivotal in giving us the knowledge and belief that Jesus Christ had introduced the end of the world through his resurrection from the dead and that the whole basis of Christianity is communicated through apocalyptic language, to the point that faith today remains incomprehensible without the apocalyptic dimension. If one removes this apocalyptic component then there is no longer any continuity between modern faith and the witness of the disciples.

Despite the incompatibility between the two positions, both Dodd and Moltmann would agree on the intrinsic significance of eschatology to Christianity. In the same way, the failure of Christmas to bring about an enduring model of human perfection—to apply Robin Cook's example here, for Christmas to really amount to a time when perfection was accomplished, strangers would say hello in the street all year long, not just for a few short days—does not diminish or undermine that hope. Would the potency of Charles Dickens' *A Christmas Carol* be any less effective if it transpired that Ebenezer Scrooge's Christmas redemption was merely short-lived as, within a period of days or months, he reverted to type as a materialistic, spendthrift, and miserly employer? Just as the efficacy of the Book of Amos need not be undermined because not everyone who reads the injunctions of the eighth-century BCE prophet is disposed to give their money to the poor afterwards, so the absence of a causal relationship between the quest for perfection at Christmas-time and any durable fulfilment or actualization of that hope does not mean that Christmas is predicated upon false or quixotic dreams.

Christmas may be a consumer festival but it is also, paradoxically, the one day in the year when (with the exception of online) retail outlets are closed, people stay at home rather than go to work, and there are no newspapers, theatres, cinemas, or public transport (see also Deacy 2013: 199).[2] A different sort of protocol is operative, as betokened by Kuper's claim that the 'establishment of a special Christmas economy—marked by the absence of work and the giving of presents and charitable donations—inverts the economy of everyday life' (Kuper 2001: 167). It may be that at New Year we 're-enter a secular, competitive, workaday, class-ridden, sexual world' (Kuper 2001: 166), but during the Christmas period at least we experience a time of the year that has its own distinctive religious, and specifically eschatological, ontology. It is not a 'secular' analogue of Christian 'sacred time'. It is 'sacred time' per se (see also Deacy 2013: 199). Rather than work in terms of linear, chronological time Marling sums up the *telos* of Christmas when she writes that the festival provides

> points of entry into a state of happiness and abundance that transcends the present and stretches back endlessly into the past. Christmas is a special time, a suspension of the workaday order of things, but it is also a doorway connecting the present to earlier eras (Marling 2000: 129).

This is pivotal to understanding how Christmas functions as there is a sense in which the participant is, simultaneously, temporarily detached from actual time and transported to a prelapsarian state, a promised land, where he or she dwells in a form of holy community

---

[2] I am conscious, however, that not everybody has the luxury of being off work on Christmas Day. Many of my students, for example, work on Christmas Day in restaurants or pubs though this is often to cover for colleagues who need the day off to spend with their families.

where release from everyday problems is facilitated. Waits categorizes this as 'a special time: festive, conflict-free, and imbued with a mystical glow' (Waits 1993: 7), and, as Restad puts it, at Christmas we are enabled to recall 'some past and more perfect moment of faith and transcendence' (Restad 1995: 179). Restad is thus only partially correct when, paraphrasing Durkheim, she refers to how (religious) holidays punctuate the rhythm of the year and are essential to the formation of a cultural identity by helping us to define and reflect the needs of the societies in which such special units of time exist (see Restad 1995: 17). What such an account lacks is the transformative, even redemptive, state of liminality or *communitas* afforded by Christmas, along the lines of Victor Turner's understanding of how subjects involved in ritual transformation will 'pass through a liminal phase in which the structures of the society are temporarily suspended, even upended and mocked, and where intense experiences of *communitas*, or a sense of communion of equal individuals, occur among participants' (Mazur and McCarthy 2011d: 104–5).

Whereas Durkheim saw holidays as providing clearly demarcated boundaries between sacred and profane time, Turner's analysis is the more germane to our discussion as, for him, 'the norms that govern structured and institutionalized relationships' are transgressed or dissolved, and this is 'accompanied by experiences of unprecedented potency' (Turner 1969: 128). In other words, Christmas is not just descriptively different; it is ontologically different from the rest of the calendar and comes equipped with a different set of opportunities, even values, to the extent that, as Rachel Wagner sees it, 'Abiding in such a liminal (in-between) space can give people the freedom to do otherwise taboo things, giving them an outlet and voice so that when they return to ordinary time they are more content with existing social structures' (Wagner 2012a: 164). In the specific case of Christmas, it might be found, for example, that in the unique opportunity afforded during the season to indulge in the supernatural and magical world evoked by Santa Claus, his reindeer and elves, core ingredients, as we shall see in chapter 5, of Christmas movies such as *The Santa Clause* (1994)—where the line between the rational and the irrational, the terrestrial and the metaphysical is shown to be porous and traversable, so that workaholic and divorced fathers can transform into Santa Claus and in the process become closer to their estranged children—and *One Magic Christmas* (1985)—where Father Christmas can even raise the dead and reunite a deceased father with the rest of his family who are struggling to cope at Christmas with his absence—we can come to understand this ordinary, mundane world better. It might be that in entering such a sacred space we learn how to cultivate or eradicate certain character traits or emotions that are unwholesome or unedifying, and so return afterwards 'to our daily lives with greater acceptance of the limitations in them' (Wagner 2012b: 130).

This may not be as wide of the mark as it might at first appear, not least because there is a rich body of literature on the transformative, even redemptive, possibilities engendered by escapism, which operates in much the same way. The supernatural and magical world as evoked in Christmas films may on one level be trite and diversionary, but, as Lyden has demonstrated with respect to escapism more broadly, there can be something theologically efficacious at work if the delineation of a fantasy world can come to be qualified within the context of life *as a whole*. In other words, rather than see the 'magic' of Christmas as immature or irrational, and suitable only for children who alone believe in the possibility of the existence of Santa Claus, a more profitable area for exploration would be one which sought to focus on the transformative possibility engendered by the fantasy-realism dichotomy. Is there any new insight to be gained from any such dialogue or exchange? If we take the line that audiences of Christmas films are passive and docile consumers then there may be little or no such transformative opportunity. But, as Lyden puts it, 'One escapes to the world of film in order to return better equipped to this world, and so even the "idealist" aspect of film serves a "realist" function' (Lyden 2003: 50; see also Deacy 2008: 18).

The effect need not be seen as wholly distinct from a religious ritual, wherein a worshipper enters sacred space with a view to seeking an encounter with another dimension of existence which he or she knows is not the empirical world but which nevertheless charges the empirical world with meaning and value following the experience of transcendence and an encounter with, to borrow Rudolf Otto's term, the *numinous* (Otto 1959: 21; see also Deacy 2008: 21). Both cinema and church thus enable people to achieve a degree of separation, or escape, from the restrictions and limitations of the 'real' world before their 'return' to the everyday which is, subsequently, imbued with new significance (see Segal 1999: 127–8, also cited in Deacy 2008: 21). As Lyden puts it, 'We desire alternate worlds because we find our own imperfect; but such desires to flee also entail a desire to return, renewed and refreshed, to the everyday' (Lyden 2003: 53; see also Deacy 2008: 21). Applied specifically to Christmas movies, it may be that, not least due to their very alterity, such films are capable of *enriching* our apprehension of the empirical world rather than *distancing* us from them. Rather than a literal model to emulate in every respect, the supernatural and magical world of Christmas movies may function effectively as what Lyden, writing in the context of a discussion of gangster films, refers to as 'a challenge to our ordinary ways of seeing and doing things' (Lyden 2003: 156; see also Deacy 2008: 22).

This is very much akin to what Turner has spoken of, not least because his understanding of liminality and *communitas* does not require there to be any evidence of a sudden, empirically demonstrable and dramatic transformation at work. Rather than a Damascus moment, Mazur and McCarthy paraphrase Turner to the effect that 'To identify ritual as a site of transformation is simply to note that we are somehow different after partaking in the ritual from how we were when it began' (Mazur and McCarthy 2011c: 105). Lyden's work on escapism works well here as he is suggesting that the process of engagement with fantasy is necessarily a protracted one. When he writes of the need to 'find ways to bring that ideal into relation with the real, however partially or fragmentarily' (Lyden 2003: 104; see also Deacy 2008: 16), we can see how in relation to Christmas it might be understood that a steady diet of magical, supernatural, escapist fare might entail not a rejection of such movies because they are contrary to the way the world 'really' is. Instead, a deeper and intangible process may be at work, which might entail asking why it is that in celluloid constructions of Christmas—even in the atypical, more subversive offerings as in the case of *Bad Santa* (2003) where Billy Bob Thornton's anti-hero identifies himself as 'an eating, drinking, shitting, fucking Santa Claus' and insists that 'I'm living proof that there is no Santa Claus'—the same conventions always apply. John Mundy sums up the formula when he refers to how 'the "miraculous", "magical" power of Christmas' is invariably 'triumphant over acknowledged dystopian elements of the festive experience' (Mundy 2008: 166). Whether we are talking about Bill Murray in *Scrooged* (1988), Tim Allen in *The Santa Clause* (1994), or indeed Thornton in *Bad Santa*, Hollywood gives us the dependable trajectory of seeing 'its heroes taunted and tested before coming good on Christmas Eve' (Brooks 2005: 43). Christmas is a site of transformation—no one is irredeemable at Christmas—and there are role models and ideal constructions at work with the inclusion of supernatural (or at least not-quite-human) agents such as angels, elves, and Father Christmas who characteristically represent values of joy, peace, love, and hope which rub off on the human—adults and children alike—characters in the film. Hence, like the rational psychologist played by Judge Reinhold in *The Santa Clause*, by the film's denouement they will have shed their aversion for the empirically unproven or unprovable and so are able to affirm something along the lines of 'There *is* a Santa Claus' or 'I *do* believe in Father Christmas', becoming 'better', more 'enlightened' people along the way.

Yet, what is significant here is the temporary scope afforded for such an experience or encounter. Lyden's escapism model has no demarcated boundaries—whenever we watch an escapist film the models proposed in the movie can always 'serve as an ideal to which we aspire, however inadequately' and there are no limitations to how they may be able to help us 'partially resolve the conflict in our daily lives' (Lyden 2003: 76). Escapism is a powerful and universal tool as there are no calendrical constraints around how by encountering an alternative, fantasy world the inadequacies of the empirical world can be brought into relationship with the world of the everyday, or how the imaginary constructions of escapist worlds can 'serve to convey real truths about the nature of reality and how it is believed to be' (Lyden 2003: 54; see also Deacy 2008: 22). In the case of Christmas, however, the escapism not only takes a different, more specialized form but it can only function within a more limited time frame. Classic escapist fare might relate to a romantic comedy with its stock-in-trade 'happy ever after' sensibility or an action film in which Batman endeavours to save Gotham City from a motley crew of villains and outlaws. But, these tend not to be supernatural tales. Batman may have resources open to him that seemingly defy nature and which exceed the boundaries of human endurance, but there are explanations—usually of a psychological kind—which account for his particular methods and motivations in choosing to act in the way he does and which are grounded in real world traumas, such as witnessing the death of a parent and seeking to exact vengeance.

Even Superman, though descended from another planet, requires the adoption of a very human persona, in the form of Clark Kent, in order for the less obviously human features of his personality to be grounded. Superheroes tend to be weak, tortured, dysfunctional figures suffering from personal struggles and self-doubts who will be forced to confront their ambiguous characters and behaviours and battle their inner demons (see Deacy 2001: 149), as epitomized in the Tim Burton rendering of *Batman* in 1989. In Christmas films, on the other hand, the existence of a miraculous other world—usually identified as Lapland—containing immortal creatures who bestow grace and good will on the films' terrestrial-based characters is a familiar staple of this genre. Even in a film such as *The Night They Saved Christmas* (1984) in which Art Carney's Santa Claus lives in a North Pole that is at risk of being destroyed by the oil-drilling and land-exploitation of an acquisitive, capitalist corporation, where the North Pole can be accessed geographically by adventurous humans, Santa is nevertheless a mysterious, supernatural figure who can manipulate matters temporal due to the existence of a time-deceleration device and whose *raison d'être* is to deliver presents to all the children around the world in one night in his magical sleigh. It is, in other words, the otherness and metaphysical construction of Santa's abode that is brought to the fore. The metaphysical, even celestial, otherness of Santa films differentiates them from standard escapism where it might be the implausibility of the romance or the ability of the hero to withstand so many encounters with mortality that predominate.

    Not only, then, is the form of escapism in Christmas films more pronounced than it is in any other genre but it only works within a concentrated and clearly demarcated period of time. If there is anything transformative, or liminal, about Christmas films it is the very specificity of the timing and nature of the ritual experience that alone brings that about. It is this sense of the supernatural being an integral part of the Christmas ritual but only within a narrow parameter that comprises one of the central paradoxes of Christmas. It is an oasis of the transcendent within a festival that is itself characterized by a surfeit of consumption. Contrary, then, to the idea put forward by deChant that Christmas is a religion of materialism, my position is that such a thesis needs to be countered by the no less acute role played by the magical and the supernatural. On one level, of course, Christmas films are made by studios for financial profit and so it is difficult to see the emphasis on the miraculous as being antithetical to the prevailing norm whereby a film will be made because it can be expected to perform credibly at the box office or on DVD or Blu-Ray. To that end, Hollywood might be said to have subsumed and harnessed the spiritual element of Christmas for its own profit-oriented purposes.

But the picture is more complicated than this. For, the same separation that exists between Christmas and the profane applies in other contexts. The celebration of the miraculous birth of the baby Jesus to a virgin mother—the Nativity story—is strongly synonymous in the Christian calendar with the Christmas period, to the point that the Nativity is not functionally transferable to another date in the calendar, say, the month of June. By the same token, radio stations, whether commercially run or broadcast by the BBC, have strict boundaries around which Christmas music is transmitted. In the case of BBC Radio 2, for instance, there will be a gradual build-up from the beginning of December of designated Christmas fare, with the third week of the month redolent with festive tracks until, but not significantly beyond (the occasional sprinkling on Boxing Day is the limit) 25 December. On 4 June 2012 Radio 2 marked the sixtieth anniversary of the Queen's accession to the throne by counting down the sixty bestselling artists of the previous sixty years (which opportunely coincided with the year of the first singles chart in the United Kingdom). For three hours on that Bank Holiday afternoon, in a live show, veteran presenter Tony Blackburn played the biggest-selling hit of each of the sixty bestselling artists in the UK—but with one notable (though not explicitly identified in the programme) exception. If the bestselling song concerned was a Christmas one it was simply omitted from the playlist. So, there was no air time given to Mariah Carey's 'All I Want for Christmas' at number 39 or to Slade's 'Merry Xmas Everybody' at number 31. Curiously, though, on the following Saturday, 9 June, in a countdown of the top-selling singles of the 1980s, Blackburn *did* play Band Aid's 'Do They Know It's Christmas?', the Christmas number 1 from 1984 and which topped the chart of the bestselling single of that decade. But, this was, significantly, a pre-recorded programme as Blackburn was suffering from pneumonia and his regular *Pick of the Pops* show, due to air live at 1pm that afternoon, had to be pulled at the last minute. The programme that was broadcast had been recorded in advance and had been made as a stand-by in case of such an eventuality and so in theory could have been transmitted at any point in the year, including Christmas-time.

The message is clear—Christmas has distinct and immovable contours and is not transferable to any other time in the year. Indeed, to play a Christmas record, to show a Christmas movie, or to celebrate the Nativity at any other time in the calendar is a taboo. Yet, within the correct framework and context it amounts to a form of 'sacred time'. As we shall see in chapter 3 in relation to Eliade, such practices amount to ritual space and time which construe and maintain our way of being in the world (see Price 2005: 202). It is the very intensity of 'play', in the respect that the religious celebration or the playing or screening of Christmas music and movies are festival-specific and take on a heightened form during this period, that makes their ability to engage and transform their participants so potent. When Joseph Price thus writes in relation to the performance of sports that the actions that take place are not just meaningful within the time frame but may, in addition, 'express meaning beyond the block of sacred time or provide release from the strictures of ordinary time' (Price 2005: 202–3; see also Deacy 2013: 199), it is clear that Christmas has something quite new and distinctive to offer even than sports as it is the very specificity of Christmas rituals that make them so efficacious.

In language redolent of Turner, Kate McCarthy makes a similar claim with respect to music concerts (with specific reference to Bruce Springsteen) when she implies that the opportunity for spontaneous *communitas* is made possible by the intensive, specific nature of the event or ritual where, in addition to the content of the music '*depicting* a kind of promised land' it also 'conjures it', thereby making it 'temporarily real for those participating' (McCarthy 2011: 33). I will pay close attention to the way music radio is involved in the same sort of *communitas* in chapter 3 when I will be examining whether the fact that *Christmas Junior Choice* is broadcast once a year, with no guarantee of future scheduling, makes its *communitas* dimension even more intense as, for its listeners/adherents/participants, it is a rare and special occasion to recapture the music and presentation associated with another era (neither the 'children's' music nor the presenter, Ed Stewart, are any more a regular feature of radio broadcasting in the UK), and the fact that the programme is transmitted live has the effect that it is not replicable, recyclable, or transferable to any other time in the year. To paraphrase what McCarthy writes about Springsteen's music, might *Junior Choice*, as with Christmas films, be able to 'reorient experience so dramatically that only the language of religion is adequate to expressing it' (McCarthy 2011: 27)? Might it, further, amount even to 'both source and medium of holy community, in which the radio transports the listener into a virtual, temporary promised land' (McCarthy 2011: 27)?

The great irony of Christmas, though, is that, while the festival can entertain such transformative rituals and experiences, it is often characterized as a period of acute anxiety and disenchantment. As Tracy puts it, 'Americans are bombarded with a flurry of marketing imagery that leads them on an annual consumerist chase after a chimera', and, he asks, 'How many people standing in line at the malls would say that their Christmas season is replete with warmth, affection, and neighborliness' (Tracy 2001a: 1)? Christmas is experienced, rather, 'by most adults as a time of intensified stress' (Tracy 2001a: 1). Schmidt also makes the instructive observation that 'Modern holidays and their rituals are often thought to be sadly insubstantial, ersatz, or hollow' (Schmidt 1995: 6), and Nissenbaum characterizes the problems as amounting to 'the greedy materialism, the jaded consumerism, the deliberate manipulation not only of goods but also of private desires and personal relationships into purchasable commodities' (Nissenbaum 1996: loc. no. 6441; see also Deacy 2013: 196). The assumption, here, is that there is a causal link between the pursuit of happiness and the spending on and acquisition of consumer goods. Accordingly, Belk sees the tension at Christmas as emanating from the fact that it is 'at once the greatest religious holy day and the greatest commercial holiday in the Christian world' (Belk 2001: 75; see also Deacy 2013: 196). But, it is not just a tension between two different types of religious observance—the one spiritual, the other material, as if we are all somehow devotees and celebrants of either one or the other (and as though 'both' were not an option). For, at one and the same time for each of us we have the competing tension of wanting to show our affection and to express private sentiment to our friends and family members while the very 'vehicle of affection' amounts to 'a material object, usually a commodity bought in a crowded, garishly decorated store' (Carrier 2001: 55). We may be purchasing mass-produced commodities from the marketplace—and 'as the result of capitalist exchange based purely on the cash-nexus' (Myers 2001b: 190)—only to give them to those within our 'domestic circle as personal, unique tokens of [our] individual affection' (Myers 2001b: 190). But, what is the alternative? As Miller sees it, the ritual of Christmas shopping may 'deaden the senses and crush our individuality' but it is also seemingly 'essential to the resurrection of the family and wider sociality' (Miller 2001: 21). Indeed, Christmas may be the most materialistic holiday in the year but, as Marling attests, it is 'also the year's primary occasion for considering the harsh realities of the world', and a festival that 'demands attention to outsiders and strangers' (Marling 2000: 159).

There is also the paradox that despite being bound up with the world of commerce and capitalism, Christmas is also synonymous with 'the home, handmade gifts, and spontaneous giving—the opposite of modern commercial activity' (Myers 2001b: 190). Miller also makes the instructive point that 'your shopping is dominated by your imagination of others, of what they desire of you and their response to you; it is about relationship to those who require something of you' (Miller 1998: 3). So, though unquestionably a celebration of consumption, Christmas is simultaneously an occasion for celebrating a quite different set of values, one in which the quest is one of perfection, akin even to that of the New Jerusalem, so that, rather than materialism per se Christmas functions rather as, in Restad's words, 'the last widely celebrated public recognition of the miraculous' (Restad 1995: 162). Christmas is thus the supreme paradox—a contested site of ideas, values, and hopes, the language of which crosses boundaries between the sacred and the secular, the holy and the profane. In the chapters that follow, this ambivalence will be examined in detail, to the point of enquiring whether Christmas is not simply a religious or a secular festival but whether the very category of religion is itself in need of more scrupulous and finely-tuned revision.

2

Revisiting the Religious Origins
and Essence of Christmas

THE ORIGINS OF CHRISTMAS

One of the curiosities of Christmas is that, notwithstanding the alleged Christocentric basis to the festival as alleged by Flynn, there is no written record of an annual celebration on 25 December that marks the actual birth of Christ until 354 CE when Julius I was bishop of Rome.[1] For the early Christians, birthdays were seen as pagan customs—emphasis was placed on the date of one's death rather than on one's birth as typified by the records surrounding early Christian martyrdoms—and there is nothing in the Gospels which gives us any indication of when Jesus was actually born (see Golby and Purdue 2000: 23). Indeed, although the Nativity story is so inextricably linked in people's imagination to the Christmas festival, it is ironic that only two of the four Gospels report it. It does not even feature elsewhere in the New Testament, where it is not the birth but the death and resurrection of Jesus that predominates. The first written material was by St. Paul and his letters give no indication of the birth of Jesus. As Forbes puts it, 'Perhaps Paul knew nothing about a nativity story of Jesus, or perhaps he did not consider it important' (Forbes 2007: 18). It was thus the Easter rather than the Christmas message which held supremacy, and it was not until the Middle Ages that Christmas emerged as the other major date in

---

[1] Not all sources agree on this date, however. According to John Storey, 'In AD 336 the new Christian Church of Rome established 25 December as the date of the Nativity, the central event in the developing Christian calendar' (Storey 2008: 17). See also Parker 2005: 21.

the Christian calendar (see Tallman 2010: 186). As far as the early Church was concerned these were not comparable festivals: 'Christmas came a poor second in the liturgical year' (Connelly 2000a: 1).

The very date of 25 December is itself arbitrary. A century and a half before 25 December was first identified as the birthday of Jesus, there is an earlier record dating from 200 CE by Clement of Alexandria where the date of Jesus' birth is given as 20 May (Tallman 2010: 186). Other dates that have been given over the years include 21 March (the Vernal Equinox), 29 March (which correlates with the Jewish Passover), 29 September (the Feast of Tabernacles), and 6 January, which is the date when the Armenian Church, who do not follow the Roman calendar, celebrate the festival.[2] The (eventual) reason given for 25 December would seem to be because the date coincided with the pagan winter solstice, specifically the great feast day of the Mithraic mystery religion, Dies Solis Invicti Nati, or Birthday of the Unconquered Sun, named after the god of light, Mithras, whose birthday was 25 December and which was initiated by Emperor Aurelian in 274 CE. As Harrison puts it, it was 'the practice of the Church in early times to seek rather to give a sacred significance to established pagan festivals than to abolish them altogether' (Harrison 1951: 11). Rather than a unique, unprecedented, and stand-alone festival, Christmas is, on this interpretation, 'the classic example of the Christian church coming to terms with the traditional customs and rites of the people, superimposing a Christian festival upon the pagan mid-winter holiday' (Golby and Purdue 2000: 23).

The correspondence between Christmas and the winter solstice was established after Christianity, whose origins were in the Mediterranean region, steadily spread northwards by early medieval missionaries towards Europe where they became fused with long established winter festivals, to the point that even in warmer climes today 'Christmas decorations and cards show a snow-covered roof or people bundled up for a sleigh ride' (Kelly 2004: 131). The birth of Jesus in a manger in Bethlehem thus became synonymous with a 'festival of lights to counter the darkness' at a time of the year when the days were shortest, 'with candles, torches and burning logs, and evergreens . . . used as symbols or decorations to symbolize life in the midst of apparent death' (Forbes 2007: 5). We see this particularly

---

[2] Writing in 1951, Michael Harrison looks at a range of such dates, including also 1 January, 10 January, 9 April, and 16–17 May (Harrison 1951: 15–16).

with respect to the northern European feast of Yuletide, also known as the Teutonic 'Midwinter', which by the ninth century CE had fully assimilated with Christmas, from which Golby and Purdue attest that 'many of the associations of our Christmas come: the warmth and good cheer around the Yule log, while outside there is darkness' (Golby and Purdue 2000: 23) and cold. Since Christmas and the solstice take place at the very time of the year when, in Waits' words, 'the seasons turned back from the deepest part of winter toward the planting season of spring' (Waits 1993: 9), then on a symbolic level the festival was able to mark the transition from death (as typified by the lack of plant growth) to new life, thereby representing 'the victory of lifeward trends over deathward trends' (Waits 1993: 9).

On one level, there is a distinctively Christological reason for celebrating the birth of Jesus, in that, in view of the Arian controversy in the early Church which emphasized the human side of Jesus' nature—specifically that the Father and Son existed on different levels such that, as only the Father is 'unbegotten', the Son was merely a creature—the decision to assign Jesus a birthday could be construed as a concession to Arianism without at the same time compromising the Church's emphasis on his divine status (see Restad 1995: 3). But, the uniquely Christian dimension of Christmas is more of a moot point. As one popular source puts it, the festival began 'so long before [Christ's] coming that we find its hero arriving on the scene after more than half of the time of the story has gone by' (Count and Count 1997: 15). Similarly, according to Clement Miles in 1912, relatively few people 'have any idea of the process by which the heathen elements have become mingled with that which is obviously Christian, and equal obscurity prevails as to the nature and meaning of the non-Christian customs' (Miles 1912: 19). The syncretic Christian–pagan nature of the festival certainly camouflages a central paradox. Although the two celebrations may have been assimilated, they embrace two antithetical perspectives about this world. On the one hand, the pagan winter festival was life-affirming and entailed a positive 'affirmation of man's relationship with the forces of nature and his ability to placate and encourage them' (Golby and Purdue 2000: 20). For early Christians, on the other hand, the ultimate goal in the period before Christianity became the official religion of the Roman Empire following Constantine's conversion in the early fourth century was heavenly afterlife, with this world merely a provisional and temporary, even inconvenient, precursor to the riches of what the next life had in store. Miles even went so far as to attest that Christianity was 'pessimistic as regards this earth, and valued it only as a place of discipline for the life to come; it was essentially a religion of renunciation that said "no" to the world' (Miles 1912: 24). So intrinsic was the afterlife to the early Christians that, as Badham and Badham put it, it was the 'absolute assurance of the reality of heaven which made the first followers of Christ so ready to suffer and die as martyrs to their faith' (Badham and Badham 1984: ix). Notwithstanding the important role that terrestrial and this-worldly understandings about the afterlife have played in Christian theology, which I have covered at length elsewhere,[3] there does seem to be a certain tension between the 'naturalistic' and the 'supernaturalistic' contours of what paganism and Christianity have traditionally encompassed to make their fusion something of an anomaly.

There may have been ways around this. Whereas in the pagan Saturnalia[4] and Kalends[5] festivals the focus may have been on revelry, by way of food, alcohol, and games, the focus of the Christian celebration of Christmas was functionally similar as it was focused, as Forbes tells us, on village gatherings, feasts, and special masses to mark the birth of Christ (see Forbes 2007: 112). Similarly, the pagan symbols of fertility and regeneration were appropriated by Christians, so that greenery came to represent Jesus as the Tree of Life (see Restad 1995: 56) and holly became a symbolic reminder of the crown of thorns worn by Jesus at his crucifixion (see Golby and Purdue 2000: 26),

---

[3] See *Screening the Afterlife*, chapter 5.

[4] Beginning on 17 December, and lasting for up to a week, Saturnalia was one of the biggest pagan winter festivals, named after the Roman god of the harvest, Saturn, and was characterized by indulgence, as well as the exchanging of presents such as candles, fruit, and clay dolls. It was also a period of the inversion of the established social order, with masters waiting on slaves at meals and slaves allowed a few days of relative 'freedom' to do as they wished. See e.g. Kelly 2004: 68, Forbes 2007: 9, and Golby and Purdue 2000: 26. Such behaviour continued in medieval times where in the Christian festivities of that period the so-called 'lords of misrule' were allowed an albeit temporary jurisdiction over their own affairs. See e.g. Mundy 2008: 171.

[5] This festival began on 1 January and inaugurated the New Year, involving the giving and receiving of presents. Such gift-giving gradually became associated with Christmas by the 1860s, though as Austin points out in France it is New Year rather than Christmas 'which is the primary occasion for gift-giving and general festivities' (Austin 2000: 165). Indeed, it is significant that it was not until the seventeenth century that the figure we now know as Father Christmas or Santa Claus became associated with the giving of presents at Christmas (see Tallman 2010: 187).

just as the celebrations that marked the rebirth of the sun could be given a Christian veneer by ensuring that adherents praised God as the source of new life and Jesus as the Light of the World. By identifying God with nature, 'pagan festivals could be ... transformed into Christian ones' (Harrison 1951: 14).[6] The irony is that some Christians were venerating the sun on 25 December as late as the fifth century (Kelly 2004: 67), causing figures such as Tertullian, Augustine, and Pope Leo I to have to offer rebuttals to claims that Sol was synonymous with the Christian God (see Hales 2010: 166) in the context of a winter festival which saw the birthday of the 'Sun' God being replaced by a focus on Jesus as the 'Son' of God. As Hales mentions, 'Clearly, it was a durable confusion' (Hales 2010: 166). For Forbes, too, it is not surprising that there were problems as 'Christians used solar symbolism to promote messages about Jesus Christ, and yet, at the same time church leaders struggled against worship of the sun' (Forbes 2007: 31).

Ultimately, the decision to schedule Christmas on the Birthday of the Unconquered Sun was political and expedient. As Parker contends, the 'Church authorities evidently felt the pagan festivities were too seductive, and needed a Christian rival if converts were to be attracted to the infant faith', the result being that 'the birth of Christ was offered in place of the rebirth of the sun' (Parker 2005: 21). In this respect, Christmas comprised an antidote to the debauchery that characterized Saturnalia, promoting what Kelly calls 'prayerful or at least moral behavior, in sharp contrast to pagan license' (Kelly 2004: 70). The so-called 'Christianization' of Christmas may not have been without complication. As Nissenbaum tells us, 'From the beginning, the Church's hold over Christmas was (and remains still) rather tenuous' as the number of people seeing the festival as a time of 'carnival' rather than 'pious devotion' (Nissenbaum 1996: loc. no. 255) were always in the majority. For Golby and Purdue, similarly,

---

[6] It came at a price, however. As Coffin sees it, 'It surely would have made sense had all gift-giving duties been conferred upon the Christ-child and all pagan sprites and Christian saints dismissed. But precision is not what the Church wanted in the early days. . . . [T]he Roman Catholic method had never been to eliminate pagan ritual or even change the time of pagan worship, but rather to allow the converts to continue what heathenish practices were dear to them, requiring only that the symbols and names of the Christian deities be introduced. Because of this leniency, bunny rabbits and colored eggs have become associated with Easter, hearts and flowers with St. Valentine, yule logs and mistletoe with Christmas' (Coffin 1973: 82).

'Despite the best and most creative endeavours of the Church, the essentially secular nature of the English Christmas persisted and was to endure into Tudor and Stuart times' (Golby and Purdue 2000: 29). Hence, when we read today of campaigns by conservative Christians to 'Keep Christ in Christmas' or to remind people that 'Jesus is the Reason for the Season' (see Forbes 2007: 32), we are witnessing a continuation of the idea to establish rectitude, discipline, and asceticism at this most profligate of seasons.

We see an even more extreme version of this distrust of the decadence of Christmas in the Reformation period when extreme forms of Protestantism denounced the festival 'as a popish, uncanonical extravagance' (Connelly 2000a: 2). In the seventeenth century, the Puritan founders of America even went so far as to ban Christmas—indeed, in 1644 Christmas was proclaimed a day of penance rather than a day for idle feasting—on the grounds that there was no reference to it in the Bible and it was not celebrated in the Early Church and was of dubious, pagan provenance (see Forbes 2007: 56). In Britain, too, Parliament at the time of Cromwell met as on any other day of the year and Christmas was struck from the list of 'holy days', with ministers who preached on Christmas Day even risking being sent to prison (see Restad 1995: 6). Even after the Commonwealth period, it was not until the Victorian era that Christmas experienced a revival, even if, as Connelly reminds us, 'it never totally lost its grip on the popular imagination' (Connelly 2000a: 2) following the Puritan clampdown. By the early nineteenth century, Golby and Purdue attest that Christmas 'was neither a major event in the calendar nor a popular festival' (Golby and Purdue 2000: 40), deemed less important than, say, Valentine's Day or New Year's Day (see Golby and Purdue 2000: 44), with many newspapers before the mid-1830s failing to give it anything other than the most cursory attention.[7] This all changed, however, by 1834 when Christmas Day became a Bank Holiday in Britain (see Belk 2001: 76) and in the United States Christmas Day was recognized as a public holiday by

---

[7] A different picture is presented, though, by David Parker who writes that at the start of the nineteenth century 'Christmas had become a festival more plebeian and bourgeois than patrician. It was looked forward to eagerly and celebrated ardently more by the have-nots than by the haves. But it was nonetheless thriving' (Parker 2005: 15).

every state starting with Alabama in 1836 and ending with Oklahoma in 1890.

What is striking, however, is the lack of any clear ecclesiastical or Christian reason for its resurgence. Ironically, in the Puritan era it was the very *absence* of a supposed Christian basis to the festival that resulted in its suppression, whereas in the Victorian age it would *seem* that the festival could not have been less Christian-centric. Schmidt writes, for instance, that 'by the end of the nineteenth century Christmas had come to stand out as a major religious event in American culture—a time to recount biblical stories of the Incarnation, sing religious hymns, stage Sunday school pageants, view Nativity scenes, decorate church interiors, hold special services, and contemplate God's mysterious work of redemption' (Schmidt 1995: 182). Yet, the contours of what was happening are far from this definitive. Golby and Purdue are not the only authors who take a far less categorical view of the reasons for Christmas's late nineteenth-century revival, as when they contend that 'The late Victorian Christmas had a spiritual significance but it was less a Christian spirituality than one which drew upon the warm but sentimental humanitarianism epitomised by Charles Dickens; it saluted and celebrated the family, childhood and the extended family of the nation' (Golby and Purdue 2000: 80). For Forbes, also, 'It is interesting to note that the return of Christmas was *not* the result of any concerted church-based campaign. Instead, it arose from efforts by cultural leaders and drew on broader cultural forces encouraging the general themes of generosity, family activities, and festivity in the middle of winter' (Forbes 2007: 66). In other words, it was more of a secular and commercial festival, and the Church was if anything on the back foot, responding to rather than initiating events outside of its control, to the extent that it was no less surprised than anyone else when, as Forbes puts it, the pews suddenly started filling up on Christmas morning (Forbes 2007: 66).

THE DICKENS CONNECTION

It is thus as a cultural, even a folk, rather than as a quintessentially Christian festival that the emergence of the modern Christmas should best be understood. What characterized Christmas by this period was not going to church per se but the communal event of carol-singing, the exchange of presents and cards and, especially, the focus on the importance of the domestic sphere and the coming together of hitherto (geographically) separated families. The extent to which Christmas as we celebrate it today was fashioned, even invented, in the Victorian period, rather than in any prior incarnation (pagan or otherwise), is an important factor to address. Indeed, for Connelly, the idea of Christmas that is most often explored in film is one which owes its origins to the vision which emerged in the nineteenth century wherein 'The Victorians took up Christmas and all its trappings and used them to celebrate home, family and charity', so that it was '[d]omesticated Christian values' (Connelly 2000a: 3) that preponderate. This fusion of Christianity and wider cultural and ideological values in the Victorian era reaches its apex in the Christmas literature of Charles Dickens which has been both acclaimed and adopted, even usurped, by Christians as epitomizing the essence of the Christian story of redemption while also, albeit subtly, offering a creative reworking of that narrative in a way that accommodates peculiarly Victorian tastes and tensions. On the one hand, Paul Davis has argued that 'Victorians of the 1870s read [Dickens'] Christmas story as a retelling of the biblical Christmas story' (in McCracken-Flesher 1996: 100) and, writing in *The Dickensian*, J. Hillis Miller went so far as to claim in 1993 that *A Christmas Carol* 'is Dickens's version of the New Testament miracle of the loaves and fishes or of Jesus's parable of the sower' (Miller 1993: 199). He wrote, further, that 'the basic story line of the *Carol* would support an argument that it belongs to the venerable genre of the conversion narrative' (Miller 1993: 200), the template of which is Paul's conversion to Christianity on the road to Damascus.

On the other hand, it is significant that Marling should see the *Carol* as, ultimately, 'a secular narrative, almost totally lacking in conventional religious references' (Marling 2000: 139). The short story was written in 1843 and in that decade it even managed to outsell the Bible in American bookstores (see Marling 2000: 150), with Russell Belk categorizing Dickens' tale of the miserly Ebenezer Scrooge who learns the 'true meaning' of Christmas after being subjected to visitations on Christmas Eve by the Ghosts of Christmases Past, Present, and Yet to Come, as the most prominent and most repeated *secular* Christmas tale in both Britain and America (see Belk 2001: 85). It is a moot point as to whether Dickens was explicitly creating a 'secular' version of the Christian Nativity story or whether his motivation was to mould Christmas into a framework that he thought would reaffirm 'the values of the family and the joyful inno-cence of childhood', espousing in the process 'qualities of human warmth and kindness, charity for the poor and moral regeneration' (Chapman 2000: 12)—attributes hardly anathema to a Christian sens-ibility but not exclusive to them either. This brings us to the heart of the matter. Chapman, for example, is emphatic: 'the Dickensian Christmas is not an explicitly religious one: it centres on the family and the hearth rather than the church and the pulpit' (Chapman 2000: 12). This does not of course mean that it cannot be construed in religious or theo-logical terms, and to this end Russell Belk is quite right in his affirm-ation that Dickens' story remains a 'sacred Christmas text' (Belk 2001: 85). Belk is quick, though, to qualify his position by arguing that its sacredness should be understood 'in a strictly non-religious sense involving myth, ritual, hierophany (showing itself to be supernatural), communitas (provoking a transcending camaraderie), and mystery' (Belk 2001: 85).

So, questions of religious definition need to be high on the agenda if we are to properly appreciate the extent to which the resurgence of the celebration of Christmas in the nineteenth century can be straightforwardly identified as an affirmation of *Christian* beliefs and values. What particularly stands out, for instance, in Dickens' classic is the private rather than communal dimension of the 'redemption' experienced by Scrooge. In lieu of the traditional social rituals and festivities associated with the season, Parker adroitly observes that for Dickens 'the festival was more important for the place it could assume within private narratives' as a time for 'inward contemplation, self-discovery, and personal redemption' (Parker 2005: 53). As Parker continues, the *Carol* 'explores a man's relation to his own past, his readiness or otherwise to live with it' and 'explores the consequences of choices he makes in the matter, upon his under-standing and his conduct' (Parker 2005: 177). Dickens' 'take' on Christmas is thus quite radical and revisionist. In Forbes' words, 'Dickens was not simply telling us about Christmas . . . ; he was also trying to change it, selectively re-creating Christmas' (Forbes 2007: 61). Any transformation or salvation achieved at Christmas is thus far removed from the pagan Saturnalia with its overturning of the estab-lished social order but is all about the resolution of inner, personal conflicts and feelings. None of this is strictly Christian in its frame of reference. The Nativity story is not a celebration of a misanthrope's realization of his need to change the way he spends his money or interacts with wider society. It is for this reason that Garrett goes so far as to blame Dickens' *Carol* for the way in which it conflates Scrooge's personal redemption 'with his willingness to celebrate Christmas', to the point that 'our occasional inability in twenty-first-century America to tell the difference between Christian redemption and Christmas spirit comes to us directly from "A Christmas Carol"' (Garrett 2007: 156). This may not be antithetical to the Christian narrative—indeed, as Garrett argues, if 'the story shows us a grace-driven redemption through supernatural intervention that drives a self-centered lout like Scrooge to treat his neighbors with justice and give to the poor' (Garrett 2007: 156–7) then there is nothing wrong with that. But, even if we are disposed to use the language of redemption, conversion, or salvation, it would be inaccurate to characterize what happens to Scrooge—the miserly businessman who 'learns from his memories and from the trials of his own past that charity is expedient' (Marling 2000: 139)—as synonymous with the birth and life of Jesus Christ.

What Dickens thus did was to fashion a narrative at the heart of which lies something 'very like the Christian ideal of emphasis on charity and community overcoming antisocial emphasis on the self' (Belk 2001: 88)—but, Christianity itself does not play an explicit role in Scrooge's trajectory. Dickens may have avowed that his books were Christocentric—Tara Moore even quotes him as having claimed that in every one of his novels 'there is an express text preached on, and the text is always taken from the lips of Christ' (Moore 2009: 38)—but there is scant evidence to suggest that Dickens was writing out of Christian conviction. In *A Christmas Carol*, there is no specific mention of Jesus or of Christianity, besides a few tangential references to church, as when we learn that 'the chimes of a neighbouring church struck the four quarters' (Dickens 1987: 32) and that 'the steeples called good people all to church and chapel' (Dickens 1987: 59). That said, when Scrooge awakes on Christmas morning and discovers that it is not too late to change his ways, Dickens underscores this decisive moment by informing us that 'He was checked in his transports by the churches ringing out the lustiest peals he had ever heard' (Dickens 1987: 101), and in between donating money to charity and spending Christmas afternoon at his nephew's house, we learn that Scrooge 'went to church' (Dickens 1987: 104). It is a moot point, however, as to whether Scrooge's newly-found 'redemption', if we can call it that, is a consequence of his having been set free by Christ's atoning blood on the Cross for the sins of the world, entailing as it does the restoration of the torn fabric of personal relationships between God and a fallen humanity due to Original Sin, or whether the presence of 'church' merely provides a rich symbolic background for what is a purely individual character arc and has happened independently of any Christological activity. If anything, Christianity's gospel of redemption is subsumed within Dickens' 'gospel' of social and humanitarian reform with the concomitant need to extend compassion and charity to the poor and disadvantaged. The Christian Gospel does not direct or dictate the parameters of Dickens' story, even if it would be less efficacious without that background adornment.

Indeed, it could be argued that it is precisely because of the albeit marginal backdrop of Christianity that Dickens' narrative has been able to assume the mantle of what James Chapman calls 'the most definitive of all Christmas stories' (Chapman 2000: 13) besides the Nativity. As Parker points out, for example, prior to *A Christmas Carol* 'redemption was something entirely new to Dickens's art', in the respect that his previous protagonists lacked the intensity of the transformation ascribed to Scrooge: 'Mr. Pickwick is not redeemed. He stops being silly. Nicholas Nickleby is not redeemed. He grows up' (Parker 2005: 198). What for Parker singles Scrooge out from his literary forebears is that, though they may change—'they improve, they reform'—they are not 'made anew' (Parker 2005: 198) in quite the same way. There may be a Christian veneer to *A Christmas Carol*, but it may be that Moore is right in her analysis that for all of Dickens' attempts to persuade others that 'the gospel dripped from every Christmas text he wrote' (Moore 2009: 124), the values that inform his writing are quintessentially Victorian, in their sentimental focus on the importance of the home and family and what Moore calls 'the myth of ideal Englishness' (Moore 2009: 43) where '[f]ragmented families were reunited, and the home nation was reconstituted as a caring place preferable to opportunities abroad' (Moore 2009: 25), rather than overtly Gospel ones.

Crucially, all of this works to Dickens' advantage. The net effect of his modern redemption story is that it connected with readers in a way that superseded what the Nativity story was able to accomplish. Flynn refers to a plethora of contemporary accounts 'in which stolid

Victorians whose families had not kept Christmas in generations sent for their first holiday turkey after reading *A Christmas Carol*' (Flynn 1993: 102). There was an immediacy and vehemence to Dickens' Christmas literature which led Robert Louis Stevenson to write to a friend in 1874 that he was persuaded to want to 'go out and comfort some one; I shall never listen to the nonsense they tell one about not giving money—I shall give money' and 'shall do it with a high hand' (in Moore 2009: 46). Dickens had effectively presented a vision of a world as it could be in which charity and generosity supplanted the qualities hitherto encapsulated in the barren, parsimonious life of Scrooge. Dickens' was a call to social action and, as Moore puts it, his literature 'offered the reader a chance to experience the Christmas utopia and consoled him with the hope that utopia could exist in reality if the so-called English precepts couched in the texts were carried out in real life' (Moore 2009: 46). Christmas is pivotal to this dynamic as it encapsulated nostalgia for a past that may never have existed in actuality but whose values of stability and order were the prototype for present and future action. As Golby and Purdue see it, indeed, in *A Christmas Carol* 'Christmas becomes a bridge between the world as it is and the world as it should be' (Golby and Purdue 2000: 45).

Yet, at the same time, there is rather more to Scrooge's 'redemption' than a spiritual transformation or conversion. For, aside from the quixotic and utopian (though undoubtedly heartfelt) odyssey that Stevenson was inspired to undertake upon reading Dickens, much of the literature on *A Christmas Carol* points to the rather more prosaic and material nature of the narrative on display, as when McCracken-Flesher detects that Dickens' story 'has become conflated with our culture's dominant economic narrative, the Christmas narrative of corporate sales' (McCracken-Flesher 1996: 93). As she sees it, 'Almost every year since the tale's publication . . . , a new stage production, radio performance, television show or movie has served to demarcate the month of December as ritual space reserved for Christmas', with the irony that a tale whose achievement has been to designate 'sacred time' has ended up setting 'that time apart for secular spending' and in stimulating the economy by coercing the 'spiritually needy' to 'participate in transactions redeeming primarily to corporate and national economies' (McCracken-Flesher 1996: 94). A different form of redemption may thus be on offer to what Dickens himself may have intended, and it is fitting to this end that in one of the most creative cinematic interpretations of *A Christmas Carol*, the Richard

Donner-directed *Scrooged* (1988), starring Bill Murray as a mercenary TV executive whose goal is to stage a live Christmas Eve spectacular of the Dickens story with an eye on the huge advertising revenue that will accrue, should be set in a world of rampant commercialism, materialism, and greed. As one reviewer from the period, John Pym, states, Murray's character is a 'two-dimensional Dickensian cipher, obsessed with the faintly sadistic pleasure of making heaps of money from the abhorrent sentimentality' (Pym 1988: 370–1) of his project.

There may be a conversion at the heart of Dickens' tale, but, on such a reading, it takes the form not of a spiritual revelation or encounter but the realization that it is what one does with one's money that matters most. Scrooge does not simply come to renounce (his former dependence on) material possessions. Quite the opposite, in fact. He chooses to give up the hoarding of money and to spend it instead on those who might benefit from it, as betokened by his decision on Christmas morning to provide a Christmas turkey for his clerk, Bob Cratchit, and his family. For Storey, however, this is no radical or revolutionary episode: 'Charity is a temporary redistribution of wealth which does not disturb the hierarchies of wealth; in fact, it safeguards the hierarchies of wealth' (Storey 2008: 26). Storey's premise, here, is that Scrooge's 'conversion' to charity poses no threat to the status quo. Scrooge is simply choosing, quite arbitrarily, to share some of his wealth with those with whom he has come into contact. This is no upturning of the social or economic order, the government does not need to intervene, and we can only speculate as to whether Scrooge's new-found penchant for charity is even a permanent fixture. Tristram P. Coffin is withering in his contempt for the supposed transformation that is ascribed to Scrooge, in the respect that there is no change in the working conditions of his employee, Bob Cratchit, who merely receives a (deserved) raise in his earnings. According to Coffin, Cratchit 'merely gets a raise quite in line with "reasonable" demand without being offered better opportunities or any basic change in his lot. What, logic asks, about the other unfortunate "cratchits" around town' (Coffin 1973: 157)? Scrooge's redemption is thus quite a conservative one. As Miller puts it, 'No suggestion is made that the class and gender arrangements of Victorian England should be fundamentally altered' (Miller 1993: 204). The most that Dickens has done, on this interpretation, is to be critical of, but not to oppose or seek to dismantle, the edifice of capitalism. All that is entailed is the 'personal patronage' (Restad 1995: 146) of a wealthy individual to ameliorate the plight of one less fortunate, and not due to any objective criteria. Rather, it is down to the discretion (or whim) of the patron, and, in any case, the Cratchits 'had first to demonstrate that they were worthy objects of Scrooge's new found charitable attentions' (Restad 1995: 146).

The most we can therefore say is that Dickens' *Carol* makes a 'powerful argument for Christian charity, but it does not appear to advocate any substantial changes in the social system of Dickens's time' (Miller 1993: 205). The first half of the nineteenth century was a time when 'the bitterness of ordinary life in the hovels' where families had to live 'and in the factories and mines' where they often had to work 'for insufferable hours' (Vidler 1988: 91) often went unacknowledged, and although, as Vidler informs us, individual churchmen were active in promoting social reform it tended to be on the grounds not of justice but of charity (Vidler 1988: 98). If there were social evils then it was thought that they could be 'cured by voluntary action, either by stimulating the benevolent sentiments of the rich and powerful, or by persuading the poor to help themselves' (Vidler 1988: 98), as exhibited by the endeavours of Wilberforce and Shaftesbury who were passionately concerned to fight social ills but did so very much within the present system, taking for granted the current social hierarchy as existed between the factory master and his workers. Scrooge very much fits into this mould. There is no radical social conscience in Dickens' novel along the lines of the precepts of the Book of Amos or, indeed, anything resembling what Miller calls the following of 'Christ's injunction to give all he has to the poor and follow Christ in poverty' (Miller 1993: 204).

Rather, one of the abiding memories of the 1970 cinematic adaptation, *Scrooge*, starring Albert Finney in the title role, is the sight of Scrooge running 'wild in a series of shops' and parading 'the streets to the accompaniment of massed voices that celebrate the joys of buying and getting' (McCracken-Flesher 1996: 101). Indeed, we see him at the end of the film dressed up as Father Christmas, dancing down the street and bestowing gifts (see Chapman 2000: 26), which very much brings us to the heart of the paradox of Christmas. On the one hand it is an opportunity for those who have it to enjoy their wealth without what Miller calls the concomitant 'reification and asocial abstractions of goods as commodities' (Miller 2001: 19). Scrooge's acceptance of the importance of family values—expressed both through his being a benefactor to the Cratchits and his decision to finally take up his own nephew's offer to celebrate Christmas with his relations—is Dickens' way of showing that materialism need not be a barrier to the possession and manifestation of a social conscience. As Nissenbaum puts it, Scrooge 'becomes ready to transform the emotionally hollow culture of sheer greed into a more fulfilling culture in which everyday activities and relationships are softened by family values' (Nissenbaum 1996: loc. no. 4562).

Yet, on the other hand what stands out throughout is that Dickens' tale is centred far more on Scrooge's personal redemption, which he achieves by ameliorating the plight of the Cratchits and making an anonymous donation to two charity collectors that he had previously rebuffed, than on the recipients of his new-found patronage. The *Carol* even, arguably, embeds Scrooge's own redemption so indissolubly in the heart of the narrative that we have the ironic spectacle of Scrooge himself being a recipient of a gift from Cratchit, rather than simply the other way around, as, in Restad's words, 'the example of Cratchit's life helped Scrooge realize his own humanity' (Restad 1995: 146). The story thus has more to do with 'Scrooge's rescue from a solitary and miserly life' than with 'the Cratchit's poverty of hard currency' (Restad 1995: 146). When J. Hillis Miller thus writes that 'Each reading of *A Christmas Carol* can make possible (though by no means inevitable) a small break in history that allows a new start changing the future' and that the fact that 'a somewhat more equitable distribution of property and privilege has occurred in the hundred and fifty years since *A Christmas Carol*'s first publication' may be a result of 'all those innumerable readings of the *Carol*' (Miller 1993: 206), this is to overplay the emphasis of Dickens' novel which is, at its heart, about the redemption of a rich man into a philanthropic (but still rich) one. It is hardly tantamount to the radical thrust of, say, the Christian Socialist movement of 1848–54 which 'speedily attracted public attention, and the scorn of the privileged orders of society' (Bowen 1968: 315), and whose leaders, which included Charles Kingsley and F.D. Maurice, were churchmen who realized that, in Vidler's words, 'the Gospel of Christ must have something better to say to the working men of England than what the official Church was saying' (Vidler 1988: 95). Whereas proponents of Christian socialism attacked the competitive, commercial nature of the status quo, and specifically its prevailing laissez-faire ideology on theological grounds (see Vidler 1988: 96), and sought to usher in a new era of social cohesion and national purpose, so that, for

Maurice, a nation of competing shopkeepers would be converted into a family of loving Christians (see Bowen 1968: 316), the supremely individual nature of the redemption that Scrooge has the luxury to undergo does seem somewhat remote from the very real and pressing needs of the age.

It is all the more significant therefore that, as Paul Davis wrote in 1990, *A Christmas Carol* 'has been adapted, revised, retold, reoriginated and modernised more than any other work of English literature' (in Collins 1993: 173). In particular, Hollywood has taken more than a passing interest in the Dickensian Christmas, with films ranging from *It's a Wonderful Life* (1946) in the 1940s to *Mr Destiny* (1990) and *Groundhog Day* (1993) in the 1990s to *The Family Man* (2000) and *Click* (2006) in the first decade of the twenty-first century, all recycling facets of the Scrooge parable as various short-sighted, selfish, egocentric, or money-hoarding protagonists undergo transformative experiences, often as a result of some supernatural or magical *deus ex machina*, into more enlightened, compassionate, and sagacious individuals. Walsh sums up the connection between *A Christmas Carol* and *It's a Wonderful Life* as follows:

> In both stories, on Christmas Eve, supernatural beings (an angel in *Life*, spirits in *Carol*) visit a man of business who is in serious peril. Each man has until now misunderstood the significance of his life and career and needs correcting. Both must review and reassess their past lives (and their possible futures) in order to come to the truth, although neither of them desires to do so. In neither story can the man intervene in the scenes the supernatural beings allow him to see. In both cases, the reassessment brings wisdom, happiness, and salvation (Walsh 2001: 58).

Obviously there are differences in the respect that, unlike Scrooge, George Bailey is a caring and philanthropic businessman who puts people before profit (rather than the other way around)—Mamet calls him 'a banker-altruist, dedicated to the community' (Mamet 2002: 22)—and in his struggle to make ends meet and the love he receives from a large and caring family he seems somewhat closer in essence to Bob Cratchit than to Ebenezer Scrooge.[8] The setting of such films

---

[8] Walsh makes the astute point to this end that '*Carol* ends with an enlightened Ebenezer doing deeds of generosity, whereas *Life* ends with an enlightened George *receiving* (at last!) generosity' (Walsh 2001: 59).

may also be different, in that they tend to be oriented around small towns (Bedford Falls in *It's a Wonderful Life* and Punxsutawney in *Groundhog Day*) rather than the metropolis of London. But, the Dickensian emphasis on the Christmas spirit looms large, even if, as Munby points out, the 'darker implications' of Capra's film, where the Scrooge-like figure of Mr Potter (Lionel Barrymore) is not redeemed at the end but remains 'an immanently evil presence', beg 'questions about the redemptive power of Christmas even as it appropriated Christmas to manufacture a happy ending' (Munby 2000: 53).

We see a similar dynamic at work in *Groundhog Day*, which, as Gilbey points out, 'borrows the idea of a decayed soul getting the chance to pick himself up, dust himself off and start all over again, although here it's millions of chances, millions of starts' (Gilbey 2004: 9), as the protagonist, Phil Connors (Bill Murray), awakes each morning to find that it is the same ice-cold wintry day in the same small town which he is destined to repeat until he finally changes his character.[9] In both cases, though, a spark of their former selves remains. In the case of Scrooge, Parker observes that he 'remains as mischievous and manipulative as ever' (Parker 2005: 214), as when he plays a game with Bob Cratchit on Boxing Day by pretending to be aggrieved that his clerk has arrived for work a few minutes late—'I am not going to stand this sort of thing any longer' (Dickens 1987: 107)— before announcing that he is going to increase his salary. Connors, likewise, still acts in a supercilious and impish fashion at the end of *Groundhog Day*, as shown by the banter he shares with Rita (Andie Macdowell) around how fortunate she is to have 'won' his services for a night in a charity bachelor auction at the Groundhog Festival Banquet, the difference being that he is now open to the needs and concerns of others rather than just caring about himself.

To be fair, not all commentators have shown great enthusiasm towards the repetitive use of the Dickens formula in popular culture. In his review of *Ulee's Gold* (1997) in the April 1998 edition of *Sight and Sound*, Philip Kemp expressed his disappointment that the story line, in which a Florida beekeeper who has hitherto rejected the

---

[9] There is a difference, though, in that whereas Scrooge had three ghosts to show him the error of his ways, Phil Connors in *Groundhog Day* has to work it out for himself. In Gilbey's words, 'While ghosts accompany Scrooge, commenting helpfully on his torment, Phil is abandoned without instruction or insight in his icy, isolated hell' (Gilbey 2004: 11).

advances of 'outsiders' into his enclosed and isolated dysfunctional home finally becomes receptive to the intervention of others when his family is threatened, should be so 'predictable', especially after having devoted 'so much attention to lived reality' (Kemp 1998: 56). In Kemp's words, 'The parable of the misanthropic loner, forced to relate to others and discovering the joys of emotional openness, was hardly new when Dickens used it in *A Christmas Carol*, and we've seen it a thousand times since' (Kemp 1998: 56).[10] Such 'narrative overdetermination' (Kemp 1998: 56) is certainly a staple Hollywood device and Dickens' *Carol* has provided the template for just about every film set at Christmas time. In *Miracle on 34th Street* (1947/ 1994), the ghosts of Dickens' story have simply been replaced by Santa Claus who brings about what Connelly calls 'the quasi-religious epiphany' (Connelly 2000b: 121), in the form of an 'unbelieving' mother slowly coming round to seeing what her young daughter has known all along—that magical things can happen, as betokened by the tag line of the 1994 remake which beseeches audiences to 'Discover the Miracle'. A sense of wonder and surprise may conclude that picture, but it is not that far removed from Kemp's indictment of Hollywood wherein 'Closure is absolute; nothing can be left tentative and open' (Kemp 1998: 56). Everything is neatly tied up at the denouement with the possibility of a fresh start and a new life (literally in the case of the 1994 *Miracle* as we learn that the mother of the tale might be able to give her daughter the present of a new brother or sister, to complement the new house and the new step-father that had hitherto been missing from her world). We do not know what the future will hold as the film, as with all Christmas films, concludes on Christmas Day, but the tone is immeasurably upbeat and optimistic.

Yet, for all of their emphases on miracles and redemptive journeys, Christmas films, whether explicitly or implicitly influenced by Dickens' formula, lack a crucial ingredient which makes their straightforward Christian identification or pedigree difficult to ascertain. Without disputing that the possibility of divine intervention plays an

[10] The analogies come thick and fast. Sara Vaux writes illuminatingly, for example, about the link between Dickens' *Carol* and Clint Eastwood's *Gran Torino* (2008) in the respect that Walt Kowalski (Clint Eastwood) 'confronts his poisonous memories to cleanse his guilt by giving his love and his life to his new friends, the outcast Hmong family' (Vaux 2012: 204), having hitherto refused that gift.

instrumental role in many Christian theologies, and is certainly compatible with the work of Karl Barth for whom God's infinite freedom entails that God is free to act in ways that lie beyond the parameters and limitations of our finite human comprehension (see Barth 1968: 310), the differences between more traditionally Christian and Hollywood delineations of divine intervention are far-reaching. In Christmas films, the intervention of an angelic or supernatural character, usually Santa Claus, is normally enough to bring about the transformation that we see via the intervention of the three ghosts in Dickens' *Carol* as unreconstructed, reclusive, or misanthropic individuals are transformed into their opposites. But, as we saw from the brief example in the previous chapter of the sudden transformation of the Judge Reinhold character in *The Santa Clause* from disbelieving sceptic to unalloyed believer in the existence of Santa Claus, this is rarely entailed by any great character arc or trajectory or by anything resembling how in the case of Christianity redemption is not simply a passive process but entails a fundamental and decisive break with one's past life and the concomitant entry into a new covenant or relationship with the Divine (see Deacy 2005: 26). In Christianity it is not enough for the individual to be submissive in the face of God and to abdicate all responsibility in the favour of angelic or messianic beings who will shoulder the burden for us. So, if there are such stark differences of approach, why even attempt to correlate Christmas with Christianity? In order to understand this, the next section will explore the way in which Santa and Jesus have often been fused in the popular imagination, and, as we shall see, it is the differences rather than the convergences which prove most illuminating.

FROM SCROOGE TO SANTA . . . TO JESUS?

On a functional level, Scrooge, Santa, and Jesus all play completely interchangeable roles. We have already examined how for Dickens *A Christmas Carol* was intended to be consonant with the Nativity story (even if the differences are insuperable), and it is revealing that in *Scrooge* (1970) the protagonist, played by Albert Finney, literally dons Santa's outfit. Strictly speaking, this is an anachronism as it was not until 1863, two decades after Dickens was writing, that the illustrator Thomas Nast established in *Harper's Weekly* the image of Santa that

we associate with him today: 'a large, jovial, white-bearded figure
dressed in a red suit with white fur trimmings and a matching cap'
(Golby and Purdue 2000: 73). It would not have been possible,
therefore, for Ebenezer Scrooge to have dressed in this fashion,
though for the makers of the 1970 musical historical exactitude is
less important than the symbolism afforded by this correlation. For
Santa's association with generous present-giving to deserving children is quite the antithesis of the pre-reformed Scrooge who responds
to the invitation to give to the poor and deserving by asking the two
charity collectors he encounters early on in the narrative: 'Are there
no prisons?... And the union workhouses... Are they still in operation?... Those who are badly off must go there', and 'If they would
rather die' then 'they had better do it, and decrease the surplus
population' (Dickens 1987: 16–17).

In truth, questions of historicity are especially problematic when it
comes to any discussion pertaining to the figure of Santa Claus, who,
the Scrooge factor aside, 'seems to be descended from a hodge podge
of figures, none of whom have any connection to Christmas or Jesus
of Nazareth' (Lowe 2010: 2).[11] Rather, for Lowe, a more fitting
association is with the Greek god of the sea Poseidon or his Roman
counterpart Neptune than anything from Christian tradition, not
least in terms of his being the patron saint of sailors and fishermen.
Yet, the Christian roots of the modern Santa are well documented (if
hardly based on a sound factual footing). His origins can be traced to
the fourth-century Christian saint, Nicholas, who was bishop of Myra
in Asia Minor from 280 to 342 CE.[12] As with his modern incarnation,
Santa Claus, he was as far removed from the early Scrooge as would
be possible to countenance, in his generosity, particularly towards
families and children, and as the special patron, even the patron saint,
of unmarried women, orphans, students, poets, travellers, seafarers,
pawnbrokers, bankers, butchers, millers, merchants, grocers, brewers,

---

[11] As Schmidt puts it, 'As a figure of hagiography, folklore, and legend, Santa Claus
was a motley compound of European traditions and American embellishments'
(Schmidt 1995: 130). He continues: 'All in all, it is something of an understatement to
say that American Santa Claus lore through the middle decades of the nineteenth century
was a heterogeneous jumble of images, stories, and legends' (Schmidt 1995: 132).

[12] deChant gives us this date, but it is not shared by all writers. According to Count
and Count, for example, St. Nicholas died on 6 December 326 CE (Count and Count
1997: 65).

tanners, candle makers, firefighters, apothecaries, the falsely accused, and childless couples (see deChant 2002: 186; Bennett 2009: 71, 74; Ebon 1975: 2). He is also alleged to have exorcized demons and performed miracles, most notably bringing the dead, including three students, back to life. It is only in later centuries that the records of his life accumulated (see Ebon 1975: 4)—during the late Middle Ages, for example, a number of legends accrued surrounding how he had 'snatched babies, children, and students from the jaws of disaster' (Bennett 2009: 75) and by the end of the fifteenth century over 2,500 churches, chapels, monasteries, hospitals, schools, and works of art had been dedicated to him in Western Europe alone[13] (Bennett 2009: 67–8)—so we are hardly dealing with reliable source material.

Indeed, rather than an historical figure who lived during the reigns of the Roman Emperors Diocletian, Maximilian, and Constantine, St. Nicholas appears to be a synonym for just about every type of cause and person. As Bennett puts it, the history of St. Nicholas 'crosses oceans, deserts, and frozen arctic climes', becoming 'an adventure tale complete with emperors, knights, villains, shipwrecks, kidnappings, treasure, and dark dungeons' (Bennett 2009: 3). At one time, as Ebon records, St. Nicholas was behind only Jesus and the Virgin Mary 'in frequency and intensity of worship' (Ebon 1975: 2), particularly in Russia. Within this context it is not surprising that he is alleged to have been not just present at the Council of Nicaea in 325 CE but had led the charge there against the Arian 'heresy' according to which Jesus was no more than a creature, even though no ancient historians actually place him at the Council (see Coffin 1973: 78). Even when the Protestant Reformation sought to eradicate the worship of saints, Nicholas managed to survive, albeit as a figure of folklore whose domain moved into the domestic sphere, where he was especially popular with children, rather than as an ecclesiastical personage (see Bennett 2009: 87; Ebon 1975: 87).

Concomitant with this change of setting were local variations surrounding the name that was ascribed to him, from Père Noël in France to Kris Kringle[14] and then Santa Claus in the United States

---

[13] We also learn that the Viking cathedral in Greenland is dedicated to St. Nicholas, that Christopher Columbus dedicated a port to him in Haiti and Jacksonville, Florida, was named after him by Spaniards (see Coffin 1973: 81).

[14] As Martin Luther objected to the practice of presents being given to children in the name of St. Nicholas, Kris Kringle emerged as the agent who brought forth presents at Christmas. He was initially known as Christkindlein (or 'messenger of

(via those Protestant immigrants who settled in Pennsylvania from Europe) to Father Christmas in Britain. In some traditions, in parts of Belgium, Germany, and Scandinavia, children to this day hang up their stockings on 6 December, on the anniversary of his death, rather than on 25 December (see Walsh 2001: 6), a tradition that began as early as the Middle Ages (Bennett 2009: 83). On this day, St. Nicholas, who was much more of a disciplinarian figure, would bring presents for those children who had been good and, in some customs, an alter-ego called Ruprecht or Pelznickel (or in some writings Belsnickel [see Restad 1995: 49]) would punish the children that St. Nicholas deemed to have behaved badly (see Waits 1993: 123), until in due course the figure of Santa Claus rewarded all children equally. The break between St. Nicholas and Santa is brought out most effectively in terms of their iconographical depictions. Although both have white beards and hair and don red ceremonial attire, Nicholas was a tall, lean, and ascetic figure whereas Santa is overweight and the personi-fication of indulgence (deChant 2002: 186). As Ebon points out, despite 'all its admixtures of European symbols and memories, today's Santa Claus is clearly the creation of nineteenth-century America' (Ebon 1975: 99).

The association between Santa and Scrooge is thus not quite as discrete as might at first appear, with both emerging in the same decade, albeit in New York and London respectively. Washington Irving even referred to Santa as the patron of New York (Restad 1995: 46). Writing under the pseudonym Diedrich Knickerbocker, Irving wrote in 1809 in his *History of New York* that the first Dutch colonists had sailed to New Amsterdam in a ship which boasted 'a goodly image of St. Nicholas' (in Bennett 2009: 97) and appeared to one of the settlers in a dream to show them where to build their new city. The Christmas connection arose when in an 1821 poem in an illus-trated book called *The Children's Friend* St. Nicholas appeared for the first time (as 'Old Sancteclaus') not on 6 December but on Christmas Eve (see Nissenbaum 1996: loc. no. 1554), and then Clement Clark Moore's 1822 poem 'A Visit from St. Nicholas' (also often

---

Christ'). See Belk 2001: 77–8. As Harrison points out, however, 'so little resemblance does "Christ-kind" bear, either to episcopal Nicholas or to divine Christ, that "Christ-kind" often appears as a tall young girl, with long flaxen hair, dressed in white!' (Harrison 1951: 213), and so appears as a sort of good fairy.

known as 'The Night Before Christmas'), where Santa is referred to as 'a right jolly old elf' (Moore 1912: loc. no. 70), introduced his reindeer and sleigh and his ascent up chimneys to deliver toys in children's stockings.[15] This developed by the 1860s into Thomas Nast's illustration in *Harper's Weekly* of the familiar image we have today of Santa Claus living at the North Pole, from where he could spy on the world's children through a telescope (see Bennett 2009: 103) and where the lists were kept of all the children, good and bad. So endemic is this representation of Santa that, in America at any rate, the Bishop Nicholas had been completely eradicated by this time[16] and replaced by a tangible (not least by his appearance in shopping malls) and congenial grandfather figure.

The irony is that, despite his virtual creation in the nineteenth century, Santa Claus was also the embodiment of a decidedly old-fashioned Christmas and, as Nissenbaum tells us, 'a figure of great antiquity' whereby, in introducing him into their households, Americans 'were carrying on an authentic, ancient, and unchanging Dutch folk tradition' (Nissenbaum 1996: loc. no. 3509). Though his origins were in a very particular, commercialized environment he was at the same time seen to be a figure who transcended time and place and stood for the nostalgic longing (on the part of adults) for a happier, utopian past. Paradoxically, therefore, he could be both very real, as a corpulent distributor of material goods, and also the personification of selfless giving. In Ebon's words, 'we are perpetuating an altruistic image of ourselves', so that 'despite the pressures of a materialistic civilization' we can demonstrate to ourselves, via the creation of Santa Claus, that we are 'capable of giving for giving's sake' (Ebon 1975: 114). Moreover, we can even do it without seeking any reward or gratitude as the credit for the gifts is assigned to someone else, prompting Hales to call the act of giving 'in the name of Santa . . . the holy act of sacrificial offering' (Hales 2010: 170).[17]

---

[15] There is much controversy surrounding the authorship of this poem, as it was first published anonymously in the *Sentinel* in 1823.

[16] Golby and Purdue go even further: 'Santa Claus swept aside all rivals, such as the German Pelz-Nickel and Kriss Kringle (the Christkind), in America and he rapidly imposed his personality and customs upon the English Father Christmas. The names Father Christmas and Santa Claus became interchangeable in Britain . . .' (Golby and Purdue 2000: 73).

[17] To this we can add Jacques T. Godbout's acknowledgement of one of the paradoxes of Christmas: 'Why, after having indebted, if not ruined, themselves in

There may be detractors from this position, as when Flynn counsels that 'Where Santa Claus is concerned, parents are persuading their children to accept as fact a legend that, in their own minds, consists of little more than repressed memories of their own childhood disappointments' (Flynn 1993: 141). But whereas Flynn is concerned that Santa is merely a fabrication and someone that parents duplicitously choose to lie about to their children, his point overlooks the more complex mythology surrounding Santa as he is able to tap into and embody our ultimate hopes, fears and aspirations 'as a symbol of assurance, trust, piety, kindness, and selflessness' (Ebon 1975: 113). Indeed, as Schmidt writes in the context of the emergence of Santa in the Victorian period, 'The Victorian Santa Claus (and all he promised) roused the religious imagination.... His superabundant bag of toys ... condensed into an overflowing pack, was the embodiment of a blessed childhood' (Schmidt 1995: 140).

Crucially, Santa mediated between two sets of seemingly incongruous worlds—the material and the spiritual on the one hand and the utopian past vs. the unstable and inauthentic present on the other. These competing values could then be played off against each other, so that any suggestion that Santa was the ambassador of materialist greed, as epitomized by his association with department stores in American cities, could be offset by the sort of picture presented by L. Frank Baum whose *The Life and Adventures of Santa Claus*, published in 1902, emphasized his origins within nature (specifically from within an enchanted and magical forest). Lévi-Strauss thus had the wrong end of the stick when he wrote in his 1952 article 'Father Christmas Executed' that 'He is not a mythic being, for there is no myth that accounts for his origin or his function' (Lévi-Strauss 2001: 43). In many films Santa's mythological backstory is a recurring

---

this ever-growing potlatch of Christmas presents that pile up under the lit tree, do parents go to the trouble of denying the gifts come from them, of making the children who receive them think their parents had nothing to do with it all, of attributing the act to a personage who has no merit other than that of bringing presents ... ? It's as though the parents are trying to prove to themselves that they expect no gratitude for the gift, that they are not "real" donors, not the only ones at any rate, that the only things that count for them is the child's pleasure, that they are giving only for the pleasure of it, not even for gratitude. They accept the fact that this gratitude will be directed towards an unreal individual, and they even arrange things so that this will be the case. The donor's pleasure is important, but it is dissociated, thanks to Santa Claus, from any gratitude aimed towards the true source of the gift' (Godbout 1998: 43–4).

feature, as when in *Santa Claus: The Movie* (1985) attention is given to his special, even divine, origin with Santa learning that he is an immortal and able to fulfil the prophecy of the 'ancient one' by delivering toys in a single night, Christmas Eve, to all the children of the world, and where the North Pole is synonymous with heaven (Belk even writes that in this movie 'North Pole is situated in Heaven' [Belk 2001: 81]).

Santa is thus a fluid, even slippery, figure who navigates antithetical realms, bestowing a sense of order, cohesion, and paternal wisdom wherever he goes. Mundy, for instance, refers to him 'as a benign materialist deity capable of addressing the contradictions between scarcity and indulgence, between sentimental parental knowingness and innocent childhood expectations, between belief, imagination and their absence' (Mundy 2008: 169). The paradoxes come especially to the fore in Christmas movies where he can be both omniscient and godlike and at the same time in need of saving from unscrupulous and even evil forces, as when in *Santa Claus: The Movie* his toy factory is under siege from a cutthroat, rival manufacturer who even manages to coax one of Santa's top elves into working for him. In *Fred Claus* (2007), similarly, the North Pole is in danger of being closed down because Santa's factory is not as efficient as those of his more capitalist-orientated counterparts, and the film engineers a crisis as a manic depressive Santa is in need of rescue by an assortment of friends and family. In an animated short from 1991, *Father Christmas*, we are even introduced to a Father Christmas, voiced by Mel Smith, who tries to escape recognition on the other 364 days of the year when he is not working and finds it difficult to 'fit in' anywhere—a case, perhaps, of being in the world but not of the world. Finally, in Palestinian director Elia Suleiman's *Divine Intervention* (2002), we have a Santa who may be of divine origin but, as S.F. Said wrote in his article on the film in the January 2003 edition of *Sight and Sound*,

> He's being chased by a gang of vicious-looking children. The sack of presents on his back is slowing him down, so he throws some shiny parcels out to his pursuers. But they're not after presents. They're after him. Speeding up, they run Santa to ground by a hilltop church. He stands there, cornered, gasping for breath—and it's only now that the camera moves in close enough for us to see the knife sticking out of his guts (Said 2003: 17).

RELATIONSHIP BETWEEN SANTA AND JESUS

In all of these cases there is a curious juxtaposition of competing Christological elements, as a Santa who is omniscient, omnibenevolent, and able to perform miracles is also a conflicted and, as epitomized in *Fred Claus*, an unstable personality. Indeed, in *Fred Claus*, Santa may be a timeless, saintly, miracle-worker, but, as Jane Lamacraft puts it, we also observe him 'fretting about delivery quotas and comfort-eating his way to ill-health and obesity' (Lamacraft 2008: 62), and who is unable to deliver presents to all of the children of the world on Christmas Eve because he has injured his back after fighting with his older brother. In *Miracle on 34th Street* (1947) the protagonist's claim to be Santa Claus results in the ignominy of being incarcerated and then undergoing a mental competency hearing on Christmas Eve. In each of these instances we find a perhaps surprising analogy with how a twofold conception of the nature and person of Jesus Christ lies at the very heart of the Christian tradition, where debates concerning the divine and human facets of Jesus' personality resulted in the definition of faith that was drawn up at the Council of Chalcedon in 451 CE which endeavoured, albeit paradoxically, to hold together and synthesize these fundamental tensions by speaking of Jesus as both fully human and fully divine. Literature on the Christological provenance of comic book superhero films, for example, is extensive, as betokened by a 1997 article in *Media Development*, 'Batman Crucified: Religion and Modern Superhero Comic Books', in which Bruce David Forbes, a Professor of Religion, writes that 'The symbolism of a Christ figure rests not only on his divinity but also on his humanity' with the vulnerability of comic book superheroes, most obviously Batman, making them particularly suitable examples of Christ figures and redeemer figures in contemporary culture, not least because 'to serve as a Christ figure, one has to be vulnerable, which the humanized superheroes are' (Forbes 1997: 12).

Writing more recently, Adele Reinhartz has argued that in superhero films the heroes 'have extraordinary powers which they usually use to save others; their exploits nevertheless involve some risk to themselves', and that 'Like Jesus, they often have mysterious parentage, eschew romantic relationships, and fight the forces of evil' (Reinhartz 2009: 432). We see similar dynamics at work in literature on biblical epics and Jesus films, in which, as I have argued before, films about Jesus can be divided into different Christological camps.

On the one hand we have the divine, transcendent Jesus of *The Greatest Story Ever Told* (1965), which fits into the 'high Christology' category as represented by Apollinaris of Laodicea's understanding of Christ as 'not a human being' but merely 'like a human being, since he is not coessential with humanity in his highest part' (in Deacy 1999: 330). On the other hand, *The Last Temptation of Christ* (1988) might be construed as the epitome of a 'low' Christology in its delineation of a neurotic, tormented, even schizophrenic, Jesus, who succumbs to temptation and who is conflicted about his messianic calling, in a manner that conforms to the sort of picture proposed in the early Church by Theodore of Mopsuestia of the Antiochene school, in which emphasis was placed on 'a human nature which is complete and independent, which undergoes real growth in knowledge, and the discernment of good and evil as well as in physical development' (Kelly 1968: 304).

Significantly, although Santa conforms to both of these Christological positions, there is limited literature available on the nature and extent of this relationship. There have been attempts by scholars to draw parallels between the two, but they tend to remain at the superficial level. Nissenbaum writes, for example, about how 'In their hearts, many people today probably love Santa Claus more than Jesus Christ' (Nissenbaum 2010: x), while Marling refers in broad terms to how in the 1930s, at a time when the person of Santa was a permanent fixture on the retail scene and caught in the crossfire between material and spiritual values, his defenders painted a picture of him as 'an abstract personification of love and the love of the Christ Child', and thus as symbolic of 'the invisible spirit of Christmas' (Marling 2000: 206). Restad makes the instructive point that, in the domestic sphere, 'Santa combined characteristics of God, Jesus, and human parents into a presence embodying love, generosity, good humor, and transcendence' (Restad 1995: 50). But, again, there is an absence of specificity or detail, as further evinced by Restad's claim that 'Nineteenth-century American families invested in Santa Claus qualities they had come to associate with Jesus and thereby introduced children to the possibility of the miraculous' (Restad 1995: 51). Restad seems to be suggesting that Santa and Jesus function symbiotically, so that in learning via Santa about the virtues of good behaviour and the possibility of miracles then the gateway could open towards learning about how Jesus performs many of the same functions. Santa, on such a reading, is a benign and user-friendly conduit for instilling in (especially) young people teachings about Jesus to which they might not otherwise be receptive—indeed, 'The Santa myth made available a personage that could further the child's understanding of religion and fortify symbolically the parents' own sense of the same' (Restad 1995: 51). The inference, however, is that by 'believing' in Santa then the 'truth' of Christianity is in some way able to sneak through the back door, suggesting that Santa is not important in his own right, but he is a patsy and a propaganda tool— there to soften the impact of discovering (or rediscovering) the importance of religion in the modern world and even to covertly convert devotees of Santa into followers of Jesus.

Inevitably, not all commentators have seen the relationship in quite such positive terms. In 1909, the *Sunday School Times* asked whether we have 'been chiefly honoring Santa Claus instead of Christ' (Schmidt 1995: 187), and Schmidt refers to a Catholic priest who claimed in 1917 that 'In America, Santa Claus is rapidly usurping the Babe's throne in the children's affections' (Schmidt 1995: 187). Waits refers also to how Santa and Jesus had been mixed up in children's minds in such a way that was deemed to be inimical to Jesus: 'In order to clear up such confusion, they favored a strong emphasis on the differences between the two holiday figures and discouraged such practices as talking about Santa Claus in Sunday school' (Waits 1993: 132). Aiken has also written more recently that 'Santa myths verge on blasphemy, if not outright idolatry' (Aiken 2010: 56), as children are being taught to recognize a second god.

These, though, are outnumbered by those sources which draw vague comparisons between Santa and Jesus, and which tend to suffer from the same problems that beset those scholarly attempts that seek to identify certain film protagonists as 'Christ figures'. According to Adele Reinhartz, for example, 'it may be said, with only slight exaggeration, that Jesus Christ, or someone who resembles him, is on view at every Cineplex in North America at any given moment' (Reinhartz 2009: 430). William Blizek, a former editor of the *Journal of Religion and Film*, also works on the assumption that straightforward connections can be drawn between a character in a film and the Jesus of the Christian tradition: 'one does not have to be a religious studies scholar to see that R. P. McMurphy is betrayed and killed and that he then rises from the dead in *One Flew Over the Cuckoo's Nest*' (Blizek 2009: 31). Blizek's assumption is that a game of pin the tail can be played here, and that whenever anyone finds a visual or thematic connection between something they see on celluloid and something that they have read in the pages of the New Testament then everyone profits: 'It is interesting, enjoyable, maybe even challenging, and it attracts many people to the study of religion and film, people who are not scholars but who enjoy movies and know something about religion' (Blizek 2009: 31).

Yet, it is hard not to feel that what is taking place here lacks erudition. We see this strongly, for instance, in Blizek's concession that 'The miracles of Kal-El/Clark Kent are not the same miracles as those performed by Jesus, but they do not have to be exactly the same miracles in order to show that both are miracle workers and that this is a significant part of their identity' (Blizek 2009: 35). While he thus seems to acknowledge that there may be dissimilarities as well as similarities, he is only interested in forging the parallels, the result of which is that 'Superman becomes a version of Jesus and what we learn from Superman and his actions may indicate what it means to be a follower of Jesus' (Blizek 2009: 36). This is precisely where the problems arise as what lies behind Blizek's, and Reinhartz's, analysis is the implicit assumption that in finding a film character saying or doing something that is reminiscent of Jesus then such characters in some way *point to* or *fulfil* Jesus. What they do not do is show any awareness of the possibility that such a process may work in reverse, and that Jesus may be a Superman figure rather than that Superman can only be a Christ figure. Underlying the literature, in other words, is a tacit assumption that Jesus is the pre-eminent bestower of salvation, or justice, or hope, or wisdom, and that anything that a film character does is merely a second-order approximation of such virtues. But, when, as Reinhartz writes with respect to romantic comedies, that movies in which 'a man or woman saves his or her romantic partner from loneliness, low self-esteem, a life of promis-cuity, or some other negative emotional state' can be categorized as 'Christ-figure films' (Reinhartz 2009: 433), the criterion is too broad to be efficacious and only film-goers specifically seeking to discover Christology in film will see this as a profitable enterprise.

In the case of Santa, we find exactly the same one-direction paral-lels. Restad, for instance, writes that 'Anthropologically and socio-logically, the essential characteristics of Santa match those associated with Jesus', as when she gives the example of how 'St. Nicholas's birth and the ongoing embroidery and ritualization of tales of his magical appearances, generosity, and immortality parallel Jesus' story' (Restad

1995: 51). On one level, such a claim could be construed as being value-neutral as it merely seeks to draw a connection without spelling out what the consequences might be of bringing them together. But, as with the literature on Christ figures, Jesus is assumed to be paramount, even if there is no explicit or ideological prioritizing of Jesus over Santa (or indeed the other way around). If Jesus were not pre-eminent, how would we explain Aiken's point that in Christian households parents expect their children to eventually grow out of belief in Santa—and as Aiken puts it 'are disappointed if they don't'—whilst when they tell their children about Jesus (whose story for Aiken is equally unbelievable) they hope that their children will never grow out of it—and, again, in Aiken's words, 'are disappointed if they do' (Aiken 2010: 58).

The anthropologist Russell Belk has written one of the best pieces on the relationship between Santa and Jesus in his chapter on 'Materialism and the Making of the Modern American Christmas', first published in 1993, in which some instructive parallels are outlined. Belk writes, for example, that both Santa and Christ perform miracles (in Santa's case he has his flying reindeer and a bottomless bag of toys which he delivers in a single night to all of the world's children) and just as Christ brought gifts of love and salvation on Earth before ascending to heaven, so Santa brings gifts of (material) toys to homes before ascending up the chimney from which he entered (Belk 2001: 82). Belk also identifies that children's letters to Santa are tantamount to prayers that offer a sacrifice of good behaviour (Belk 2001: 82)—a point further developed by Schmidt who not only refers to the giving of presents in the nineteenth century as 'the answer to children's prayers' but identifies Santa 'as a focus of real veneration; praying to him or through him became a recognized piety of Victorian childhood' (Schmidt 1995: 139). Belk further writes that Santa is omniscient in the sense that he knows which children have been bad or good and holds them to account for their behaviour and is also 'immortal, is normally unseen, and is capable of forgiveness' (Belk 2001: 82). Finally, Belk suggests that there is an analogy between Santa's elves and Jesus' apostles, that Christmas songs about Santa are effectively secular hymns, and he sees it as more than a coincidence that 'Santa lives in a heavenly place of whiteness and purity' (Belk 2001: 82).

In many ways, we see the same problem mirrored in the debates surrounding H. Richard Niebuhr's 'Christ of Culture' model, the second of the five typologies he proposed in his 1952 publication *Christ and Culture*. Belk's talk of how Santa and Jesus are functionally indistinguishable corresponds to this model, according to which theology is so firmly embedded in culture that it is inevitable that Christ will be discerned through the agencies of that culture. As I have written elsewhere, Christ will always be the dominant motif 'but secular thought-forms and agencies have the capacity to resonate with, and even amplify, the extent to which the Christian message can be discerned' (Deacy 2008: 27). The literature on cinematic Christ figures certainly fits in here as if, as Niebuhr believes, 'Jesus often appears as a great hero of human culture history; his life and teachings are regarded as the greatest human achievement; in him, it is believed, the aspirations of men toward their values are brought to a point of culmination' (Niebuhr 1952: 54), then it is hardly surprising if film characters seem to be bearing more than a passing resemblance to the figure at the heart of the New Testament.

The problem with this model, however, is that, so reductionist is it in its scope—it sacrifices Jesus to the interests of the prevailing culture (see Deacy 2008: 28)—that there is no opportunity for a critical conversation around the efficacy of forging the parallel in the first place. For, if 'Santa = Jesus', then wherever Santa can be found what we have 'really' found, this argument would go, is Jesus (and, *ipso facto*, the 'secularization thesis' has been disproven and Christianity is found to be not just alive and well but actually at the very heart of the Christmas festival, whether we can 'see' it or not). There is no doubt that for Belk Santa's sacredness would not exist were it not for the Christological association. Even if one were to argue that Santa has supplanted Christ, the key point is that it is through his resemblance to Christ that he is accorded such special status. As Belk sees it, 'the development of the Santa myth has made him increasingly Christ-like'—indeed, he is not only a 'hero' but a 'god', which the Christ-connection has given him—and, he continues, 'Santa Claus is a sacred figure for a secular world' (Belk 2001: 82). Even when Belk proceeds to outline differences between the two, they are far more superficial and inconsequential than the correlations. Belk tells us, for instance, that in terms of physical image Santa is old and plump whereas Christ was young and thin (though, surely, the claim could be made that they are both perceived as bearded); Santa wears rich reds and furs whereas Christ wore humble white robes; and Santa is jolly whereas Christ is serious. The only significant difference is where

Belk outlines that whereas Santa gave (material) toys and luxuries, Christ offered (spiritual) health and necessities, and, indeed, condemned the sort of material focus that belief in Santa's gifts promote (see Belk 2001: 83).

This, however, is dubious territory. Attractive though it may seem to construe the Santa story as 'a pocket-sized Christian allegory' (Hales 2010: 167), with Santa operating as a kind of 'practical, this-worldly sort of demigod' (Hales 2010: 168), there is a certain irony that Jesus and Santa operate in quite discrete, ontologically different realms. Santa may be a secular version of Jesus but Christmas has a number of mythologies, rituals, and norms which do not customarily dovetail with those of the Christian story. It may be that the Nativity has played a role in forming the backdrop to the modern Christmas celebration, but, according to Kathleen M. Sands, it is 'neither what we are chiefly remembering nor what we are laboring most vigorously to forget' (Sands 2001: 56). Sands' point is that in a film such as *White Christmas* (1954), nostalgia for past Christmases plays a pivotal role (indeed, the first lines of the Irving Berlin song 'White Christmas' performed by Bing Crosby are 'I'm dreaming of a white Christmas/ Just like the ones I used to know'), harking back as it does to a past that was 'decent and wholesome' (Sands 2001: 55)—yet this is a completely religion-free (and, indeed, Jesus-free) zone. Rather than 'count against the credibility of our Christmas products and productions', she makes the instructive point that in *White Christmas* 'it does not' (Sands 2001: 56). Across the whole spectrum of Christmas movies we have precisely the same dynamic. If there is a heroic, messianic, or supernaturally-tinged character it is Santa who alone fulfils this role. Even where traditional religion appears in the film it is merely there to buttress the Santa myth, as when in *Christmas with the Kranks* (2004) we see a Roman Catholic priest, Father Zabriskie (Tom Poston), spending his Christmas Eve not at Mass but at the Kranks' annual festive house party where images of Santa are everywhere but Jesus appears nowhere. Even in a scene set in a traditional religious building, as when in *Home Alone* Kevin (Macauley Culkin) pays a visit to his local church and witnesses a choir rehearsal, Jesus is not specifically referenced, and, as Agajanian pertinently observes, 'it is Santa rather than God who Kevin asks for help in restoring his family' (Agajanian 2000: 153).

Quite simply, as Connelly perceives, 'the stark truth is that Christmas films, like much of the modern Christmas itself, are not directly interested in the birth of Christ' (Connelly 2000a: 7). Significantly, though, as Sands points out, 'the emotional efficacy of Christmas artifacts is reduced not a whit by the absence of Jesus, nor even by the absence of "religious" referents as such' (Sands 2001: 56). Any reference to religion or, specifically, to Jesus has been removed from the equation, without this even being cited as a problem, and indeed for many people today the iconic image of Christmas is not Jesus in the manger but Santa in the department store. Certainly, as Myers puts it, 'there are certainly more visible and credible images of Santa Claus in our malls and in the mass media than there are of the Nativity or any other single image' (Myers 2001b: 189). Bennett similarly attests that 'Most tiny tots with their eyes all aglow spend Christmas Eve wondering about the mystery of flying reindeer, not the mystery of the Nativity' (Bennett 2009: 108).

Instructive though it may therefore be for Belk and others to draw parallels between Jesus and Santa, and to imply that in discerning such correlations Santa is effectively accorded a sacrality he would not otherwise have possessed, what really stands out is that they rarely inhabit the same space. Indeed, they remain separate, *competing* mythologies. Nissenbaum referred in 2010 to a website which lists 231 different Christmas products which show Santa kneeling before Jesus (including figurines and Christmas tree ornaments) (Nissenbaum 2010: xii), and Schmidt has written about the appearance in one holiday trade card—effectively a souvenir token given by merchants to their customers—from the nineteenth century which featured an illustration on the front by Thomas Nast of Santa, while on the back Schmidt writes that

> Jesus and Santa Claus are mixed together in a jumble of successful petitions for Christmas toys. The children's invocation of a gentle Jesus and an indulgent Santa Claus breaks the 'stern heart' of a cold, angry father who, softened, learns to purchase presents for his children with glad abandon (Schmidt 1995: 140).

But it is the novelty and kitsch value of such enterprises which stands out, as in the popular imagination at any rate it is highly unusual for Jesus and Santa to be juxtaposed (see deChant 2002: 1). In the twentieth century, there were some attempts by American merchants to insert Santa into the re-creation of the manger scene in department store displays, but, writes, Nissenbaum, 'It didn't work and their efforts were ridiculed' (Nissenbaum 2010: xii). The reason for the failure of this venture is put succinctly by deChant who tells us that the 'two figures are simply from two different religious worlds' (deChant 2002: 1), and that it would be akin to inserting the (Jewish) menorah—or, we could add, the figure of the Buddha or the Prophet—into the nativity scene. An interesting analogy is provided by Mazur and Koda in the context of a proposal in Virginia to build a Disney theme park near a Civil War battlefield which was rejected due to an incompatibility between the two different sacred mythologies on display (see Mazur and Koda 2011: 319). Curiously, where there have been attempts to bring Santa and Jesus together they have been done for satirical purposes rather than out of veneration for two religious 'leaders'. In 1995, for example, a video short was produced called *Spirit of Christmas*, by the same team which went on to make *South Park*, in which, as *Sight and Sound* describes the plot, 'Jesus returns to earth to duke it out with Santa Claus for ruining his birthday. The two of them have a knock-down kung-fu fight and, in the process, teach the kids the true meaning of Christmas: presents' (Anon. 1998: 4).

It is not therefore sufficient to argue that Santa owes his sacredness to his association with Jesus when it is their separation from one another that paints a more accurate picture. To make the picture even more nebulous, it is not traditionally even Santa Claus who, in Spain, distributes gifts. Rather, it is the three wise men, Melchior, Caspar, and Balthasar, who, as Peter William Evans tells us, distribute gifts in Spanish department stores—even if, in more recent years, Father Christmas

> has been steadily encroaching on the Wise Men's territory, encouraged of course by all retailers, a situation that now often means not one but two spending sprees, one to coincide with the aged patriarch's Christmas Eve chimney visits and another with the royal Easterners' later arrival (Evans 2000: 211–12).

In terms of such a scenario, the connection is not between Santa and Jesus but between Santa and the three wealthy, foreign kings who, in Matthew's Gospel, are the first to pay homage to the baby Jesus, bestowing on him gifts of gold, frankincense, and myrrh (Matthew 2: 11). This, indeed, problematizes the Santa–Jesus relationship still further as whereas Santa is the *manufacturer* and *deliverer* of gifts, Jesus is the *recipient* of wealthy presents from Eastern dignitaries. Jesus may be able to bestow on the human race gifts of salvation and love, but when it comes to the exchange of material presents, as is synonymous with the Christmas holiday, Jesus' role is marginal at best.

Whatever analogies can be forged, it is Santa (or even the *magi* in terms of the above example), not Jesus, who has the monopoly on Christmas gifts, even if, in his previous incarnation as St. Nicholas, Santa is (albeit loosely) connected to a fourth-century bishop. So integral is Santa to the modern Christmas that, in deChant's words, 'Trying to have our children ignore him is even more difficult, more difficult perhaps to shield them from Santa than to shield them from Christ' (deChant 2002: 196)—should one even wish to, of course. It is not, then, the case that Santa is becoming more prominent while Christ is receding in importance, in what might be construed as a Christmas-specific version of the secularization thesis, as if people are transferring their allegiance directly from Jesus to Santa in an age when Christianity is purportedly dwindling in significance. A more accurate picture would be one which sees not the replacement of one religious icon or hero by another, as when a Christian converts to Buddhism or Islam and finds the Buddha or the Prophet a better role model or exemplar than Christ, but one which sees Santa and Jesus as inhabiting incommensurate religious realms which for the most part have nothing to do with one another. Christians may transfer their faith away from Christ to another religious figure or deity, but even if, as deChant believes, Santa is no less a god or the apotheosis of the sacred than Christ (deChant 2002: 185), and even if it is as inappropriate to juxtapose Christ and Santa in Nativity displays as it would be to juxtapose Santa and the Buddha, there is a crucial difference here as it is customary for Christians to believe in the existence of both Santa and Jesus at one and the same time, without conflict or contradiction.

Whereas belief in Christ or Buddha would be an either/or decision—one is either a Christian or a Buddhist—the same dichotomy does not apply in the case of Christmas when Christians will still erect displays of Santa on their roofs and children will be taken by their parents to visit Santa in his grotto in department stores or will be told on Christmas morning that the presents that sit under the tree were put there in the course of the night by Father Christmas after he came down the chimney and stopped to consume a glass of milk or sherry and a plate of mince pies before making his way to the next home in his magical reindeer-pulled sleigh. The crucial difference is

that the two figures arc not interchangeable, so that in church services
at Christmas it is the birth of Jesus that is celebrated and when
children write their 'thank you' letters they send them to Santa
Claus at the North Pole. They may hold discrete roles, but they are
also uniquely complementary ones, and to this extent both Santa and
Jesus are profoundly religious figures—even if, as deChant indicates,
one is the embodiment of 'our culture's greatest religious myth: the
myth of success and affluence, right engagement with the economy,
and the acquisition and consumption of images and objects' (deChant
2002: 194).

   That the two religious icons, Jesus and Santa, exist in their own
designated spaces and without the one treading on the territory of the
other is simply a given in contemporary society. As Golby and Purdue
see it, for example, 'if the newspapers or television stations wish to tug
the heart-strings in the interests of a charitable cause or a hard-luck
story, Santa Claus rather than the infant Christ is likely to be invoked'
(Golby and Purdue 2000: 88). Jesus may be integral to Christian
religious devotion but this does not impact on Santa's status 'at the
sacred center of every shopping mall in the post-modern world'
where we find him sitting in 'palatial splendor' (deChant 2002:
197). This does not mean that Jesus' role is denigrated or usurped;
Christians, for example, no more have to choose between celebrating
the birth of Jesus and the presence (and indeed the presents) of Santa
than they do between going to church and going to the cinema. They
may indeed perform complementary roles as when both church and
cinema comprise 'places where dreams are projected', with both
amounting to '"inside" places where images of an "outside", other
than that from which the viewers have come, are shown' (Loughlin
2007: 340). The crucial point is that participation in one does not
exclude presence at the other. When Schmidt thus writes that 'Santa's
Toyland throne' might be construed as 'a place of mysterious and
sometimes frightening presence, a place of fantastic gifts, perhaps the
closest thing for the modern child to a place of grace' (Schmidt 1995:
141), the language that is used may mirror that used in Christian
discourse, but there is no suggestion that Santa has the monopoly
on grace, any more than the sense of wonder, enlightenment, even
redemption, that a film may be able to engender means that the
Church has forfeited its right to teach or preach about such matters.
As I have written previously, indeed, even though the doctrine of
redemption has a Christian foundation it is curious that throughout

history this doctrinally-specific concept has been open to a rich and heterogeneous assortment of expressions (Deacy 2011: 37), and that neither the theologian nor the filmmaker has privileged or exclusive access to its sphere of activity (Deacy 2011: 38).

Max A. Myers is thus right when he attests that 'The chief icon of the American Christmas, Santa Claus, is a symbol of a very different kind of grace than is preached by Christianity' in the respect that, as he sees it, 'The grace preached by Christianity is connected with the execution of a leader whose message threatened those who held political and social power' whereas the 'grace represented by Santa Claus legitimates the institutions of political, economic, and social power' (Myers 2001b: 188). The former may entail 'a life of sharing' and 'a lifestyle of self-sacrifice to meet the needs of the other as the highest virtue' while the latter may be bound up with 'meeting the needs of the self' and the celebration of 'inordinate consumption' (Myers 2001b: 188). But, crucially, both values are often held together in the case of each individual and family. After all, Christians hardly live privileged and rarefied lives exempt from the marketplace of global capitalism, and nor would they necessarily choose to do so.

The scenario would seem to be comparable to when H. Richard Niebuhr developed his dualist 'Christ and Culture in Paradox' model in 1952 in which it is taken as a given that Christians are constantly having to negotiate between two sets of conflicting demands—that of Christ's injunctions on the one hand and those of secular authority on the other. As Niebuhr saw it, 'man is seen as subject to two moralities, and as a citizen of two worlds that are not only discontinuous with each other but largely opposed' (Niebuhr 1952: 56). It is possible, in terms of such a position, for the Christian to, albeit reluctantly, acknowledge and accept the norms of secular culture, even while recognizing the inherent limitations of living a life that is not explicitly informed or imbued by Christian beliefs, teachings, or doctrines. But, whereas Niebuhr saw an inevitable tension between Christianity and culture, my position is that Jesus and Santa can exist simultaneously and even harmoniously while at the same time their roles do not straightforwardly go together.

Niebuhr's model works to a point as it shows that, applied to the present discussion, Christ and Santa belong to separate spheres and that there are different authorities and values at work (as betokened by Myers' understanding of how they both utilize grace but do so in divergent ways). The key difference with Niebuhr, though, is that for him Christianity is primary and we simply have to learn to live with non-Christian competing sources of authority. While I agree with his emphasis on the need to understand the differences, the problem with his model is that it sees the tension as being one-directional, whereas in practice most Christians celebrate Christmas (and Santa) no differently from non-Christians. Niebuhr's position is also too simplistic in the respect that his model works on the assumption that we can draw a distinction between 'Christianity' on the one hand and 'culture' on the other, as if both were separable, monolithic categories. In the case of Christmas, it is not just that Christians can go to church to celebrate the Nativity and then return home to indulge in more 'secular' pursuits on Christmas Day, as even then there is still an assumption that our time is demarcated and compartmentalized in such a regimented fashion that we are at any one time either worshipping Jesus *or* Santa.

That life is far more nuanced than this is borne out by some of our everyday activities where we are constantly assimilating various possible competing tensions. The rise of Megachurches particularly in the United States is a good example of how there is an interflow between traditional religious worship and new, potentially rival activities such as going to a music concert or watching a film. In Megachurches, such 'secular' pursuits are fully subsumed within the auspices of the Church so that, as Ostwalt tells us, 'In any particular week, a member of a megachurch might go bowling, attend an aerobics class, play basketball, seek family counselling, and attend a multimedia presentation—all within the church's confines' (Ostwalt 2003: 30). In the case of Islam, recent research has been conducted into the way Muslim students at the University of Kent are increasingly using electronic media, especially YouTube, as a way of listening to the recitation of the Qur'an.[18] Accordingly, rather than simply attend a mosque for religious worship it is common practice for a student to hear the sacred words on one's headphones in the library while working on an essay. It is difficult in terms of such a scenario to separate out traditional religious celebrations or forms of worship from their 'secular' counterparts. Churches, mosques, or synagogues may not customarily screen Christmas films

---

[18] One of my undergraduate dissertation students in 2013, Sandra Maurer, undertook an ethnographic participant observation case study that examined how Islamic practice might be influenced and reshaped by religious communities through their use of media, as the recitation of the Qur'an is accessible through the internet.

but there are plenty of instances whereby religious communities are using new media in order to facilitate worship and communication among congregations, as when in March 2005 Heidi Campbell informs us that 'MIRS Communications, an Israeli wireless company, announced the launch of a cellular phone designed specifically for the Orthodox Jewish community' (Campbell 2010: 162; see also Deacy 2013: 200).

It is not a case of *either* traditional religious worship *or* their modern, secular counterparts—the two can quite comfortably function together. The very idea, therefore, that in the specific case of Christmas we should see Jesus and Santa to be either synonymous with or different from one another paints only an incomplete picture. The argument is as specious as one that concluded that, because Christmas trees not only adorn people's homes at Christmas but are a staple decoration in churches also, it amounts to proof that Christmas is a Christian festival. This position is inadequate as it suggests that the traffic only flows in one direction. Indeed, it has often been claimed that Martin Luther invented the Christmas tree (see Marling 2000: 177), and, as we learn from Marling, in the mid-nineteenth century the tree was 'the cornerstone of Christmas exercises for Sunday school classes', and 'Nativity pageants staged around the tree ended in a mass distribution of toys, candy boxes, and warm mittens' (Marling 2000: 177). This is all well and good but the argument could just as well be presented in reverse, to the effect that because the 'secular' Christmas tree has encroached on the life of Christians to such an extent that the tree is an intrinsic part of church décor then Christianity's distinctiveness has been usurped and its values distorted or compromised. In reality it is never quite this black or white.

It is thus ironic that Belk, who has provided such a rich and helpful outline of the functional similarities (and, to be fair, the dissimilarities also) between Santa and Jesus, should conclude that 'Santa Claus is to American material faith what Jesus Christ is to Christian spiritual faith' (Belk 2001: 85). Whereas in one sense this is a perfectly legitimate argument—after all, Belk also writes that 'Christ reigns in the realm of the spirit' whereas 'Santa's realm is that of material abundance' (Belk 2001: 83)—what is at fault is the clear-cut assumption that Christ operates in one set of discourses and Santa in another when in reality, as we shall see especially in chapter 6, the capitalist-oriented Christmas is itself a pivotal site of religious activity.

Accordingly, it is problematic when one hears the familiar refrain that the 'Christian' Christmas has been 'lost' to commercialism, as if Christianity (or indeed 'religion' more generally) exists in some sort of economy-free zone without compromise or contamination where all that matters is the unadulterated attachment to, and love of, matters spiritual. For a start, it is significant that in the 1994 remake of *Miracle on 34th Street*, Kris Kringle (Richard Attenborough) uses language that seems more redolent of Jesus than that of an ambassador for consumerism:

> I'm not just a whimsical figure who wears a charming suit and effects a jolly demeanour. I'm a symbol of the human ability to be able to suppress the selfish and the hateful tendencies that rule the major parts of our lives. If you can't believe, if you can't accept anything on faith, then you're doomed for a life dominated by doubt...If I can make you believe then there'd be some hope for me. If I can't then I'm finished.

Whether Santa is thus 'a secular version of Christ' (Belk 2001: 83) or whether he may in fact embody characteristics that are no less integral to the 'religious' sphere (as if such binary realms exist in the first place) to the point that he is a quintessentially religious, and not 'merely' secular, figure confirms the importance of using the right definitions. As a result, in chapter 3 I will pay close attention to questions of religious and theological definition with a view to asking whether Christmas may comprise a rich site of religious activity because of rather than in spite of its material and consumerist pedigree. While Connelly thus makes the highly judicious point that, in the light of the above quotation from *Miracle on 34th Street*, 'The tenets of Christianity, of love and selflessness, are here given expression by a figure associated with Christian mythology, but it is a figure that has become increasingly secular' (Connelly 2000b: 120; see also Deacy 2013: 196), I would suggest that Connelly's point would be no less efficacious or accurate were the word 'but' changed to 'and' and the final word 'secular' changed to 'religious'. It should thus now read: 'The tenets of Christianity...are here given expression by a figure associated with Christian mythology, and it is a figure that has become increasingly religious.'

3

Is Christmas a 'Secular' Religion?

A REFRAMING OF THE PARAMETERS

Any suggestion that Christmas may comprise a site of religious activity, or at the very least that there may be something analogous at work between the celebration of Christmas and what happens in traditional religious discourse, is the corollary of recent trends in the evolution of the category of religion. Rather than see Christianity, for example, as an autonomous, clearly demarcated religious tradition with a pre-established and distinctive set of values in relation to which a 'secular' festival of consumption must necessarily fall short, the culturalist turn in the study of religion since the 1970s has identified the relationship between religion and culture to be one of decentring and deregulation (see Morgan 2008: xiii; Lynch et al. 2012: 1; Deacy 2013: 197). When it comes to understanding 'the symbols of meaning and the order of life, the establishment and cultivation of individual and collective identity, and the generation and cultivation of moods and motivations' (Horsley 2001a: 182), it would be a retrograde step if it was assumed that any one agency, institution, or authority had a monopoly on such concerns.

The media is one of the more obvious sites of meaning-making, and this may be what Horsley has in mind when he writes that the 'high-rise headquarters of large corporations have long since come to dwarf the churches and cathedrals in the landscape of modern urban society' (Horsley 2001a: 182). But, the relationship between media empires and traditional religious institutions should not necessarily be seen in competing, binary terms. It may have been the case in the past that, as Hoover attests, the relationship between the media and religion was seen in terms of a 'dualist instrumentalism' whereby both were seen 'as autonomous historical categories', such that 'it is possible to understand them only as competing with and contesting one another' (Hoover 2005: 142). Today, though, this is too limited a view, with the focus having shifted towards looking at how the media and religious institutions intersect—'the same ground is being trod by these two areas of cultural practice' (Hoover 2005: 142; see also Deacy 2013: 197). The line of demarcation between transcendent and mundane activity has been replaced by something much more permeable in which 'religious and theological images, themes and concerns appear in surprising places' (Mahan 2007: 53; see also Deacy 2013: 197). As Mahan puts it, indeed, 'religion is multivalent and the wall between sacred and secular is clearly porous' (Mahan 2007: 52). Whereas it may once have seemed that, not least in terms of the secularization thesis, 'in contrast with traditional societies, in modern society the sacred existed within an ever shrinking circle', Mahan continues that the 'discovery of the existence of the sacred within the profane world of popular culture challenges that interpretation' (Mahan 2007: 52).

We see related ideas at work in what Marsh says about how 'people who do not profess a religious tradition nevertheless make their meaning in similar ways to those who do' (Marsh 2007: 22), the difference simply concerning the *location* of the resources that are utilized. Ostwalt covers similar ground in his assertion that 'secularization' pertains not to the decline of religion per se but to the decline in religious *authority* and to the 'shifting structures of power in society' (Ostwalt 2003: 7). As he states, 'Secularization and religious devotion are not necessarily inversely related; that is, one does not have to suffer for the other to prosper' (Ostwalt 2003: 12). Indeed, the religious and the secular spheres 'have always coexisted' and 'affect one another' and even 'feed off each other' (Ostwalt 2003: 4). Even if the content involves the transcendental and otherworldly, all cultural products, and here Ostwalt includes religion which, for him, should be labelled as 'a secular cultural form', are 'affected by and must conform to the exigencies of secular life' (Ostwalt 2003: 4). This has a serious effect on the way the category of religion is construed as the space vacated as institutional religion recedes or declines might be seen to have been filled by alternative agencies, not least by popular culture, the sources and resources of which are turned to, as Elaine Graham attests, 'as a means of rehearsing and examining questions of belief, meaning and spirituality' and 'offering alternative archetypes, myths, heroic figures or soteriologies to form the stories we live by' (Graham 2007: 68).

Within such parameters, it is clear that Christmas is a potentially rich site of contemporary religiosity, not least with its ready-made adornment of redeemer figures by way of Santa and Scrooge, flying reindeer, magical elves, and even, as delineated in the 1985 Disney movie *One Magic Christmas*, Lapland as a functional equivalent of the Christian heaven. If anything, therefore, Graham is underplaying the potential afforded by this new cultural turn when she writes that 'Popular culture is believed to constitute a central source and resource for theological understanding' and that 'questions about good and evil, life and death, what it means to be human, identity and community are mediated as much through popular cultural expressions as via the voices of "high culture"' (Graham 2007: 69). Where I differ, however, from Graham is in her assumption that because this presents a new challenge for theology then 'If theology is to respond authentically to its human situation, then it must be ready to respond in kind' (Graham 2007: 69; see also Deacy 2013: 197). Implicit in what she is writing here is that there is a separation between what goes on in theology and the rest of 'culture', as if (applied to the present discussion) we should construe Christmas and Christianity as belonging to discrete spheres. Such a position is redolent of Niebuhr's dualist, 'Christ and Culture in Paradox' model, as was discussed in chapter 2, which sees a tension between these two norms and which, while allowing for negotiation and sometimes compromise between the two, is nevertheless clear that they are not interchangeable or fluid constructs (as would be delineated, for example, in Niebuhr's 'Christ of culture' model).

Although Graham is to be commended for the way in which she sees popular culture as inhabiting the space created by the change in the way religion is mutating, I am less inclined to see the relationship between 'old' and 'new' forms of religiosity as capable of being expressed in such binary terms. Graham's position is, though, a common one in much of the literature about secularization, with Steve Bruce one of the more vocal proponents of the idea that religion has a fixed, unchanging essence and as having, as Dutton paraphrases him as construing it, 'set, unchanging properties' such that 'something should be classed as a religion if it conforms to this ideal form' (Dutton 2010: 177). What Bruce does not take into consideration is the possibility that religion has the capacity to evolve. As Dutton sees it, Bruce's way of approaching religion 'reflects the Judaeo-Christian origins of the word religion' (Dutton 2010: 177), and it also falls into the rather narrow conceptualization of religion as being apprehended and measured solely in terms of its institutional presence and function. We see this exemplified in Bruce's 2011 book *Secularization* where Bruce is insistent that when it comes to looking at people's beliefs and commitments the only 'reliable index' for ascertaining their presence (or indeed absence) is attendance, as when he argues that 'It is rare to find a large number of survey respondents who describe themselves as . . . Christian . . . but do not attend church regularly' (Bruce 2011: 16). Using such narrow criteria it is hardly surprising, indeed it is inevitable, that Bruce should reach the conclusion that 'secularization must be seen as irreversible' (Bruce 2011: 56). Bruce is only interested in 'looking for a single simple measure to convey a general impression' such that when it comes to contemporary Christian societies 'church attendance works remarkably well, which is why I have frequently used it' (Bruce 2011: 16). Another British sociologist of religion, Bryan Wilson, is another case in point as, in Bailey's words, he has 'tended to equate any change within religion with a decline in "genuine" religiosity, and simultaneously (yet paradoxically?) denied the presence of any real religiosity outside the traditionally religious' (Bailey 2006: 26). While such positions are endemic, they are also flawed, fitting as they do Lynch's critique of those understandings of religion which see it as existing 'in some precultural Platonic world of ideas separate from actual cultural histories, resources and lives' (Lynch 2007b: 163; see also Deacy 2013: 197).

One of the most prolific chronicles of the new cultural turn is in J'annine Jobling's *Fantastic Spiritualities*, published in 2010, the premise of which 'is that religious sensibility in the Western world is in a process of transformation, but that we see here change, not decline' (Jobling 2010: 2). Contrary to Bruce's approach which is to see religion fragmenting and declining, Jobling chooses to focus on the role of spirituality in modern culture where the sort of constraints that circumscribe Bruce's work, with its focus on religious institutions, do not apply. Drawing on the fantastic genre of literature which includes the *Harry Potter* series and *Buffy the Vampire Slayer*, she argues that 'the production and consumption of the fantastic in popular culture can offer an illuminating window on to spiritual trends and conditions' (Jobling 2010: 2) where narratives, characters, and motivations are 'situated consciously and eclectically within a "detraditioned" religious space' (Jobling 2010: 107). Such literature may make in some cases 'overt use of traditional Christian symbols, thought-structures and themes', but, Jobling attests, 'these are relocated into a frame whereby their potency is cultural rather than confessedly religious' (Jobling 2010: 108).

Indeed, as Jobling convincingly shows with reference to the 1990s television series *Buffy*, it is the very *subversion* of 'normative patterns of power and authority at both individual and social levels' (Jobling 2010: 196) that makes them spiritually empowering for audiences, as when she argues that the programme 'presents a model of the human which has the capacity for self-transcendence through acts of love, heroism and community-inspired action' (Jobling 2010: 200) as opposed to the foregrounding of traditional, institutional authority which, she writes, 'is presented, generally, as negative, lacking in insight' and as 'oppressive' (Jobling 2010: 195). Whereas Bruce would see the absence of institutional religion as evidence of religious decline, Jobling presents a far richer and more subtle analysis of contemporary spiritual and religious trends. She notes, for example, that in the *Harry Potter* stories 'institutional religion does not appear' (Jobling 2010: 129) but that religiosity is nevertheless crucial to the power of the texts, as when she writes that the Harry Potter story 'maps onto Joseph Campbell's hero quest, and represents a spiritual and personal transformation with distinctly Christological sub-texts in places' (Jobling 2010: 44). In *Buffy*, too, crosses, crucifixes, and holy water are much in evidence but the overarching world-view is decidedly humanistic and lacking in any metaphysical frame of reference, with all emphasis placed on 'realizing one's own authentic potential' (Jobling 2010: 201) in relationship with others.

As an analogy to what Jobling says about the fantastic, Karen Pärna has written on how the internet can also be construed as 'a modern-day, sacred object of belief' (Pärna 2006: 201) which 'would not just somehow transform the world, it would also bring about great improvements and answer a number of age-old dreams' (Pärna 2006: 190), not least in terms of how 'the Internet is expected to give us power over space and be the agent of a new kind of existence' (Pärna 2006: 197). Though a mechanism of modern science and technology, Pärna's thesis is that the internet can be understood as a site of religious activity, in terms of how, for example, 'it functions as a point of reference for values and meaning' (Pärna 2006: 198)—thus tying in with functionalist accounts of the definition of religion—as well as how, vis à-vis a substantive approach to religion, it 'appears capable of doing the impossible and realizing dreams of harmony' (Pärna 2006: 198), as well as in its 'construction of ultimate values' and 'the hopes of salvation and visions of transcendence that one can observe in the discourses about the Internet' (Pärna 2006: 200). Such perspectives clearly contradict Bruce's language of secularization in which the rational and the scientific are believed to have supplanted and replaced the world of religion, spirituality, and the transcendent. Pärna, indeed, is emphatic that the nature of the sacred may have changed but it has not disappeared (see Pärna 2006: 183), not least because, in principle at any rate, 'any object can acquire sacred connotations and take on a religious meaning, including products of modern technology' (Pärna 2006: 186), just as, as we shall see later in this chapter, for Mircea Eliade the sacred is believed to comprise an essential element of what it means to be human.

What needs to be stressed, therefore, is that, once the initial surprise has passed that popular culture or the media may be a repository of religious activity, we should be inclined to look not at how the media or popular culture illustrates or bears witness to traditional, institutionalized forms of religion but at how we can understand religion today more fully and judiciously by examining how the likes of the fantastic genre of literature, the internet, and Christmas are themselves repositories of religious meaning and activity. Useful though it may be to look at how *Buffy* is religious because characters wear crucifixes, such a limited, descriptive perspective misses the point that, as Jobling has shown, the world of the characters 'both vampiric and human' is 'not determined by traditional or institutional theologies' (Jobling 2010: 107). In the case of the internet, there is no doubt that traditional religious institutions use cyberspace for the purposes of promoting their faiths and disseminating information about, for example, their doctrines, teachings, liturgies, and service times, but Pärna's work has demonstrated that the internet can itself change the site and indeed meaning of where we think religion is located. Sarah Lawther has asked many insightful questions in this regard in her examination of how the internet has specifically impacted on the way in which religious organizations handle religion online, and whether it is the medium that shapes the message rather than the message that shapes the medium (see Lawther 2009: 232). But we could go even further and ask whether there is a difference between 'religion online', where religion is literally on the internet, in the form of web pages put up by and for the benefit of Christians, Jews, Muslims, Hindus, Buddhists, or Sikhs, and 'online religion' where new ways of doing, understanding, and reframing religion can be situated. A case in point here is the 'First Church of Cyberspace' (www.godweb.org), set up by Presbyterian minister Charles Henderson in the late 1990s, whose congregation is exclusively online, and where 'cyberspeak' has replaced traditional language of religious devotion and worship, with cyber-congregants given the opportunity to, among other things, enter and participate in an online sanctuary which contains prayers, sermons, and meditations.

Regarding Christmas, it is perfectly fine to look at how Christmas carols, songs, and movies include references to God, Jesus, or the Nativity, but it would be a limited exercise indeed if this was seen to be the extent of 'religion' vis-à-vis Christmas. At the very least, our ideas of what Christmas 'means' cannot be dissociated from the way the media shapes and directs our interpretation of the festival. In November 2013, one of the leading discussion points in the media concerned the £7 million Christmas commercial by the John Lewis store (see Hawkes 2013: www.telegraph.co.uk/finance/newsbysector/retailandconsumer/10460348/bear-and-hare-best-Christmas-ads-Lily-Allen-John-Lewis-Christmas-adverts-Xmas-ads-Steve-Hawkes.html). It even prompted the magazine section of BBC News online to identify ten possible interpretations of the animated advertisement, in which we watch a hare trying to ensure that a bear does not miss out on the Christmas celebration to the sound of Lily Allen singing a cover of the Keane song 'Somewhere Only We Know'. As the article points out, 'John Lewis's Christmas advert is now one of the most discussed parts of the festive run-in' (BBC News 2013: www.bbc.co.uk/news/magazine-24901114). Steve Bruce may be correct when he attests that formal, institutionalized forms of religion are dwindling in significance, but his approach does not allow for how, in the case of Christmas, there may be alternative sites of religiosity which are performing analogous functions. There are, of course, numerous Christmas pop songs about Jesus, most notably Harry Belafonte's 'Mary's Boy Child', the Christmas number 1 from 1957, and Cliff Richard's 'Saviour's Day', which topped the UK singles chart over Christmas in 1990.[1] For the most part, though, Christmas music

---

[1] The birth of Christ may be what is being alluded to in the 1976 Christmas number 1 from Johnny Mathis, 'When a Child is Born', though its references to the

tends to be about Santa or 'Frosty the Snowman' rather than about the Nativity, and only a narrow conceptualization of religion would exclude such phenomena from its orbit. As Whiteley sees it, Christmas records 'remind us of what we should be doing (celebrating with the family and loved ones, singing carols, decorating the tree, giving to those less fortunate than ourselves) and what we should be feeling', to the point that 'there is an ideological discourse that governs the construction of the lyrics and the feel and arrangement of the music, which draws on the sentiments engendered by the religious basis of Christmas and such familiar texts as *A Christmas Carol*' (Whiteley 2008: 108).

An entire value system is often encapsulated in the lyrics of a song such as Chris Rea's 'Driving Home for Christmas' which, as Whiteley has observed, 'perpetuate a highly idealised image of the family which is often at odds with the tensions generated by family gatherings' (Whiteley 2008: 107). Christmas pop songs are redolent with sentiments concerning the social or familial rituals of 'Rocking around the Christmas tree' in the case of Brenda Lee's top ten Christmas hit from 1962 (in a manner which, the song tantalizingly augurs, is at once new and old-fashioned), or, as in the case of the Christmas number 1 of 1985, Shakin' Stevens' 'Merry Christmas Everyone', how a season of love and understanding, parties and celebration makes us wish that every day could be Christmas. Roy Wood and Wizzard similarly wished, back in 1973, that 'it could be Christmas every day', and Slade, in their Christmas number 1 from the same year, were likewise unequivocal about the allure of Christmas and the desire for its celebrations, sentiments, rituals, and hopes to be carried forward beyond the specific time scale of the festival itself, in which they beseech us to look to the future which, the song promises, has only *just* begun. Crucially, these songs comprise a non-specifically Christian but nonetheless religiously rich repository of sentiments and aspirations, which increasingly characterize and epitomize the modern Christmas landscape. We hear these songs in restaurants, department stores, and supermarkets for several weeks in the run-up to Christmas and it is highly unusual for radio stations not to include

---

world waiting for one particular child who may be black, white, or yellow suggests that the song is more inclusive in its scope than a reference to the Christian Nativity story alone.

Wham's 'Last Christmas' or the Pogues' 'Fairytale of New York' in their playlist in the weeks leading up to 25 December.

This is very different from the simplistic sense in which Christian values can simply be disseminated on the media, as when in 1944 the archbishop of York, Cyril Garbett, wrote in the *Radio Times* that 'the wireless and the English tongue are means by which God's message of love and peace can spread through the world' and that 'From early morning to late at night on Christmas Day the wireless will carry both to those at home and to their friends and kinsfolk far away the news of God's love to mankind and His promise of peace to men of good will' (in Connelly 2012: 152). This idea of radio as an unquestioning carrier of Christian teachings is reminiscent of those approaches, quite common in the early to mid-twentieth century, which saw film as a vessel for disseminating Christian values, such that, according to a papal encyclical from 1936, cinema needed to be 'elevated to conformity with the aims of the Christian conscience' (Pope Pius XI 2007: 38). Pius XI's encyclical continued that it is thought 'necessary to apply to the cinema a supreme rule which must direct and regulate even the highest art in order that it may not find itself in continual conflict with Christian morality' (Pope Pius XI 2007: 36). Film's role, he wrote, was 'to assist in the perfecting of the moral personality' and to be 'an influence for good morals, an educator', and 'a valuable auxiliary of instruction and education' (Pope Pius XI 2007: 36). We can contrast this with how, for Connelly, the television schedules 'for the entire period from about 23 December to 1 January now seems to have the status of a custom: the bombardment of advertisements, the increased Americanisation' (Connelly 2012: 7). In lieu of the wireless as a missiological or evangelizing tool for Christianity, we can see that the media has itself become a site of religious activity in terms of Connelly's identification of how in the course of the twentieth century 'listening to festival-specific radio programmes or attending the cinema for Christmas-themed films joined a visit to the pantomime as venerable expressions of observance' (Connelly 2012: xiii). We see similar testimony to the central role played by the media in directing and setting the agenda for Christmas in Restad's assertion that 'Under media influence, millions of listeners and viewers experienced the same modern Christmas lore simultaneously, the annual rewindings and rerunnings of Christmas programs themselves becoming a nostalgic ritual for many Americans' (Restad 1995: 171). Although Connelly makes it clear from the outset of *Christmas: A History* that his book 'will hardly make any mention of religion' (Connelly 2012: 7), it is not difficult to see how, once 'religion' is allowed to encompass more than any specific reference to the institutional Church then religion actually lies at the very heart of the territory that he explicitly sees as lying outside of religion's jurisdiction.

The reason this is so significant is that both Connelly, who is writing in the context of the English national Christmas, and Restad, whose focus is on the American Christmas celebration, are implicitly aware of how TV and radio are not simply playing a background role. Rather, the media is central, indeed pivotal, to the way in which the day is celebrated and experienced. It may be a day for spending with family but the day's rituals will characteristically fit around certain key media events, whether it is the Queen's speech that is broadcast at 3 p.m. or what Connelly refers to as the 'traditional Christmas Day film' (Connelly 2012: 7), in relation to which he observes that a 'Christmas tradition has been created without it having anything to do with Christmas whatsoever' (Connelly 2012: 7). The film concerned might be *Batman* (1989), a summer blockbuster from 1989 which premiered, to much hype, on BBC1 on Christmas Day two years later, or *Jurassic Park* (1993), which was broadcast early on Christmas evening on Christmas Day in 1996, again marking the first time that it was shown on terrestrial TV in the UK. Other familiar Christmas stalwarts include *The Wizard of Oz* (1939), *The Great Escape* (1963), and *The Sound of Music* (1965). This is not a new phenomenon either. In the Christmas 1974 special of the BBC sitcom *Whatever Happened to the Likely Lads?*, Bob Ferris (Rodney Bewes) recounts to his wife, Thelma (Bridget Forsyth), his reason for preferring not to go out to his mother-in-law's next-door neighbours' charades party on Christmas evening in a repetition of the previous year—'Christmas night, full of food. I just want to sit in an arm chair and watch the box. *Great Escape* was on, wasn't it? Usually is.'

Sight and Sound may have been right when an editorial in their February 1998 edition made the instructive point that, in an age of satellite television, 'The days when the Christmas Day movie on BBC1 or ITV seemed a media event are gone' (Cathode 1998: 34), and the proliferation in the years since of DVDs, Blu-rays, pay-per-view movies and downloads if anything exacerbates the point. But, even if the Christmas day consumption of TV is not uniform or homogeneous (though the healthy ratings of Christmas Day specials of *Doctor Who*, *Strictly Come Dancing*, and *Downton Abbey* suggest that certain programmes do still enjoy mass appeal, even if in many cases they will be watched on the iPlayer after the initial broadcast time) it is the media that still determines how the day is going to be spent. Looking back over the way Christmas has been celebrated in America during the twentieth century, Restad makes the instructive comment that 'In addition to print advertising, radio, movies, books, songs, and television molded its salient images and language into a Christmas more uniform and secular than any preceding it, and found a following for it in every corner of the nation' (Restad 1995: 171). My difference from Restad is simply over the use of the terminology that is utilized. Whereas she sees radio, film, and TV as bearing witness to the increased *secularization* of Christmas, my argument is that these are new and alternative religious sites. As Lynch wrote in 2007, 'Much of the literature in the study of religion, media and popular culture proceeds on the basis of the assumption that the meaning of religion is relatively straightforward' (Lynch 2007a: 125), whereas the line between the purported 'religious' and 'secular' is much more porous than such binary definitions allow.

There are a number of different ways in which the religious provenance of Christmas TV, film, or radio can be tabulated. One would be to do down the 'substantive' definition of religion path which sees religion as possessing a core doctrinal element which needs to be present in order for something to be categorized as religious. On such a reading, the presence in a film or radio or TV programme of a church, a scriptural text, or a belief in God would be sufficient to justify the classification of the media product concerned as 'religious'. This is the approach that most closely matches the way in which the BBC defines its approach to religious broadcasting. In a press release dated 25 November 2013, the BBC Media Centre announced that 'This Christmas the BBC will be celebrating a diverse range of religious programming on TV and radio, from uplifting songs and festivities to traditional prayer' (BBC Media Centre 2013: www.bbc.co.uk/mediacentre/latestnews/2013/religious-programmes-christmas.html). Programmes specifically identified as part of its religious scheduling included *Songs of Praise* and *Carols From King's* and the BBC's Commissioning Editor for Religion and Head of Religion and Ethics, Aaqil Ahmed, was quoted as saying that

This year the BBC's television and radio output is, as always, the cornerstone of traditional religion programming over the festive period.

From the warmth of Tudor Monastery Farm Christmas to Radio 4's Christmas Service from Chester Cathedral and two evocative Eucharist broadcasts coming live from the historic and glorious setting of West-minster Abbey, the story of Christmas is at the heart of BBC schedules this December (BBC Media Centre 2013: www.bbc.co.uk/mediacentre/latestnews/2013/religious-programmes-christmas.html).

A case in point is BBC Radio 2's *The Sunday Hour*, broadcast at 6 a.m. each Sunday morning by Diane Louise-Jordan, a special edition of which would be broadcast on Christmas morning in 2013 celebrating 'the Christmas carol with a variety of special guests and a selection of carols chosen by the Radio 2 listeners', which would include the presenter delving into 'the history of the carol to tell unusual and little-known stories about some of our favourite carols' (BBC Media Centre 2013: www.bbc.co.uk/mediacentre/latestnews/2013/religious-programmes-christmas.html). There is nothing at all wrong or unusual in these programmes. They are precisely what the BBC's religious programming has historically been about and they demon-strably fit one of the examples of a substantive approach to religion given by Lynch, namely 'the representation of religion in media and popular culture' (Lynch 2007a: 127).[2] Such an approach works well when religion's contours are unequivocal and clearly demarcated, but they do pose difficulties when anything that does not conform to such an explicit and self-evident way of identifying religion must, by definition, be rejected as being non-religious. We see this, for example, in the way in which Amy Taubin looks at how the film *Taxi Driver* (Martin Scorsese 1976) is, on one level, not about religion in the respect that 'Although churches are everywhere in New York, [the protagonist Travis Bickle] never notices them (and therefore they're absent from the film)' (Taubin 2000: 19). She concedes that the film's director and screenwriter, Martin Scorsese and Paul Schra-der, 'were both raised in religious households' and she is aware of 'the Christian allegorical aspect of Travis's story' as well as that there is something in Bickle's 'language and, of course, in his dramatic trajec-tory that suggests the influence of an apocalyptic strain of Christianity' (Taubin 2000: 19). But, perhaps surprisingly, Taubin's approach is a

---

[2] The other definitions given by Lynch are a 'focus on the production, use and consumption of media and popular culture by religious groups' and 'interventions by religious groups in response to media texts and popular culture practices' (Lynch 2007a: 127).

typically reductionist one which sees the presence (or indeed the absence) of religion based purely on the presence (or absence) of the institutional church. It is because Bickle 'never notices' any churches that, in Taubin's words, 'he seems to have no interest in any religion' (Taubin 2000: 19). Taubin's point would be valid if the institutional dimension of religion were the only, or at least the pre-eminent, dimension that a religion possesses. For Ninian Smart, though, it is one of seven which he chooses not to place in any order of priority or importance. The institutional, or social, dimension is the sixth of his seven dimensions and is an important dimension insofar as whereas the previous five he looks at—the ritual, experiential, narrative, doctrinal, and ethical—'can be considered in abstract terms', the institutional and the material, which is the seventh dimension in his typology, pertain to the 'incarnation of religion' (Smart 1998a: 19) in embodied, external form. It is not, however, the one which should solely be used to characterize, and so caricature, the 'essence' of religion.

On the plus side, of course, it can be helpful, especially outside the academy, when religion's boundaries are relatively clear-cut and pre-established. If the definition of religion within such a context were to widen along the ways suggested here, then the Head of Religion would have responsibilities not just for *Songs of Praise* but for sports coverage, cookery programmes, soap operas, situation comedies, and indeed all aspects of Christmas scheduling also, including Christmas movies. It might be easy to make the case, as I did in chapter 2, that Scrooge, Santa, and Jesus possess many functional similarities, and the intellectual and theological ramifications of such approaches may be manifold. But the present configuration of what comes under the auspices of, say, 'sports' or 'religion' may be necessary to ensure that everybody knows what is being referred to when a programme is identified as being sports-, or religion-, or indeed drama-, or children-, or politics-related (there is invariably going to be a cross-over between departments—religious programmes can be entertaining, for instance, and an entertainment programme may well feature religion, such as *Citizen Khan*, a BBC sitcom about a Muslim family living in Birmingham), even if the 'religion' that is designated is artificially and narrowly limited to institutional structures and denominations. The same applies when it comes to drawing on substantive definitions of religion, for, as Lynch points out, the benefit is that they are able to delineate 'a relatively clear field of study' (Lynch 2007a: 129), involving as they do the structures,

symbols, and practices of established (institutional) religious traditions. The danger, though, is that when 'religion' is seen to be limited
to particular representations and manifestations of institutional religions one may end up missing out on the larger picture of the ways in
which people's beliefs and values take shape in modern society, along
the lines of Lynch's argument that 'Limiting the study of religion,
media and popular culture to issues related to institutionalized religions could therefore blind us to some of the most pressing questions
about the stories, values and meanings that shape many people's lives
today' (Lynch 2007a: 130).

It may be, for example, that programmes made outside the auspices
and remit of religious broadcasting are no less fecund when it comes
to exploring matters of faith, identity, beliefs, and values. Connelly
makes the point, indeed, that, in the first half of the twentieth century,
'The material produced by the BBC and American and British cinema
about, and for, Christmas tended to emphasise family values, the
antiquity of the English Christmas and a rosy nostalgia for the
Victorian Christmas' (Connelly 2012: xiii). And, he continues, the
annual observation of Christmas was even deemed to be 'a moment of
spiritual communion for English-speaking communities across the
globe' (Connelly 2012: xiii). Lord Reith, the BBC's first Director-
General, may have seen in radio the capacity to be what Connelly
calls 'the perfect complement to the traditional Christmas' (Connelly
2012: 134), as when Simon Elmes writes that from its very beginnings
in the early 1920s 'the BBC's schedules were filled with religion', it
being one of Reith's 'principal pillars . . . and the priests and preachers
who dominated the air throughout the 1920s became household
names, true *religious* radio stars' (Elmes 2012: loc. no. 506). Elmes
proceeds to write that Reith 'was raised a religious man and religion
played a big part in the early wireless schedules. Sundays were replete
with ponderous organ recitals and military bands . . . together with
sermons and addresses by padres and parsons' (Elmes 2012: loc. no.
868). But whereas the BBC in its early days saw itself as providing a
service that complemented what the Christian church was able to
do—as when the *Illustrated London News* reported in 1923 that 'The
invention of broadcasting has immensely extended the power of
music to diffuse the spirit of Christmas', in terms of the way in
which the 'range of carol-singers' voices, hitherto restricted to the
limits of a building, or a short distance in the open air, has been
increased by hundreds of miles (in Connelly 2012: 134)—so today the

function is analogous to what was being envisaged here but without the same explicitly Christian affiliation.

CHRISTMAS JUNIOR CHOICE

A prime example here is *Junior Choice*, a weekend radio programme aimed at the younger listener, first broadcast simultaneously on BBC Radios 1 and 2 in 1967 with Leslie Crowther as host, before Ed Stewart took over presentation duties from 1968 to 1980. Like its predecessor *Children's Favourites* in the 1950s, *Junior Choice* consisted of music requests in which children would write to the BBC asking to hear a particular favourite piece of music that more adult-oriented programmes would be unlikely to feature, with 'Sparky's Magic Piano', Charles Penrose's 'The Laughing Policeman', and Michael Holliday's 'The Runaway Train', stalwarts of the old-school *Children's Favourites* on the BBC Light Programme under the auspices of Uncle Mac (Derek McCulloch)[3], giving way to music very much of the era that *Junior Choice* was running. Many of the most popular songs went on to top the charts, with 'Two Little Boys' from Rolf Harris, 'Grandad' by Clive Dunn, Benny Hill's 'Ernie', and 'There's No One Quite Like Grandma' from the St. Winifred's School Choir, all reaching the coveted number 1 position around Christmas-time[4] during (or just after in the case of the latter) Stewart's tenure on the programme. When Stewart started on the programme in 1968 16 million listeners tuned in each Saturday and Sunday morning, and it had its highest listening figures on Christmas Day (Stewart 2005: 135). In his autobiography from 2005, Stewart cites a *Sunday Express* article from the late 1960s by Peter Dacre which referred to how 'In 15 months, [Stewart] has turned it into not so much a record show as

---

[3] McCulloch became head of Children's Hour in 1933, yet, as Elmes points out, by the 1960s McCulloch's 'frankly now old-fashioned style sat uncomfortably amongst the changing tastes in popular music. "You're a Pink Toothbrush, I'm a Blue Toothbrush" and "The Big Rock Candy Mountain" or "The Runaway Train" may have sounded fine in Mac's introduction, but as soon as rock 'n' roll took teenage breath away, he sounded out of touch' (Elmes 2012: loc. no. 1393).

[4] Though released in late November 1970, Clive Dunn's 'Grandad' did not reach number 1 in the UK Singles Chart until January 1971 where it remained at the top for three weeks.

a family gathering. He gets more than 1,500 requests a week and . . . has BBC radio's second-largest audience, second only to *Two Way Family Favourites*' (in Stewart 2005: 135). I grew up listening to *Junior Choice* in the late 1970s, and especially remember his successor Tony Blackburn's period as host, and in an age before e-mail or social networking sites *Junior Choice* epitomized one of radio's most distinctive characteristics—the opportunity to bring together geographically discrete audiences who shared the same interests in a virtual environment which functioned as a forum not just for record requests and dedications but for hearing about the celebrations and commiserations of children the same age as ourselves whose pastimes corresponded to our own, both in and outside of school, nursery, or family, even if we would never meet them in person. Radio supplied a gateway into a virtual world where our hopes and fears, and our idiosyncratic musical tastes, united us, if only for two hours on a Saturday morning, when our parents were (and thought we were also) still in bed or were preoccupied with adult responsibilities.

In my own case, despite growing up listening ritualistically to *Junior Choice* it is insightful to learn that Tony Blackburn, who inherited the programme, saw it as signalling the death of his own career: 'After 15 years at the top of my profession presenting various daytime radio shows [including the Radio 1 Breakfast Show for the first six years following the launch of Radio 1 in 1967] I found myself spinning *Nellie the Elephant* and *Puff the Magic Dragon*' (Blackburn 2007: 191) to an audience of 'under-eights. Really thought things were going down the pan' (Blackburn 2007: 277). For the next twenty-five years *Junior Choice* had disappeared completely from the radio schedules, with children's television having superseded radio as the place for children to congregate on a Saturday morning, with the likes of *Saturday Superstore* (itself presented by a Radio 1 breakfast host, Mike Read, who moved from weekday adult radio to weekend children's television without there being a comparable radio show) and *Going Live!* reaching the same target audience that *Junior Choice* had achieved in previous years. On 30 September 2007, however, Ed Stewart returned to Radio 2 as part of the day's celebrations of the station's fortieth anniversary with a special live sixty-minute edition of *Junior Choice* from the BBC studios in Birmingham, in which he began by playing the first ever record played by Leslie Crowther forty years ago to the day, 'Pleasant Valley Sunday' by The Monkees. Although the show had originally been aimed at children, what stood out from that anniversary programme was that the original audience now had, in many cases, children and grandchildren of their own and the programme was comprised of requests and dedications from middle-aged listeners who, like the presenter, were reminiscing about their memories of growing up both in the 1960s and 1970s with the programme as accompaniment to their adolescence.

A follow-up, pre-recorded Christmas edition of *Junior Choice* followed on Christmas Eve that year, and each year since 2008 Stewart has broadcast live each morning on Christmas Day with a two-hour *Christmas Junior Choice* which has taken the form of nostalgia on the part of listeners to the original programme, now in their forties and fifties, but with an added, perhaps unexpected, twist. While social networking sites such as Facebook and Twitter are adept at facilitating conversation between people who are physically separated, *Christmas Junior Choice* has become a mainstay of listeners who wish to interact with friends and family members who now live away, in many cases overseas, and for whom radio is the more intimate medium precisely because it is able to evoke memories of Christmases past. Many of the dedications come in from listeners who first had a dedication read out by Stewart several decades earlier and who see in the programme the chance both to supply an update on what has happened to them in the intervening years and also to enable their own children to experience the same anticipation and excitement of tuning in to a radio programme, with an audience in the millions, to hear if their own message to loved ones, and accompanying chosen record, has been selected for inclusion.

Regarding the 2012 Christmas Day programme, for example, which was broadcast from 9 to 11 a.m. from the BBC studios in London, the following is a sample of listener testimony which I have transcribed from a recording of the show:

'My wife and I are avid listeners to *Junior Choice* every Christmas morning, warming to the nostalgia of the fantastic songs from our childhood.'
'Looking forward to listening to your show every Christmas. It brings back such lovely memories of my childhood.'
'*Junior Choice* has become a new Christmas tradition in our household. It's so special to watch my two young boys George and Harry dance along to songs that I grew up with.'
'It brings back happy memories of listening to *Junior Choice* during the 70s.'
'We all love *Junior Choice*. It's becoming a Christmas tradition again.'
'We all love listening to *Junior Choice* and singing along and reminiscing to our childhoods.'

(continued)

'. . . those wonderful days of listening to *Junior Choice*. The songs have become etched in one's mind and hearing them again is one of the best bits of Christmas for me.'

'Fond memories of the show in the 60s as a boy in our old terraced house with no bathroom.'

'A request for my family who are spread around the country at Christmas . . . Your lovely programme brings us all together.'

'The radio will be tuned to *Junior Choice* at our parents' home this morning as it was when we were kids.'

'I always listened to your show at the weekend and enjoyed it so much. It was a much gentler and happy time.'

'*Junior Choice* formed a massive part of my growing up. . . . It is fabulous to have you back to play all our favourites.'

'I lost my beloved dad in July of this year and will miss him terribly this Christmas Day . . . He loved to sing [*Ernie* by Benny Hill] to me as a nipper.'

On the 2013 Christmas morning programme, broadcast from 10 a.m. until 12 noon, Ed Stewart said at one point during the broadcast that 'It reminds an awful lot of you of your youth, this programme. It's amazing how it's not so much the children of today who make the requests but the children of yesterday who remember all these.' In the words of the listeners, too, similar testimony is also elicited, again transcribed from my recording of the show:

'Listening to your show at Christmas over the last two years brought back so many happy memories for me and my wife.'

'*Junior Choice* has become as much of a Christmas tradition in our household as turkey or sprouts.'

'Found your show a few years ago and now it's firmly part of my Christmas Day.'

'*Junior Choice* is one of the best Christmas presents ever. I'm alone at work in security in Southend-on-Sea and always listen to your yearly show at Christmas time.'

'*Junior Choice* on Christmas Day has become a tradition.'

'Liz and I used to listen with our Mum in bed every weekend when we were little. Brings back so many happy childhood memories.'

'My family have been listening to your show since our children were small. We now live in Chicago and our children are grown up with children of their own. Every Christmas morning we tune into the programme via the internet and it brings back so many happy memories of our young days raising our family in Enfield in England.'

'Your show has become a tradition now in our house [at] Christmas.'

'Christmas wouldn't be the same without *Junior Choice*.'

'You're part of our Christmas morning tradition.'

In the most recent programme to date, on 25 December 2014, again broadcast from 10 a.m. to 12 noon, listener testimony included the following:

'We're planning our Christmas . . . and your show is an important part of it. Christmas Day wouldn't be the same without it.'
'Your Christmas Day show has become traditional in our house.'
'Christmas isn't Christmas without your show, Ed.'
'It's become, your show, a tradition in our house on Christmas Day.'
'I always listen on Christmas morning while in the kitchen getting the lunch ready for the family and it brings back some great memories of my childhood.'
'I used to listen to your *Junior Choice* show many years ago when my father would turn on the radio for me and my sister, leave it at the bottom of the stairs for us to awaken from our slumber.'
'We grew up listening to your show. We are both listening in different continents, in Australia and Ian in Nottingham.'
'*Junior Choice* has become essential Christmas listening.'
'Your programme is now part of our Christmas and that of my family around the country.'

This selection from *Junior Choice* is certainly an unusual and unprecedented one in academic discourse, and what is clear from the above testimony is just how devoid any of it is of explicitly scholarly or theological vocabulary pertaining to religion while at the same time testifying to something out of the ordinary and akin to Eliade's talk of 'sacred time'. It certainly accords with the notion, outlined in chapter 1, that Christmas is a time of the year when our normal rituals and schedules are disrupted and even dissolved and that the transcendence, even the transformation, afforded by Christmas is what marks it off as ontologically different from any other time of the year. It also encapsulates Agajanian's notion, as discussed at the outset of this book, that Christmas is associated with 'a feeling of nostalgia for good times past' (Agajanian 2000: 145). Certainly, when I referred in chapter 1 to how Christmas could be said to comprise the site of one's nostalgic longing for a prelapsarian universe or promised land where release from everyday problems is facilitated, this accords with the testimony of the listener who wrote in 2012 that 'I always listened to your show at the weekend and enjoyed it so much' in what is now seen, retrospectively, to have been 'a much gentler and happy [*sic*] time'. This, again, corresponds to what Marling has said about how, as mentioned earlier, Christmas comprises 'a doorway connecting the present to earlier eras' (Marling 2000: 129). Listener requests are redolent with language of how '*Junior Choice* has become essential Christmas listening' and 'a tradition in our house on Christmas Day' or that 'Christmas Day wouldn't be the same without it' in a way that links with how, to appropriate Victor Turner's vocabulary, there is a state of liminality or *communitas* at the heart of Christmas which is ontologically distinct from any other point in the calendar.

Indeed, the fact that *Junior Choice* is broadcast just once a year, with no guarantee of future scheduling, and entails the playing of music that is otherwise off-limits supplies an intensity and focus to the programme and heightens the sacrality on display. It works precisely because of the clearly demarcated boundaries surrounding the programme's transmission whereby in the *present* moment—to this end, the *eschaton* is now—listeners *look forward* to a ritual, or as one of the listeners in 2012 put it, a 'new Christmas tradition', the *telos* of which is to recapture and bring back memories and nostalgia of one's (childhood) *past*. Its effect is in accordance with Nissenbaum's wider argument that Christmas rituals 'have long served to transfigure our ordinary behavior in an almost magical fashion, in ways that reveal something of what we would like to be, what we once were, or what we are becoming despite ourselves' (Nissenbaum 1996: loc. no. 139; see also Deacy 2013: 198). *Junior Choice* may play only a temporary and provisional role in the radio schedules but it is just this interplay between past, present, and future that makes it such an enriching site of *communitas*.

Of course, on one level, there is all the difference in the world between a radio programme that indulges in childhood nostalgia and Turner's anthropological fieldwork on ritual studies in Central Africa, specifically the Ndembu tribe of northwest Zambia whom he studied for two and a half years (see Turner 1969: 4). Turner's core thesis is that there are

> two major 'models' for human interrelatedness, juxtaposed and alternating. The first is of society as a structured, differentiated, and often hierarchical system of politico-legal-economic positions with many types of evaluation, separating men in terms of 'more' or 'less.' The second . . . is of society as an unstructured or rudimentarily structured and relatively undifferentiated . . . community, or even communion of equal individuals who submit together to the general authority of the ritual elders (Turner 1969: 96).

From the outset, therefore, *Junior Choice* has no obvious contribution to make to Turner's research which is predicated on the way in which in tribal societies 'social life is a type of dialectical process that involves successive experience of high and low, communitas and structure, homogeneity and differentiation, equality and inequality' (Turner 1969: 97). It is the relationship between the individual or group and the social structure that is core to Turner's thesis and to this end the strictly *virtual* nature of community that encapsulates the milieu of *Junior Choice* is simply alien to how, for Turner, the basis for talk of liminality and *communitas* is the common characteristic of persons who 'fall in the interstices of social structure', who 'are on its margins' and who 'occupy its lowest rungs' (Turner 1969: 125). For Turner, in other words, there is an inextricable relationship between low social status and *communitas*, as when he writes that 'In liminality, the underling comes uppermost' (Turner 1969: 102) and he refers to the common attributes 'of such seemingly diverse phenomena as neophytes in the liminal phase of ritual, subjugated autochthones, small nations, court jesters, holy mendicants, good Samaritans, millenarian movements…and monastic orders' (Turner 1969: 125). *Communitas* can only emerge in the specific context of social structure—something that would be hard to see as functionally or analogically operative in a Christmas radio programme.

However, where Turner's work does intersect well with *Junior Choice* is in terms of his talk of the *liminal* state or period in which individuals or groups may be construed as 'passengers' who are detached 'from an earlier fixed point in the social structure, from a set of cultural conditions (a "state"), or from both' and whose 'characteristics' might be deemed as 'ambiguous' as they pass through 'a cultural realm that has few or none of the attributes of the past or coming state' (Turner 1969: 94). Liminality thus points to an 'in-between' state in which one leaves a social structure behind and then, following the liminal period, is reaggregated or reincorporated into society once more and is 'expected to behave in accordance with certain customary norms and ethical standards binding on incumbents of social position in a system of such positions' (Turner 1969: 95). Liminality for Turner is a 'moment in and out of time' and 'in and out of secular social structure' (Turner 1969: 96) which posits the awareness that a fissure has opened up between the way life was lived in the past and the way things are now. Crucially, the liminal state is not permanent but is a moment out of time and place which is, rather than an end in itself, a means to an end of returning to society once more, renewed and refreshed. Although on the one hand, 'from the perspectival viewpoint of those concerned with the maintenance of "structure," all sustained manifestations of communitas must appear as dangerous and anarchical, and have to be hedged around with prescriptions, prohibitions, and conditions' (Turner 1969: 109), Turner takes the line that 'communitas is made evident or accessible, so to speak, only through its juxtaposition to, or hybridization with, aspects of social structure' (Turner 1969: 127). No matter how 'elusive' or 'hard to pin down' (Turner 1969: 127) talk of liminality and *communitas* may be, that liminality or *communitas* cannot be understood outside of a relationship or understanding of social structure.

This accords with how, in respect of *Junior Choice*, no matter how aberrant or deviant the programme may be from the mainstream—even to the point that its playlist of novelty songs may be deemed a taboo, as typified by 'There's No One Quite Like Grandma' by St. Winifred's School Choir, which, despite being a number 1 hit in 1980, has, according to the *Daily Telegraph*, 'been a regular feature of "worst ever song" compilations ever since' (Jamieson 2009: www. telegraph.co.uk/culture/culturenews/6622821/St-Winifreds-choir-reunites-for-charity-version-of-Theres-No-one-Quite-Like-Grandma. html)—once the strictly two-hour annual ritual has finished there is no ambition on the part of the BBC to incorporate the programme into the regular weekend schedules, despite entreaties on the part of listeners for *Junior Choice* to become a weekly ritual once more as was the case from 1967 until the early 1980s. *Christmas Junior Choice* celebrates the marginal and appeals, uniquely in British radio, to those on the underside of the status quo whose musical tastes are not otherwise accommodated. When Turner thus attests that 'Liminality implies that the high could not be high unless the low existed, and he who is high must experience what it is like to be low' (Turner 1969: 97), this also characterizes how for the British radio establishment the regular, mainstream playlist is given legitimacy when it is juxtaposed with, or seen in opposition to, that which functions in alterity to the norm. In much the same way Nissenbaum refers to how, in the Puritan era, Christmas was an occasion when the social hierarchy was turned upside down, practices which still exist today as when in the British Army officers wait on their subordinates (see Nissenbaum 1996: loc. no. 269; Kelly 2004: 68; Golby and Purdue

2000: 26). Similarly, for Nissenbaum, charity was something that emanated at Christmas, when the rich and powerful would give the fruits of their harvest bounty to their poorer neighbours or kin: 'Christmas was a time when peasants, servants, and apprentices exercised the right to demand that their wealthier neighbors and patrons treat them as if *they* were wealthy and powerful' (Nissenbaum 1996: loc. no. 281). Crucially, from the point of view of our present discussion, Nissenbaum concludes that 'by inverting the established hierarchy (rather than simply ignoring it), those role inversions actually served as a reaffirmation of the existing social order' (Nissenbaum 1996: loc. no. 321).

It would be interesting to this end to see what effect the programme would have were it to be given a regular and permanent slot in the weekly radio schedules, such as on Saturday and Sunday mornings as used to be the case. Were this to happen then the same process that Turner espouses with respect to tribal culture would apply here. In Turner's words, 'There is a dialectic here, for the immediacy of com-munitas gives way to the mediacy of structure. . . . What is certain is that no society can function adequately without this dialectic' (Turner 1969: 129). What Turner is advocating is that structure and tradition often give way to the need for the spontaneity and immediacy that characterizes *communitas* but, once attained, after a period of time 'Maximization of communitas provokes maximization of structure, which in its turn produces revolutionary strivings for renewed com-munitas' (Turner 1969: 129). Paradoxically, then, 'Communitas itself soon develops a structure' (Turner 1969: 132). The process is recyclable and repetitive, and even though in itself *communitas* is never anything other than something 'betwixt and between' (Turner 1969: 95)—it is forever in a state of becoming and pertains to hopes, dreams, aspir-ations, and wish-fulfilment, such as that of the promised land, as when Turner argues that 'Communitas has . . . an aspect of potentiality; it is often in the subjunctive mood' (Turner 1969: 127) and wherein 'we may catch glimpses of that unused evolutionary potential in mankind which has not yet been externalized and fixed in structure' (Turner 1969: 128)—in reality regular exposure to something this transforma-tive and even life-changing would likely mean that *Junior Choice* would no longer function as *communitas* and something else would have to take on that function. Only by its presence outside of ordinary, profane time, in the form of a live radio programme on Christmas Day, is this experience of *communitas* able to be maintained.

To this end, there is a parallel with Kate McCarthy's thesis that Bruce Springsteen concerts are akin to Turner's understanding of spontaneous *communitas*—'here made possible by common connection to a particular vision of America, one in which time moves slowly, neighbors are trusted, and the good life can be had over a shared beer' (McCarthy 2011: 33). The fact that McCarthy also likens this experience to the albeit temporary manifestation and realization of the promised land (McCarthy 2011: 33) suggests that Turner's thesis has the capacity to apply to debates that lie at the very heart of contemporary media and popular culture. In McCarthy's case she is arguing that as concert-goers are temporarily removed from 'real' space and time they will be predilected to 'share beer, money, and affection with others who, outside the performance context, they would be unlikely to share a conversation with' (McCarthy 2011: 33). Accordingly, when one goes to see Springsteen perform, 'Lines of class, politics, and geography . . . seem to dissolve within the "sacred" space and time of the concert experience' (McCarthy 2011: 33). While *Junior Choice* lacks the same social and communal element that an outdoors rock concert is able to elicit, it does seem able to capture, for two hours on Christmas morning, the ideal of a happy, functional, homogeneous family unit, imbued by memories of 'perfect' Christmases past in which 'my father would turn on the radio for me and my sister, leave it at the bottom of the stairs for us to awaken from our slumber' or when 'Liz and I used to listen with our Mum in bed every weekend when we were little'.

Even less auspicious childhood experiences can be transcended and overcome as indicated by the listener in 2012 who wrote to say that he had 'fond memories of the show in the 60s as a boy in our old terraced house with no bathroom'. Similarly, for listeners who have suffered a family bereavement *Christmas Junior Choice* has proven to be a conduit for them to remember their loved ones from a happier time, as in the case of the listener from Merseyside in 2012 who wrote to say 'I lost my beloved dad in July of this year and will miss him terribly this Christmas Day'. It was the memory of her late father singing Benny Hill's 'Ernie', a staple of *Junior Choice*, to her which prompted her to contact the programme and communicate with others the love and loss she has experienced in a way which gets to the very essence of Turner's understanding that *communitas* 'is a transformative experience that goes to the root of each person's being' and where one can find 'in that root something profoundly communal and shared' (Turner 1969: 138). *Communitas* for Turner may only be 'a phase, a moment, not a permanent condition' (Turner 1969: 140) but it is all the more efficacious when applied to the milieu of *Junior Choice* as that one musical dedication for 'Ernie' encapsulates, and evokes powerful memories of a golden age, free from mortality, where fathers and daughters enjoyed such happiness together. It is far from wide of the mark to see this as corresponding to Turner's argument that *communitas* is 'accompanied by experiences of unprecedented potency' and which 'often appear to flood their subjects with affect' (Turner 1969: 128).

It is doubtful that the presenters or production team would see the function of the programme as being religious in scope, and certainly for the programme's final presenter, Tony Blackburn, religion itself is a complete anathema. He wrote in his autobiography about being turned off from religion at an early age 'and nothing has altered my opinion since. If people want to believe this stuff, then good luck to them, but please don't get fanatical about it' (Blackburn 2007: 38). Writing about the resources that we use when conducting research in religion and culture, Tom Beaudoin has called for scholars to pay close attention to their underlying motivations, attachments, and methodologies and to be upfront about what exactly our relationship is to the academic disciplines and practices that we use (see Deacy 2009: 9; Beaudoin 2009: 23, 32). He queries whether such studies are the pure and objective scholarly productions that we deem them to be or whether they say rather more than they might be prepared to allow about our own idiosyncrasies, fantasies, daydreams, and fictions— indeed, our 'fandoms' (Beaudoin 2009: 23). While academics may see themselves as being involved in objective and rational enterprises and thus in a sufficiently detached position to be able to decode the discourses of others, Beaudoin counsels that, in actuality, they have more in common than they care to acknowledge with the category of 'fandom' as developed in popular culture studies (see Deacy 2009: 9–10). This is certainly true of work that has been undertaken in the field of religion and film, for example, as we see in Robert Pope's light-hearted comment in the preface to *Salvation in Celluloid* that when he began teaching a module titled 'God in Film' at the University of Wales

> students would often remark that this would be a good opportunity for them to discuss their favourite films. I corrected them by insisting that

they would be discussing *my* favourite films instead. While this was not entirely true, there is a greater significance in this kind of argument than scholars of theology and film are often prepared to admit (Pope 2007: ix).

It is notable that many of the scholars who write on religion and film preface their books with reference to how they first became interested in bringing together the academic pursuit of religion or theology with a medium that has brought them, personally, so many pleasures over the years. It is insightful to this end that Pope begins his book by recounting his first visit to the cinema as a child growing up in Swansea in the late 1970s. For Adele Reinhartz, too, she goes to some lengths in the introduction to *Scripture on the Silver Screen* to qualify her academic study of films which draw on the Bible in the course of their narratives and plots with the confession that her 'interest in the movies is entirely amateur . . . in my pure and often uncritical enjoyment of movies, which are one of my favorite forms of entertainment' (Reinhartz 2003: 2). Some books go even further and are explicitly and transparently grounded in the films which had such a profound emotional effect on the author while they were growing up. Though an autobiographical rather than scholarly work per se, journalist John Walsh's *Are You Talking to Me?* foregrounds how specific movies he watched as a child left such an indelible impression on him that, having lost, at the age of nineteen, 'the last vestiges of religious faith' (Walsh 2003: 310; see also Deacy and Ortiz 2008: 38), it fell to the movies to supply the beliefs, hopes, and values that the Catholic church had once performed for him. I, too, am more than aware that my personal enjoyment of watching films has often been the impetus for being research-active in this area. Had I not been excited, for example, about the prospect of watching *Working Girl* (1988) and *The Shawshank Redemption* (1994) for my last publication, *Screening the Afterlife*, I would most likely have chosen to write on two different pictures instead. It is certainly true that my appreciation of these two movies preceded any academic work undertaken by me in the field of religion and film. But that is not to say that fruitful and critical scholarly enquiry cannot accrue when one is writing about films which have had a formative influence on one's life.

What is required is a recognition that our motivations are far from pure or unsullied and should not be presented as such. When Walsh thus concludes the introduction of his book with the invitation to his reader 'to raid his or her own filmic image-bank and consider what

flickering presences, what seductive scenes and passionate epiph-
anies, made them into the people they've become' (Walsh 2003: 17),
his plea is not dissimilar to how for Beaudoin academics, like fans,
are no less irrationally disposed to venerate particular passions,
attachments, and subjectivities (see Deacy 2009: 10). Beaudoin is
thus right to highlight the need for academics to undergo a self-
and communal examination of their motivations and fandoms (see
Deacy 2009: 10) before, when applied to the present discussion, they
can even attempt to adjudicate on the extent to which something from
popular culture may be found to correspond to, or deviate from, a
pre-established religious framework which the scholar has brought
to the agenda.

In my own case, *Junior Choice* would be an atypical way of
documenting contemporary religious activity, not least due to its
failure to conform to the more conventional substantive approach
to religion of which Blackburn's critique from outside the academy of
'religious mumbo-jumbo' (Blackburn 2007: 253) is symptomatic.
Indeed, a substantive definition reduces religion to the presence (or
absence) of a particular essence, creed, institutional structure, deity,
or other supernatural phenomena or belief-system, such as whether
or not heaven exists. When Blackburn thus correlates the lack of
belief in a 'magical afterlife that we all float off to' (Blackburn 2007:
252)—as he puts it, 'Why worry about life after death when in all
likelihood there isn't one?' (Blackburn 2007: 253)—with the improb-
ability that 'there is a God' (Blackburn 2007: 253), we see in effect the
operation of a substantive model of religion in everyday discourse.
Although *Christmas Junior Choice* does not therefore equate in any
way with a substantive approach to religion, it could be seen as a
prime example of a *functional* definition of religion, in which the
emphasis is on the function, and effect, of religion, rather than on its
substance or essence. As Lynch sees it, 'Functionalist definitions open
up the possibility that any socio-cultural system which serves . . . basic
"religious" needs for community, identity and meaning could be
defined as religious, even though it may fall far outside the conventional canon of religions' (Lynch 2007a: 129). Examples that Lynch
gives in this context are 'nationalism, cinema-going, sports fandom,
retail therapy . . . and the production and consumption of popular
music' (Lynch 2007a: 129). In none of these examples is it relevant
as to whether or not there is a deity or a heaven, as it is the social (and
in some cases material) value that we place on objects, rituals, and

activities which comprises the religious dimension. This is a very Durkheimian perspective, which bears witness to a shift in the way in which the sacred or religious is constructed away from the metaphysical and towards the terrestrial and social, and as Lynch sees it, it 'can provide a more flexible framework for taking the religious pulse of contemporary culture' (Lynch 2007a: 131). Certainly for Smart 'It is important for us to recognize secular ideologies as part of the story of human worldviews', especially in view of the fact that 'they sometimes function in society like religions' (Smart 1998a: 10).

In this respect it fits very well with how *Christmas Junior Choice* might be deemed to comprise a site of religious activity. If, as Smart suggests, there are plenty of people who 'may see ultimate spiritual meaning . . . in relationships to other persons' (Smart 1998a: 12) then we should take stock of the role that radio has played in fomenting this sense of community and togetherness over the last century. Connelly refers in particular to how in its early days the wireless 'quickly established its role as a companion to those who were alone, a feeling exacerbated by the communal festivities of Christmas' (Connelly 2012: 134). Responding to the question as to whether (not least on 'religious' grounds) the BBC should have closed down on Christmas Day, the corporation argued that had they done so 'thousands of lonely people throughout the country would have had no message of cheer or Christmas greeting', and 'That a little brightness may have been brought to lives all too drab and wretched is more than ample compensation to BBC officials for the sacrifice of their own Christmas festivities' (Connelly 2012: 135). This latter point is especially germane to *Junior Choice* as it is one of only two daytime programmes to be transmitted live on Radio 2 on Christmas Day, the other being the more traditional *Good Morning Christmas* with its mixture of carols, hymns, and spiritual reflection which is normally aired from 7 to 9 a.m. Connelly quotes a London vicar from the early days of radio who wrote that 'One thinks with sympathy at this time of year of lonely people, and assuredly it must be Broadcasting that will help to increase the Christmas spirit for them. . . . They know they are enjoying what is a pleasure to others; in a word, they are members of a Christmas party' (Connelly 2012: 135). Similarly, in the Christmas 1951 edition of the *Radio Times* reference was made to how at Christmas-time the presenters felt themselves to be closer than ever to the listeners: 'The friendliness and joyfulness of Christmastide find their way into the BBC's Christmas programme, at no other season is the broadcaster so closely in tune with his vast audience' (Connelly 2012: 136).

In the preface to their edited volume *God in the Details* Mazur and McCarthy attest that 'Today, people are almost silly with the exploration of religion in popular culture' (Mazur and McCarthy 2011a: xvii). Their assumption is that whole publications have been devoted to discussing religion in literary fiction, film, TV, music, graphic arts, tourism, capitalism, and sports, leading to 'some confusion over audience, purpose, and method' (Mazur and McCarthy 2011a: xvii). Their concern is that since 'some are clearly written for fun, some are clearly meant for scholarly reflection . . . and some are clearly meant for religious reflection', then publishers (and, presumably, teachers and scholars too) 'seem to have placed all of these works into the same conversation' (Mazur and McCarthy 2011a: xvii). The issue is more complicated when we factor in literature on Christmas as here, as we have been discussing, the boundaries are even more contested over where religion may be found to lie. In the case of *Christmas Junior Choice*, Mazur and McCarthy's claim that 'religious meaning can be found in activities that are often considered meaningless' (Mazur and McCarthy 2011b: 2) would certainly accord with how the programme's ostensibly trivial content—record requests for 'My Old Man's a Dustman', 'Captain Beaky', and 'Hello Muddah Hello Faddah'—yield richer meaning on closer inspection. Indeed, when Mazur and McCarthy write that 'In the visit to the dentist, the bathroom, or the hospital, we find meaning . . . that would have been missed if we had simply overlooked these areas' (Mazur and McCarthy 2011b: 2), it might be added that a radio programme that might be listened to while families are opening presents, cooking the Christmas turkey or simply as background accompaniment to as mundane a ritual as cleaning one's teeth is no less religiously fecund than 'those events traditionally plowed for "deeper" meaning, such as life-cycle and rite-of-passage events' and 'annual rituals of religious . . . communities' (Mazur and McCarthy 2011b: 2). Their talk of when 'a wide range of apparently nonreligious phenomena become religiously significant' (Mazur and McCarthy 2011b: 4) and how as 'religious institutions have lost their monopoly on the construction and maintenance of meaning, religiosity has found expression in a wide variety of human practices' (Mazur and McCarthy 2011b: 9) equates well with a radio programme whose accomplishment, if not its *raison d'être*, has been to establish a virtual community of listeners for whom the programme is a conduit for facilitating their return, if only in imagination and for one day a year, to the nostalgia and innocence of childhood when the same presenter played the same tunes and read out dedications to (in many cases) the same expectant band of listeners.

RAMIFICATIONS FOR THE DEFINITION AND STUDY OF RELIGION

The ramifications of construing *Christmas Junior Choice* as a potentially fertile site of religious activity are immense. It may be commonplace, as Jobling asserts, to identify religion with 'the institutional, ritualistic and dogmatic' (Jobling 2010: 11), in which case of course the correlation simply would not work. However, it is never possible to construe religion as some sort of pure or objective essence which exists in a vacuum, impervious to what is happening in culture at large. Clark makes the astute observation to this end that 'While it is undeniable that something we call religion "happens" quite often throughout the world, whenever something religious occurs, it does so within the confines of other cultural events, that is, within a complex cultural context' (Clark 2012: 8; see also Deacy 2013: 204). The 'sacred' and the 'profane' are not therefore clearly demarcated categories that are known to and understood by everyone—'This varies from people to people, and place to place' (Clark 2012: 8). What is present, in other words, is a functionalist way of categorizing religion where a phenomenon or event is performing a function that is recognizably religious but where the boundary between the sacred and the secular is blurred. To an extent there is a Tillichian element at work here in the respect that, as Brant sees it, 'It is not only the case that all religious actualization must be through culture; it is also true that all cultural creation is inherently religious' (Brant 2012: 54; see also Deacy 2013: 201), even to the degree that for Tillich 'a secular painting can be more religiously meaningful and potent than a painting with religious subject matter' (in Brant 2012: 86; see also Deacy 2013: 202). As we shall see, however, Tillich did not go so far as to see *everything* in culture as religious per se as in order to be authentically transcendental a cultural creation had to mediate what Brant calls 'the revelation of divine Spirit or Spiritual Presence' (Brant 2012: 66; see also Deacy 2013: 202). In its own right, and without that transcendental underpinning, culture lacks the sort of depth or ultimacy that for Tillich was necessary. For Clark, in contrast, the line is more porous than this, such that 'whenever something religious can be said to have happened, it must be understood as doing so in relationship to other things that are not considered sacred' (Clark 2012: 8) and that 'Those things in society that are considered to be either religious or secular are always being defined or redefined, in relation to one another' (Clark 2012: 9).

If this is the case, then the fact that, as Horsley sees it, Christmas 'incorporates every aspect of religion (meaning, community, identity, symbol system) at every social level of society (individual, family, community, national)' (Horsley 2001a: 168) would suggest that the festival can readily lay claim to being innately religious. Ironically, however, Christmas is one festival of the year which strongly polarizes people precisely because it is either seen as inescapably secular (due, as we shall see, to its commercialized and consumerist pedigree) or as a quintessentially religious festival in view of its Christian origins. It is worth paying attention to some of the different positions on display as in some cases it is clear that pre-established definitions are being 'read into' the celebration of Christmas, which has the effect of obfuscating the question of whether it is truly religious (and if so what sort of religion is being countenanced). Joseph F. Kelly is a case in point as he begins his book *The Origins of Christmas* with the assertion that 'Christmas has achieved the status of a national holiday. Many people who do not celebrate it religiously still observe it as a secular holiday' (Kelly 2004: xii). This is quite a problematic statement as it draws a distinction on the one hand between the 'religious' and the 'secular' while, tantalizingly, raising the question of whether a 'secular' festival might in itself be celebrated in a 'religious' manner, without, say, any Christian baggage. As Restad sees it, 'Thinking that money has overdetermined the meaning of Christmas, many premise their critiques of the holiday on the notion that its sacred meaning and its secular celebration form two separate spheres, and that profane (which is commercialization) has edged aside sacred (which has to do with the spirit)' (Restad 1995: 167).

On this basis, a functionalist understanding of religion might want to ask whether to indulge in the commercial side of Christmas might be no less classified as a religious activity than the 'spiritual' element which is identified as its polar opposite. Indeed, as Restad further outlines, not only is the Christmas season set 'visually apart from the

remainder of the year' but commerce has 'exploited the flimsy parti-
tion between sacred and profane time at Christmas, beginning its
quest for holiday profits in late November or still earlier at Halloween
and before' (Restad 1995: 168). She is quite right to identify in the
foreword of her book that 'within a culture that also values religious
freedom and separation of church and state' Christmas retains 'its
unchallenged position as the most important of national holidays'
(Restad 1995: loc. no. 64), but where I would take issue with her is
over her implicit assessment that there is a binary at work here—an
'either/or', where one is celebrating a religious festival *or* a national
holiday. To this degree I agree with Haire and Nelson that 'Christmas is the paradigm example of the increasingly blurred line
between the religious and consumerist tendencies of our society'
(Haire and Nelson 2010: 85). Kelly is not therefore wrong when he
argues that 'Christmas has always had a secular element, which can
flourish alongside the religious element and add to the season'
(Kelly 2004: 129), but here there is still an assumption that the
'religious' and the 'consumerist' are separable and exist in distinct
spheres, even if, in keeping with Niebuhr's 'dualist' model, some
element of negotiation between them is both inevitable and even,
sometimes, mutually beneficial.

One of the most extreme instances of this binary model can be
found in a 1993 publication, *The Trouble with Christmas*, by humanist author and editor of *Free Enquiry* magazine, Tom Flynn, which
espouses an atheistic critique of the Christmas festival and takes it as a
given throughout that Christmas is an indissolubly Christian celebration: 'no holiday is viewed by non-Christians as more representative
of Christian culture' (Flynn 1993: 37; see also Deacy 2013: 198). So
inescapably Christian-based is Christmas, according to Flynn, that
every facet of Christmas—'from crèches and carols to snowflakes and
sleighs'—are unequivocal 'emblems of Christian dominance' (Flynn
1993: 221) and thereby alienate anyone who does not observe the
Christian faith, including Muslims, Buddhists, and atheists, leading
him to conclude that Christmas should be 'abandoned as a *universal
public holiday*' (Flynn 1993: 209). As he sees it, 'Nothing less will suffice
to safeguard the rights of children of diverse religious (and nonreligious) backgrounds' (Flynn 1993: 223). What is curious about Flynn's
polemic is that there are no shades of grey. Clement Miles' argument, as
outlined in chapter 2, that the various ingredients which have gone into
Christmas are of pagan derivation and that few people 'have any idea of

the process by which the heathen elements have become mingled with that which is obviously Christian' (Miles 1912: 19) is foreign to Flynn, who appears to be saying that idolizing Santa, gorging on roast turkey, mince pies, and sherry, watching *The Great Escape*, or, indeed, listening to *Junior Choice* are facets of a sectarian Christian holiday and insensitive to minority groups. If Flynn had his way then American public schools which, he contends, 'have become a flash point in the Yuletide battle between traditionalists and multiculturalists' (Flynn 1993: 212) would be open on Christmas Day 'as they always have on the holy days of other world religions' (Flynn 1993: 227), and the trimming or display of Christmas trees or the exchange of gifts would be banned from the public school system (see Flynn 1993: 226).

The problem with Flynn's argument is that although for him organized gift-exchanges are of Christian provenance, most non-Christians are unlikely to be offended by the giving of presents on Christmas morning. Is the gift of an MP3 player, for example, covert Christian propaganda? Flynn may have a point when he contends that if one believes Christianity to be 'untrue' then 'the alleged birth of Christ is not something we ought to celebrate' (Flynn 1993: 232), but it is a moot point as to whether people are really celebrating Christianity on 25 December or whether they might be celebrating consumption, or the chance to spend time with their families, or simply making the most of the opportunity to take a break from the normal cycle of work. Flynn's premise is that Christmas is a monolithic event and its celebration is oppressive for non-Christians, such that 'atheists, agnostics, free-thinkers, and secular humanists' will want to 'sit out the winter holidays' (Flynn 1993: 234). In reality, though, when he extols the positive consequences of raising children 'Yule-free' it is hard to discern what is explicitly Christian about the things he says a non-Christmas celebration will positively entail: 'the fear of Santa Claus, the shopping frenzy, the immersion in superstitious thought and behavior, that corrosive acquisitiveness, and the disappointment when peace and goodwill fail to materialize' (Flynn 1993: 233). Many Christians would also be keen to forego Christmas's more crass and materialistic components, and it is a bit of a stretch to assume that non-Christians would feel liberated if they no longer had to observe the festival when what makes Christmas distinctive for many people, Christian and non-Christian alike, is the opportunity to give and receive presents, entertain family and friends, eat and drink, and relax in front of the TV.

To this end, Max A. Myers supplies a more subtle and realistic understanding of the Christian/non-Christian interface at Christmas when he writes that 'As Christmas became increasingly associated with [Santa] and with his narrative, it ceased to be identified with the specific religion of Christianity and came to be simply part of the American cultural tradition' (Myers 2001b: 197). Whereas for Flynn non-Christians 'shouldn't even get caught *appearing* to celebrate' (Flynn 1993: 232) Christmas, the dividing-line between Christians and non-Christians is in reality far more opaque. As Myers sees it, 'One had the right to celebrate Christmas merely by virtue of being an American, and one could exercise that right simply by participating in consumer capitalism', such as in the form of purchasing 'a tree, decorations, card, food, and gifts' (Myers 2001b: 197). For John Badertscher, also, the seasonal ritual of Christmas transcends any narrowly conceived Christian frame of reference and is even the 'most easily understood example of an explicitly religious expression in our culture' (Badertscher 2010: 203). Crucially, for Badertscher, it affects everyone—not only committed Christians but 'those who regard themselves as secularized', although he is a little vague about the form that it takes for non-Christians, simply writing that 'Every-one in this culture ... must deal with it' (Badertscher 2010: 203). Freya Jarman-Ivens also provides an account of Christmas which qualifies the binary nature of Flynn's delineation. According to Jarman-Ivens, although 'Christmas as a festival has an indelible association with Christianity and Christian values' (Jarman-Ivens 2008: 130), she writes that 'Each December seems to see "Christmas values" superseding Christian values, and even absorbing some along the way', with '"Charity" and "Goodwill", "Family" and "Peace"' remaining 'central tenets of the hegemonic Christmas message, while the story of Jesus's birth is relegated to a sideshow' (Jarman-Ivens 2008: 131).

In what could be seen to comprise a refutation of Flynn's argument that Christmas should be boycotted by non-Christians, Jarman-Ivens observes that 'Even the most hard-core atheist risks being drawn into the media-manufactured Christmas, and the Christmas period is seen as an immensely important time by millions of people who may not even believe in God' (Jarman-Ivens 2008: 131). This is the polar opposite of Flynn's message to Christians that 'we non-Christians should have the courtesy not to distort *your* observance, which has a deep and authentic meaning within your community of belief'

(Flynn 1993: 233) but which could not possibly have any deep or authentic meaning, Flynn presumes, outside of that faith community. Likewise, for Tara Brabazon, 'Popular culture generally, and the popular media specifically, configure a secular Christmas that circulates meanings and interpretations of goodwill, family, love, peace and generosity that are disconnected from religion' and which, crucially, 'overwrite and mediate religious discourses' (Brabazon 2008: 151). Brabazon has in mind the way in which films such as *It's a Wonderful Life* and the various re-tellings of *A Christmas Carol*, as well as soap operas, TV news, current affairs, and drama, all have their own idiosyncratic take on Christmas which may not be incompatible with traditional religion but are hardly subservient to it in their various representations of 'family, friendship, the home and consumerism' (Brabazon 2008: 151).

Finally, at the other end of the spectrum, it is possible to encounter positions which are far removed from Flynn's critique, but which retain the binary between the religious and the secular. Whereas for Flynn all the accoutrements of the Christmas holiday need to be boycotted due to their association with Christianity, William Waits, writing in the same year as Flynn, holds that 'the secular aspects of the celebration, such as gift giving, the Christmas dinner, and the gathering of family members, have dwarfed its religious aspects in resources spent and in concern given' (Waits 1993: 3). He even concludes that 'One cannot escape the conclusion that the secular aspects of the modern celebration have been more central than the religious aspects', and that one 'must not confuse the rationale for the celebration (the celebration of the birthday of Jesus) with what is central to the celebration as indicated by the behavior of celebrants' (Waits 1993: 3). Flynn holds that the whole of Christmas is contaminated by its association with a religious tradition that not everyone subscribes to, while Waits takes the line that the religious element can easily be bracketed out and marginalized as peripheral to what Christmas means to the majority of people. Although this is a more pragmatic perspective than Flynn's call for Christmas to be boycotted, there is still an assumption that somehow we can disaggregate the 'religious' from the 'secular'. The difference in a way is just on the emphasis in that whereas for Flynn everything to do with Christmas was Christian-oriented, for Waits only a tiny amount of what Christmas means to people has a sufficiently religious element to it for it even to feature in his study of how Christmas has evolved over the course of the twentieth century: 'This book does not discuss the religious aspects of Christmas' (Waits 1993: 3).

What Waits does not countenance is the possibility that the secular may itself be a repository of the religious. The religious is assumed to have clearly established contours and to be an anathema to the modern-day festival of consumption. In much the same vein, Mark Mercer has written that 'Nowadays, Christmas is, for many of us, a holiday that has no religious significance at all', on the grounds that when one celebrates 'good will, generosity, and peace among nations' (Mercer 2010: 71) and when we adorn the festival with 'Christmas trees, wreaths, colored lights, candy canes, carols and Christmas music', this does not 'put us in mind of any values or doctrines specifically Christian or religious' (Mercer 2010: 72). As with Waits, the assumption here is that religion is bound up with its institutional and specifically Christian elements, the peripheral nature of which for many people means that Christmas is therefore a secular festival. Indeed, as Waits puts it, 'Although celebrants may have had meaningful Christmas experiences in church or in other religious settings, they have spent much more time during the holiday season in such secular matters as selecting presents, then wrapping and presenting them, and making arrangements for holiday visits and feasts' (Waits 1993: 3). When Mercer defines the modern secular Christmas as being 'about everything that religious Christmas is about'—and he specifically has in mind here the accentuation of 'good will, generosity, peace and children'—but, crucially, 'save religion' (Mercer 2010: 72), we see just how restricted, deficient, and distorted the definition of religion is in so much of the literature pertaining to the festival.

The way forward is thus to lay to rest the secularization thesis, with its simplistic assumption that religion in Western society is undergoing a period of escalating and irrevocable erosion. Perhaps what we should be marking is not the disappearance of religion so much as its 'de-institutionalization' (Ter Borg 2004: 111) and its re-framing using the language of, for example, the category of Implicit Religion (as we shall see in chapter 4). The problem with the secularization thesis is that it sees the trajectory as being one-sided, with the decline in religious worship and membership of institutional churches seemingly evidence of religious decay. Schmidt offers a better model when he suggests with specific reference to Christmas that tempting though it might be to view the festival 'as a tale of woeful secularization', this sort of trajectory, if allowed to go unchallenged, camouflages 'an equally important story—that the sacred and the secular have been ceaselessly combined and recombined, that these categories have regularly dissolved in lived experience' (Schmidt 1995: 297; see also Deacy 2013: 203). Schmidt identifies the marketplace, for instance, as 'a realm of religious enchantment' and he draws attention to 'how secular much of the sacred is and how sacred much of the secular is' (Schmidt 1995: 297).

In following this approach the advantage is that we do not fall into the sort of trap of delimiting the presence (or indeed absence) of religion before undertaking the research or examining the evidence (or purported lack thereof) in a way that has marred too much of the literature in the field. Richard Dawkins is a classic case in point. For Dawkins, religion is a virus and the antithesis of rational and 'true' scientific discourse, and as he wrote in *The God Delusion*, 'one of the truly bad effects of religion is that it teaches us that it is a virtue to be satisfied with not understanding' (Dawkins 2006: 152). Dawkins' argument may be persuasive in the context of having to adjudicate in debates over the relative merits of evolution vs. creationism where Dawkins takes the line that 'Any science teacher who denies that the world is billions . . . of years old is teaching a preposterous, mind-shrinking falsehood' (in Deacy 2009: 3), but it has little to offer debates on the religious character of Christmas. For Dawkins 'religion' is synonymous with a God that does not exist, and if that were the extent of what religion is then it would make no sense to construe, say, *Christmas Junior Choice* as having religious properties or characteristics.

Too narrow a definition can thus exclude phenomena that demonstrably contain or bear witness to various functionalist or even substantive types of religion, but by the same token if a definition is too broad then the opposite happens and religion ends up being found everywhere. Melanie Wright has made the judicious point to this end in the context of debates about religion and film that if 'films are about "life" and its meaning' and 'religion is about "life" and its meaning' then, as a corollary, 'all films are "religious", or are amenable to some kind of religious reading' (Wright 2007: 16). Such a syllogism is no less futile when applied to Christmas as, if religion is associated with something as diffuse as that which gives us meaning or that which we consider special, then it is hard to see how Christmas would not automatically qualify as a religion. The mere act of exchanging gifts, decorating a tree, hoisting a Santa on the rooftop, inviting loved ones over for lunch, or indulging in a traditional Christmas afternoon film are all special, distinctive, meaningful acts and, *ipso facto*, religious. Neither of these approaches is without its problems, but the fact that some definitions are too narrow and others too wide establishes something that too few of the contributors to the debate have tended to acknowledge, namely that religion is not an objective, self-evident essence or the prerogative of any one theoretical, ideological, or scholarly constituency. On the contrary, as Will Sweetman puts it, 'When we attempt to define religion . . . we are not making a claim about what religion "really" is, or is not—*there is no thing that religion is*, it is not a substance—but merely about how we use this particular part of language' (Sweetman 2002: 13). To call Christmas a religion is thus analogous to what Sweetman says in the context of Hinduism: 'To say that (what we call) Hinduism is a religion is to say something about how we intend to approach it, not about what Hinduism is' (Sweetman 2002: 14). In the same way, Christmas cannot be 'proven' to be religious. It is a tactical way of looking at things which perhaps says more about the person making such an assertion than it does about the category of religion per se (see Deacy 2013: 203). Indeed, as Jonathan Z. Smith sees it, 'Religion is solely the creation of the scholar's study' and is 'created for the scholar's analytic purposes by his imaginative acts of comparison and generalization' (Smith 1982: xi; see also Deacy 2013: 203).

These are not merely abstruse considerations, however. On the contrary, questions concerning where religion can be apprehended and encountered often lie at the centre of public debates. Guy Ménard draws attention, for example, to how in 2004 the decision by the French government to ban the presence of all religious symbols in the public sphere (especially in schools) raises questions about the parameters of what we mean when we use the language of religion in this context. For, as Ménard puts it,

> If it is specifically religious signs—as such—that one wishes to exclude from the public sphere, then, it is not only the *hijab*, the *kippa* or the bells of Krishna that should be the target of the French state. Indeed, one should include virtually any sign that marks men and women of our advanced consumer societies; that is, their clothes, the music they listen to, the games they play, the objects they consume (Ménard 2004: 251).

Ménard's concern is that if it is only explicitly religious symbols, such as the *hijab*, that are prohibited, then the approach taken is 'narrow-minded and unjust... because it does not take into account, or recognize, the actual fragmentation of the more *implicit* forms of religion' (Ménard 2004: 253). Ménard has in mind here the fact that when teenagers turn up at school 'in Nikes, or with piercings everywhere, or with a queer haircut or dress' (Ménard 2004: 254), this no less says something about where religion might be encountered: 'for *one* case of a *kirpan* placed in the public spotlight... how many other youths are reprimanded every day for dressing like Britney Spears or any other of their idols, without it ever becoming a national debate, or moreover, without raising the slightest hypothesis among the vast majority of scholars in Religious Studies that these behaviors could have something to do with *religion*' (Ménard 2004: 253)? Ménard's position, in other words, is that in only targeting 'the presence of *explicit* forms of religion in the public sphere' (Ménard 2004: 253), one ends up being oblivious to 'a growing number of expressions which, though not explicitly religious, are nevertheless themselves bearers of a genuinely religious experience' (Ménard 2004: 255).

There is thus a disjuncture between what 'religion' is officially taken to mean—in this case by the French government—and the way scholars are inclined to define and appropriate the term. This sort of contestation has led some scholars to feel the need to drop the term 'religion' altogether as it is not a term that adequately encompasses the full set of meanings and values ascribed to it. As Lynch sees it, for example, researchers are 'becoming interested in how concepts, symbols, and practices associated with "religion" circulate through contemporary society beyond the boundaries of traditional religious institutions, as well as the ways in which different social institutions (such as the legal or educational systems) play an active role in the construction of "religion"' (Lynch 2012: 5). Accordingly, for Lynch, the category of the 'sacred' more accurately expresses some of these extra-institutional forms of religiosity, not least because, as he argues at length, 'The content and structure of sacred forms range much further than the conventional conceptual boundaries of "religion"' (Lynch 2012: 6). What thus becomes clear is that it is very much a matter of which language we use and which questions we ask when drawing on the category of religion for any conversation involving 'religion' to be meaningful or fruitful.

Abby Day recently found when undertaking qualitative fieldwork within the sociology of religion that it was important not to select potential interviewees 'on the basis of their involvement or articulated interest in religion or spirituality' on the grounds that if in a survey someone is asked what their particular religious affiliation or belief might be (such as whether they believe in God) this raises problems as such approaches which ask explicitly religious questions 'cannot reveal nuances of meaning, as what is meant by "belief" or "God" is not apparent' (Day 2012: 444). Indeed, she has Steve Bruce's work in mind when she points out that such 'surveys tend to demand closed answers to closed questions' (Day 2012: 444) and that a better approach is one which avoids pigeonholing people into pre-established categories of the religious vs. the secular which take the secularization thesis as a given: 'I did not, therefore, lead my fieldwork with definitions of what is religious or secular, and then set out to discover if informants conformed to [these] definitions' (Day 2012: 445). I will look at the work of Edward Bailey in more detail in chapter 4, but his work in initiating the study of Implicit Religion is germane here as Day found that his approach of asking interviewees questions along the lines of 'What do you enjoy most in life?' (in Day 2012: 444) was more helpful when it comes to ascertaining someone's religious (or for that matter non-religious) affiliations or predilections than simply correlating religion with belief in God or membership of institutionally-based religious traditions.

In the specific case of Christmas, Horsley makes the instructive point to this end that in America especially it is often overlooked that 'the grand American holiday festival expresses and embodies community in civic affairs, whether in small towns, large cities, or the nation as a whole' (Horsley 2001a: 169). *Christmas with the Kranks* (2004) is a good, albeit caricatured, illustration of this sort of process, inasmuch as an entire community, ostensibly set in the Chicago suburbs, comes alive in the run-up to Christmas by each household conforming to the requirement to erect gaudy displays of snowmen, flashing lights, and Christmas trees for all the other neighbours to witness and appreciate (and even out-do). Just as Abby Day writes that the period of national census data gathering every ten years in the UK has become 'a performative moment for many, when the act of choosing the religious category of Christian brought into being a specific sense of identity' (Day 2012: 441), so in *Christmas with the Kranks* social cohesion and identity comes about each December (only) when a particular (conformist) ritual is enacted, failure to do so leading in the film to a souring of community relations and a rupture in the fabric of society. The film is of course a work of fiction, based on a novella, *Skipping Christmas*, by John Grisham, but it does present in stark terms an instance of what Horsley is referring to when he writes that 'the holidays as a whole have become a prolonged expression of the "civil religion" in the United States' (Horsley 2001a: 169).

It is not just in Christmas films, though, that we see such profane spaces as sites of religious ritual and community. Sara Anson Vaux has written at length, for instance, about how in Clint Eastwood's *Million Dollar Baby* (2004) the Hit Pit fighting gym, managed by Eastwood's protagonist, Frankie Dunn, is a place where the socially marginalized and dispossessed can come together to enjoy a sense of comfort and community that is not otherwise available in the world outside. It is, as Vaux puts it, 'a protected space to nurture human interactions' (Vaux 2012: 105). This may be the role that churches might conventionally be expected to perform, and Vaux's discussion of how the nourishing, community-oriented arena of the gym—a site, indeed, of 'luminous transformation'—stands in contrast to the 'profane' and 'contaminated' space of the boxing ring 'where bodies are meticulously prepared for display before injury and possible death' (Vaux 2012: 105) certainly suggests that traditional religious institutions do not have the monopoly on the functional aspects of religion such as group solidarity. Religion, for Durkheim, may have comprised 'a unified system of beliefs and practices relative to sacred things . . . that unite its adherents in a single moral community' (Durkheim 2001: 44), but when Jonathan Rosenbaum wrote in relation to Eastwood's Oscar-winning picture that 'In a bleak world, where neither family nor religious faith offers any lasting respite, *Million Dollar Baby* offers redemption that derives from the informal and nameless loving relationships people create on their own rather than inherit from family, church, or society' (in Vaux 2012: 113), it is clear that the boundaries of what religion is and where it can be located are porous to say the least.

If the focus is on what religion *does* rather than on its substance or essence then it is simply not meaningful to say that the community rituals associated with sporting clubs or Christmas are *alternative* or *analogous* forms of religious expression. They are religious per se. This is a crucial distinction as it means that religion is no longer seen as an ontologically distinct phenomenon to wider social and cultural practices and events but, as Horsfield sees it, as originating, developing, and adapting itself 'through the same mediated processes of creation, conflict, and negotiation within itself and in relation to its wider environment that all of life participates in' (Horsfield 2008: 114). Accordingly, as Horsfield goes on to attest, 'The study of media and religion . . . needs to be broadened to include the messy, diverse, and at times contradictory individual and group practices of mediated daily life to which religious meanings are ascribed' (Horsfield 2008: 114). The net effect may be that religion lacks definitional specificity but, when construed in this way, it becomes possible to see how Dell deChant is able to claim in *The Sacred Santa* that Christmas can be categorized as a religious festival in its own right and not because of any causal relationship to the Christian tradition.

Published in 2002, deChant's thesis is that in place of the religious-secular dichotomy and what he calls the 'simplistic' assumption of the secularization thesis that 'with the rise of modernization Christianity became increasingly marginalized in the West as secular institutions began to replace it as the source of cultural meanings and values' (deChant 2002: xiii), Christmas is the epitome of a struggle between two different *religious* systems. Indeed, his premise is that 'rather than being secular and nonreligious, America's late capitalist, postmodern culture is actually intensely religious, and best classified as a contemporary version of ancient cosmological religiosity' (deChant 2002: xiii). This is the thinking that whereas in the ancient world everything depended on the life cycles of nature and fertility (see deChant 2002: 30; Deacy 2013: 201), today there is an analogous ultimate sacred power in the form of the economy: 'As the ancients participated in rituals and temples and shrines, we participate in similar rituals at malls and department stores' (deChant 2002: xiv). deChant does not dispute that Christmas is, functionally, 'secular' in nature, but he argues that it is precisely the festival's 'secular' components, as typified by its materialist, commercialized, and consumerist ethos, that gives it a religious character 'in the context of postmodern cosmological culture' (deChant 2002: xiii). In other words, despite being, for all intents and purposes, 'secular', on closer inspection 'our entire culture system begins to look profoundly sacred' (deChant 2002: xiv). We could not therefore be further away from the traditional 'secularization thesis' as, here, the 'secular' *is* the 'religious'. As Christmas is the quintessence of materialism and consumption, and thus a more intense and profound version of what goes on throughout the rest of the year where the workings of the economy are paramount, so Christmas lays claim to being the most religious event in our culture.

This may be far removed from the traditional correlation between religion and transcendence or theism, but it is no less religious for that. Shopping and retail spending are thus innately religious activities and, even, to paraphrase Tillich, 'late capitalism's ultimate concern' (deChant 2002: 5; see also Deacy 2013: 202) as it 'serves as the Ultimate Power or Principle of a culture', its 'ground of being and source of meaning and purpose' (deChant 2012: 38).

This is a distinctive and innovative thesis, although I disagree with deChant over his forthright conclusion that this cultural shift 'serves to delegitimate the foundational faith claims of transcendental religions while simultaneously offering new and contrasting claims about the ultimate meanings and values of life' (deChant 2002: 4; see also Deacy 2013: 203). deChant's oversight is to assume that the 'transcendental religions' he talks about are inextricably transcendental at heart. As I have argued elsewhere, it is quite common for theologians to espouse what is known as a realized eschatology, in which it is believed that eternal life refers to the quality of life in present existence (see e.g. Deacy 2012b: 72–4; Deacy 2012a: 79–85). Since the Enlightenment, for example, there has been a re-orientation of eschatological beliefs away from a traditional emphasis on a future judgement, heaven and hell, and towards a reading which understands that a person can undergo a transformative experience in the here and now, within the present dimensions of space and time (see Deacy 2012b: 72). As Don Cupitt has argued, 'in the modern period we have come more and more to explain events in this world in this-worldly terms' and that we 'no longer seem to require the old idea that there is an invisible world of supernatural beings lying behind this world' (Cupitt 2003: 35). It is, rather, in the present moment that the believer has passed through judgement and entered upon eternal life. Such perspectives have also been taken seriously within the Church of England (the Anglican Communion in England), whose Doctrine Commission reported in the mid-1990s that 'in the twentieth-century West, across a whole spectrum of types of Christianity, there seems to be a fairly consistent emphasis on salvation here and now rather than after death' (Church of England Doctrine Commission 1995: 29; quoted in Deacy 2012b: 72–3). A number of New Testament commentators have also taken this view, with C.H. Dodd writing, for example, that 'for the New Testament writers in general, the *eschaton* has entered history ... the Age to Come has come' (Dodd 1944: 85; quoted in Deacy 2012a: 80) while John A.T. Robinson questioned in

Honest to God 'how far Christianity is committed to a mythological, or supranaturalist, picture of the universe' (Robinson 1963: 33; quoted in Deacy 2012a: 85), preferring the idea that through Jesus Christ the goal of history has already become present *in history* and that the rule of God *has already begun* (see Deacy 2012a: 85).

deChant is thus going too far when he sets up a dichotomy between the *transcendental* nature of Christianity and the *cosmological* dimension of Christmas. The boundaries between the two are not that clearcut. Although the concept of transcendence is understood as referring to 'other-worldly, godly realms', Pärna is right in her reformulation of the term which sees it as referring to 'the surpassing of boundaries and crossing the limits of particular sets of truths and values' (Pärna 2006: 188). This ties in with how for Robinson the transcendent can be found deep within the human person *in the immanent sphere* rather than above and beyond the world, akin to how for Tillich God can be understood as the 'Ground of our Being' (see e.g. Tillich 1964: 163). On this basis, God can still be radically 'other' and transcendent, but not as a being who dwells in the celestial firmament. The key point is that there is more to transcendence than the supernatural. To be efficacious it must pertain to the here and now. deChant's understanding of the transcendental-cosmological binary is thus too narrow in its frame of reference as it misses how, as John Hey has shown, for example, 'the concept of transcendence can properly be understood as a secular notion' (Hey 2012: 81). Hey's thinking here is that although the 'transcendent traditionally is conceived of as some reality or realm beyond' (Hey 2012: 82), it can only ever be conceived with reference to *this-worldly* vocabulary, experience, and encounter. He argues, for instance, that when Bultmann or Tillich refer to the 'transcendent' they do so not on the basis of the reality of the transcendent but 'from the power of the existential conviction' (Hey 2012: 87) with which they endow it: 'It is the existential encounter with the gracious transcendent "other" which transforms my existence in the secular world' (Hey 2012: 84).

Even Karl Barth's neo-orthodox theology, with its emphasis wholly on the otherness of God, is not immune, according to Hey, from secular manifestations of transcendence. As he puts it, although 'Barth is well known for his insistence upon a "wholly-other" metaphysical transcendence, and an insistence that there can be no natural theology' (Hey 2012: 87), he 'does not see faith's metalanguage as being distinct from either the world or secular language' (Hey 2012:

88), such that any transcendence that is spoken about must pertain to the salvation of the *secular* world of our experience which is the only domain in which we can partake as we cannot transcend the human. Hey's position is clear: 'there is no *prima facie* reason to assume some supernatural or metaphysical or transcendent reality as [the] cause' (Hey 2012: 92) of our meaning-making. To this end, we can compare the work of Abraham Maslow who used the language of 'sacred', 'divine', 'holy', 'salvation', 'transcendence', and 'spiritual' to talk about subjective experiences (see Gollnick 2002: 87). The sacred is not, then, ontologically different from the secular but in some instances may arise from, and lead to the transformation of, secular, human experience (see Swatos Jr 1999: 36). Ter Borg expresses similar sentiments in his talk of how 'the vertical transcendence of Christianity, aimed at God, has been replaced by a horizontal transcendence, aimed at improving the world' (Ter Borg 2008: 236). We can also compare Robert Bellah's work on American Civil Religion with its combination of Protestantism with a discernibly worldly form of salvation in which, as Wender sees it, we see 'a bold demonstration of transcendence being experienced, in the form of a nationalist consciousness, within a secular, social and political milieu' (see Wender 2007: 251), where 'the transcendent source of salvation' has been relocated 'within the mundane realm of proprietorship and economic activity' (Wender 2007: 252). Indeed, according to Wender, 'It would seem that perhaps nowhere more than in US nationalism . . . are the boundaries between sacred and secular so indistinct' (Wender 2009: 290).

THE NEED TO MOVE AWAY FROM BINARIES

With this in mind, it is fair to say that there is no consensus among theologians and others as to how to approach the concept of transcendence, and deChant's method of drawing a clear line of demarcation between the metaphysical-transcendental nature of traditional Christianity and the immanent and this-worldly character of contemporary postmodern culture is no less problematic than Flynn's simplistic binary between Christianity (and for that matter Christmas which he deems to be indissolubly Christian in essence) and atheism. The way forward in this debate is to move beyond the tendency to foreground pre-determined binaries, whether construed in terms of deChant's approach of differentiating between the transcendent and the material/economic or Flynn's separation of Christmas and the non-religious, which are being applied to Christmas from the outside. The fact that Flynn associates Christmas with traditional transcendence and deChant with the realm of the material highlights the danger of pigeonholing religious phenomena as religion as a whole, and the Christmas festival in particular, are far more subtle and nuanced than either dichotomy-based model permits. Everyone brings their own baggage to the phenomena that they are studying. When William Waits looks at Christmas through the lens of the history of gift-giving and receiving and its wider ramifications for the economy, or Mark Connelly studies Christmas through the lens of English social history, or indeed when Flynn seeks to ban Christmas from the public sphere in the light of his secular humanist predilections, it is clear that they all have distinct agendas and backgrounds which enable them to focus on particular manifestations of the festival in idiosyncratic, even partisan, ways.

There is nothing wrong with this, but the problem arises when it is assumed that 'because religion is x then Christmas must be y', or indeed (as is the case with both Connelly and Waits) that because their pre-established understanding of what religion is does not fit with what they believe Christmas to be about then religion is extraneous to the debate altogether. deChant's model, which will be the focus of chapter 6, while not perfect, is one of the most illuminating approaches to the festival that we have seen precisely because it seeks to reframe the debate in terms of what religion is and where it can be apprehended. deChant may be beholden to a binary model but it is a necessary starting point in any attempt to move the debate forward from how, for Eliade, the world can simply be separated into two categories of people—the religious and the non-religious, whereby, as Mazur and Koda put it, 'nonreligious people go through life without distinguishing varieties of time or space' while 'religious people observe and maintain sharp distinctions between the sacred and the profane' (Mazur and Koda 2011: 310).

Revisited through the lens of deChant, when Eliade saw the sacred as the wholly other that gives our lives depth, meaning, and purpose—indeed bound up with matters 'extraordinary, memorable, and momentous . . . eternal, full of substance and reality' (Pals 2006:

199)—that could no less be applied today to a festival of materialism, consumption, and consumerism which on Eliade's model could only pertain to the realm of the (deficient) secular. Eliade may have seen the sacred as the polar opposite of the profane, but it is its very secularity that makes Christmas such a compelling, and even transcendental, religious holiday. If, as Pärna says in the context of Eliade, the sacred is by its very nature 'subject to other laws than the ones applicable in the ordinary world and ... capable of acts that transcend human limitations' (Pärna 2006: 186) then it would be hard to see Christmas, a festival marked by its separation from, and indeed its rupturing of, the rhythms and conventions of the everyday—an event that, in Nissenbaum's words, has 'long been a special ritual time when the ordinary rules of behavior were upended' (Nissenbaum 1996: loc. no. 2847; see Deacy 2013: 199)—as anything other than an intensely sacred event. Yet, unless the boundaries of what constitutes religion are allowed to expand in this way, the sacred or religious designation of Christmas would make no sense. For, as Wagner puts it, 'sacred time has virtually no relationship to time as experienced by the nonreligious' (Wagner 2012a: 311). Certainly for Flynn or Waits where the boundaries of religion are already assumed to be fixed, such language would be unintelligible.

When Durkheim similarly concluded that the sacred is the realm of the perfect while the secular comprises the realm of the imperfect (see Heelas 2012: 479), a false distinction is set up which bears little resemblance to the reality of how Christmas is experienced and celebrated. If the sacred amounts to an ideal, transcendental world that is set apart from everyday life (see McDannell 2012: 135) and which is marked by its polar opposite, the profane, then on this reading Christmas would be the anathema of Durkheim's understanding of religion. For, if, as is Durkheim's premise, the Church is sacred territory while the home or workplace is the site of the profane (see Deacy 2013: 200) and that these two places are necessarily ontologically separate—'The religious life and the profane life ... cannot exist in the same place' (in McDannell 2012: 136)— it would be impossible for *Christmas Junior Choice* to be construed as religious due to its profane 'home or workplace' setting. The real distinction when it comes to Christmas is, of course, between 'home' and 'workplace' rather than to conjoin the two, as Durkheim does, as equivalent profane sites that are distinguished from the (exclusively) sacred space of the Church. The recreational time afforded by Christmas when offices and businesses tend to be shut means that the home becomes the key site at Christmas around which the quest for (if not the attainment of) perfection is executed whereby, as we discussed in chapter 1, the focus is on children and families, the strictures of 'ordinary time' are overcome, the economy of everyday life is inverted, and a state of liminas or *communitas* can be achieved.

To appropriate Durkheim's language, the profane arena of home can thus be the site where the sacred is at its most pronounced. This is not to decry the role of the conventionally sacred sphere of the church as, once we remove the binary, it becomes possible to see the dissolving of the sacred and the profane as widening our understanding of how and where the sacred or religious may be found to operate. There is no reason, for example, as to why one cannot attend a service at their local church on Christmas morning before returning home to enter the no less sacralized milieu of *Christmas Junior Choice* (see Deacy 2013: 201). Robert Cipriani argues, for instance, that this is precisely the sort of thing that already happens in the context of sporting rituals and events, whereby, as he points out, 'there is no clear barrier between the spiritual and the sporting event, between the temple and the pitch', as 'one goes first to the service in church, later to the football match in the stadium' (Cipriani 2012: 142). Instead of a tension between the sacred and the profane what we have instead is a 'temporal *continuum*' (Cipriani 2012: 142). Seen in these terms, Durkheim's conviction that the sacred is a stand-alone and immutable category 'removed from all other forms of life' (Lynch 2012: 23) is no longer a credible option. Indeed, in Lynch's words, 'the radical separation of the sacred and the profane reflects a tendency towards binary oppositions in Durkheim's thought that do not always adequately reflect empirical data or provide sufficiently nuanced theoretical tools' (Lynch 2012: 26).

Swatos Jr thus proposes a more accurate and nuanced position in his affirmation that 'We do not think that sacredness lies in being set apart, but in penetration', in which the 'sacred takes meaning precisely as it runs in and through everyday life in constant dialogue with the mundane demands of everyday existence' (Swatos Jr 1999: 34). It is this oscillation rather than separation between the two categories, and the dissolving of pre-established boundaries as to what comprises the sacred and what comprises the secular, that must be the way forward for debates in the category of religion. Rather than take the line that the sacred is always superior to and more efficacious than the secular, as lies at the heart of Eliade's and Durkheim's typologies, a more sophisticated approach is to focus on what Swatos Jr calls 'the *duality* of sacred-secular' in which the 'one cannot exist without the other' (Swatos Jr 1999: 35). More than anything else, such talk is simply commonsensical. As we will see in chapter 4 in relation to Implicit Religion, most people, even those who possess fervent and inflexible religious affiliations, are in reality motivated by wider and additional attachments and principles. Lynch, for instance, has shown how 'The individual human subject in late modernity . . . rarely lives in relation to a single sacred form, but rather in relation to multiple forms in contingent and complex ways' and that even 'religious groups who believe themselves to be oriented simply around a particular sacred form of their tradition are in reality influenced by other sacred forms' (Lynch 2012: 135; see also Deacy 2013: 200). Although the 'sacred forms' that Lynch has in mind are nationalism, human rights, and the care of children (see Lynch 2012: 135), Christmas with all of its distinct (and distinctive) accoutrements may be a no less fecund fit. There is no reason, for example, why someone should not have an allegiance to a traditional religious organization or community which entails spending Christmas morning at their local parish church while also passing their day involved, no less trenchantly or fervently, in other sacred activities. Rather than an 'either/or', it may be that 'sacred time' is actualized *both* by going to church or mass *and* through the nostalgia of Christmases past which is evoked in *Christmas Junior Choice* through listeners sharing memories and requesting children's records, such as 'Sparky's Magic Piano' and Clive Dunn's 'Grandad', from their own childhood.[5]

I am thus in agreement with Mazur and Koda who conclude that 'Eliade's vision of the sacred is far too simplistic—religious people live in the real world just like the nonreligious person' (Mazur and Koda 2011: 314). Moreover, even Eliade, despite seeing 'sacred time' as having set and specific boundaries, acknowledged that it was possible to be religious in what Price calls multiple and competing ways (see Price 2005: 208–9; Deacy 2013: 201). This indeed is the central

---

[5] I first tentatively examined the relationship between 'sacred time' and *Christmas Junior Choice* in Deacy 2013: 199.

paradox in Eliade's work. While on the one hand he associated the sacred with the 'wholly other', he also saw that it is often 'found in the most familiar matters' (Pärna 2006: 187)—a sacred stone or building, for instance, remains 'just' a stone or 'just' a building while also acquiring sacred meaning (see Pärna 2006: 187) when, as Wagner characterizes it, 'the sacred enters into it and "saturates" it with "being"' (Wagner 2012b: 123). When Pärna thus concludes that, in line with this 'paradox of the sacred', the internet can be 'both a familiar, banal tool and an extra-ordinary, emotionally charged object to admire' and even 'a point of reference for values and meaning' (Pärna 2006: 198), so I would suggest here that Eliade can help us to understand how a product as 'trivial' as a Christmas film or *Junior Choice* might be a sacred site for others.

This is not to say, of course, that Eliade himself would have appreciated the analogy. Eliade's own view was that all sacred things on earth 'have an extraterrestrial archetype, be it conceived as a plan, as a form, or purely and simply as a "double" existing on a higher cosmic level' (Wagner 2012b: 124; see also Deacy 2013: 200). This would then rule out *Christmas Junior Choice* from Eliade's typology as it is not modelled after a celestial prototype, in the manner of the New Jerusalem being modelled on the earthly Jerusalem, nor is the programme situated in a celestial region of eternity (see Wagner 2012b: 123). At the end of the day, though, even Eliade conceded that the sacred–profane distinction lies in the eye of the beholder (see Pärna 2006: 187) and we should bear in mind that the categories of the sacred vs. the secular or the profane are, as with binary distinctions more generally, artificial constructions and, as McDannell puts it, 'not always part of the awareness of those involved in practicing religion' (McDannell 2012: 139; see also Deacy 2013: 201). Tillich similarly recognized that it was not only traditional religious symbols that could express the divine (see McDannell 2012: 142; Deacy 2013: 202). Rather, for Tillich, the sacred could be encountered *in*, rather than in contradistinction to, the secular (see Deacy 2013: 202), as when he attested that 'The "sacred" or the "holy" inflames, imbues, inspires, all reality and all aspects of existence', such that 'There is no profane nature or history, no profane ego, and no profane world' (in Brant 2012: 57; see also Deacy 2013: 201–2).

An undue emphasis therefore on what comprises the 'sacred' and what comprises the 'profane' only serves to distort rather than inform the nature of contemporary religious debate. It may have been the case for Eliade that myths and rituals enable religious people to demarcate time and space, to orient the world in terms of a God or gods, and to avoid the meaninglessness of the 'non-religious' world (see Mazur and Koda 2011: 312; Deacy 2013: 199), but he was working on the assumption that there was an actual, heavenly, otherworldly sacred that serves as the model or template for human religious activity (see Wagner 2012b: 124). If we remove this traditional transcendental dimension from the categorization of religion then a different picture emerges. deChant, for example, has shown us that Christmas is a religion in its own right, not because of the way it bears witness to, enshrines, or even approximates the traditional Christian celebration with its attendant mythological, supernatural, and transcendental world-view. Accordingly, the 'meaninglessness' that Eliade speaks of vis-à-vis the profane world could be inverted from the perspective of deChant's model, so that it is the traditional sacred, with its emphasis on a world-view that is far removed from the cosmological and worldly nature of the 'real' Christmas that should more accurately be ascribed as 'meaningless'. For the devotee of *Christmus Junior Choice,* the world of the traditionally sacred may be of less value—even no value—compared to the 'sacred time' actualized by the programme, in which something genuinely out of the ordinary takes place as it evokes the nostalgia of Christmases past and engenders even an experience of liminality or *communitas.*

At the very least, even if *Christmas Junior Choice* is not deemed to be a site of transcendence per se (and neither the programme-makers nor the audience explicitly construe the programme as a site of religious activity, which is hardly surprising since the term is too often associated with merely formal and institutionalized forms of belief) it might, to paraphrase Wagner who is writing in the context of virtual reality, profitably be construed as a space in which the transcendent could be said to appear in an otherwise 'secular' milieu (see Wagner 2012a: 97). The key thing is not to assume that in view of the programme's ostensibly entertainment pedigree it cannot function as a site of authentic religious meaning. The following from Jeffrey Scholes, written in the context of the Coca-Cola brand and religion, applies well in the present context also: 'The task is not to spurn such popular cultural expressions for their shallowness, instability, or their short shelf-lives but to learn more about how authentic religion can possibly emerge from such inauthentic processes', and that 'even secular and fleeting cultural expressions can perform this task' (Scholes 2012: 147). With this in mind, the focus in chapter 4 will be on how this focus on the unconventional and the everyday in religion applies to *Junior Choice* and Christmas more generally when examined through the language of Implicit Religion.

4

Christmas as a Site of Implicit Religion

WHAT IS IMPLICIT RELIGION?

Having established that Christmas may legitimately be posited as a rich, if surprising, site of contemporary religion because of, rather than in spite of, its consumerist and materialist pedigree, the aim in this chapter is to find a theoretical model which best fits, and indeed encapsulates, this phenomenon. Starting with the premise that the 'definition of religion is notoriously difficult' (Bailey 2006: 1), Edward Bailey's work in the field of Implicit Religion provides just such an approach as his research is predicated on the notion that what we consider to be the realm of the secular and of ordinary life may contain unacknowledged and unarticulated religious elements. Bailey first coined the term 'Implicit Religion' in 1968 and he has been at the forefront of debates in the UK since that time which ask whether our understanding of the realm of the secular is any less religiously fecund than more conventional or established domains of religious behaviour or activity. According to Bailey, 'there are as many ways of being religious . . . as there are of being human', and this, combined with the awareness that different religious traditions themselves contain many different essences and 'different *kinds* of essence' (Bailey 2006: 3), serves to establish that the boundaries of what comprise religion are far from set in stone. Bailey is keen to rule out the identification of Implicit Religion with any single tradition—as he explains, 'To be "implicitly religious", in no way implies being "implicitly Christian"' (Bailey 1998a: 14) and that the term 'religion' can 'never now be seen as coterminous with Christianity, or any other single religion' (Bailey 1998a: 15).

In its place Bailey prefers to further his understanding of the category of religion with reference to secular predilections and commitments.

The secular is thus no less viable at helping us to understand the nature and location of contemporary religious debate than the traditionally religious. To his credit, Bailey is aware that the language we use in this context is often part of the problem. In the first edition of the *Implicit Religion* journal which Bailey edited since its inception in November 1998 until his death in April 2015, Ninian Smart wrote an article, 'Implicit religion across culture', which draws attention to the ambiguity that pertains to the word 'secular'. According to Smart, although in one sense the term means 'non-religious' (and is thus the opposite of the religious, along the lines of the dualisms of Eliade and Durkheim that we looked at in chapter 3) he notes that people tend to use it in the context of having no *established* religion, as when we might refer to the United States or India as having secular constitutions (see Smart 1998b: 24). With this in mind, Bailey makes the instructive point that 'if we could find the distinctive meaning of "secular" in today's culture, we would at last know how to define religion' (Bailey 1998b: 19).

This moves the debate in an important direction as it means that the secular has an important contribution to contemporary religious debate in its own right and not simply because it stands in direct contrast to the realm of the religious (as if that were itself straightforwardly ascertainable). To this end, it would be wrong to assume that the 'secular' is quite easy to define, along the lines that 'It always means, simply, the opposite of "religious", whatever that means' (Bailey 1998b: 18). In the context of 1960s secularization debates where it was believed that religion was increasingly being relegated from the modern world, it is not surprising to find such a position in vogue. If religion is believed to be on the retreat then, according to the secularization thesis, it is obviously the secular that takes its place. The secular could not be understood, on such a basis, except in terms of its binary relationship as the polar opposite of the province of religion. Inevitably, however, the debate has moved quite a long way from here, with even Wilfred Cantwell Smith arguing in later years, in his 1997 publication, *Modern Culture from a Comparative Perspective*, that religion itself should be seen as a secular concept, on the grounds that 'human nature is fundamentally secular' (Smith 1997: 75) and that religion should be seen as an addendum to this.

Religion and the secular thus overlap much more than is usually understood, a consideration not lost on Bailey who attests that the secular can be 'a self-authenticating dimension of reality' even though in practice it is the religious that 'continues to provide the frame for living secularly' (Bailey 2006: 6). In place of the traditional distinction, as typified by Durkheim, central to Bailey's argument is the idea that in contemporary society 'room has to be found for a middle ground between the sacred and the profane' (Bailey 2006: 6). This, for Bailey, comprises the realm of the 'ordinary' where precisely because we do not frame our commitments in language redolent of either 'the sacred' or 'the profane'—because to do so would be to acknowledge that to participate in, say, *Christmas Junior Choice* is either a sacred or a profane activity, which is not the way most people think—the use of religious language to categorize such an important, meaningful commitment or ritual simply goes unnoticed. It was through considering the nature of contemporary society in this way that Bailey came up with the term Implicit Religion, after originally toying with calling it 'secular religion' (Bailey 2006: 7).

Bailey is keen to emphasize that although the corollary of his approach is that *anything* may be implicitly religious this is not the same as saying that *everything* is religious: 'To suggest that anything may be implicitly-religious, by no means suggests that everything is (implicitly or otherwise) religious; any more than the anthropological commonplace about there being no limit to what *can* be sacred, suggests that in any context *every* thing *is* sacred' (Bailey 2006: 9). There is nothing 'arbitrary' (Bailey 1998b: 13) at work here. Bailey's preference is to say that anything has the *potential* to be (implicitly) religious in a way that might be analogous to how for Tillich religion should be construed as the Ground of Being or Ultimate Concern. It is, in other words, not about the essence or ritual or even (as it is for Tillich) the goal that one is striving for so much as the mode of behaviour entailed that designates whether or not something may be categorized as religious. Implicit Religion thus contains what Karen Lord calls 'a number of named religious and quasi-religious practices within its wide-ranging definition and is not limited to only one area' (Lord 2006: 206). Although the term itself may be new, Implicit Religion is not about identifying and labelling a new *type* of religion (as if it is functionally equivalent to Christianity, Buddhism, or Islam) but a new *method* for examining 'the interconnectedness of religious and quasi-religious behaviour in society' and for enabling us 'to redraw previously accepted boundaries in order to enhance the analysis of such behaviour' (Lord 2006: 207).

THE DISTINCTIVENESS AND IMPACT
OF IMPLICIT RELIGION

In this sense, Implicit Religion is not interested in finding out or pinpointing what it is about 'secular' things which makes them religious, as in such an exercise the implicit assumption is that there is a central kernel or essence to religion which it is the job of the scholar to discover and disclose. Pärna has made one of the best contributions in this respect when she clarifies that 'Implicit religion does not exist beyond scholarship' (Pärna 2012: 395). Rather, it is 'an analytical concept, which can yield refreshing insights' (Pärna 2012: 395–6) about the way religious language might be employed in areas that depart from traditional institutional manifestations, such as by focusing on wider commitments, practices, experiences, ambitions, and skills that are not commonly labelled as 'religious' but where religious concepts (or at least those which might be deemed to resemble religious concepts[1]) serve as what Daren Kemp refers to as 'fundamental assumptions of a broad section of the population' (Kemp 2001: 37) in an otherwise 'non-religious' context—*Christmas Junior Choice* being an obvious case in point.

This ties in with how for Bailey 'the formulation of the concept was aimed at assisting in the understanding of people, not at asserting the universality among human beings of some attribute that can be labelled "religious"' (Bailey 1998a: 70). None of this reveals anything new in and of itself. It is simply the language, or method, that helps ascertain why the phenomena concerned—*Christmas Junior Choice*, for example—might be deemed appropriate to examine through this sort of lens. Using a different, more traditional institutionalized approach to religion would not pick up on the religious provenance or ramifications at work but might simply stop at seeing the phenomena concerned as an example of *secular* meaning or discourse. The reason *Junior Choice* does seem particularly amenable to Implicit Religion is in light of how in so many examples cited by Bailey and others of what constitutes a site of Implicit Religion, 'On the surface, the focus of the activity does not appear to be deeply meaningful, but it may be symbolic of more profound issues' (Lord 2006: 209). The Boy Scout movement, for instance, is an example of what Robert

---

[1] This qualification is helpfully supplied by Karen Lord (Lord 2006: 214).

A. Campbell has termed 'an implicitly religious organization', with Campbell even going so far as to propose 'that participation in Scouting programmes is a fundamentally religious experience' (Campbell 2001: 23). This is not because of any affirmation of belief in God (even though until recently its members were expected to subscribe to it) or even because of the movement's association with Christian churches 'and their other auxiliary voluntary associations', but because, as Campbell sees it, 'Scouting has developed an elaborate and rather sophisticated set of guidelines and programmes through which a series of implicitly religious principles are made explicit' (Campbell 2001: 16). He continues that it even 'provides an alternative outlet for religious expression in the world' (Campbell 2001: 19), and goes on to conclude that 'the Scout movement is not a religious organization in a formal or traditional sense, but that fact does not make it any less implicitly religious than it clearly is' (Campbell 2001: 23).

Crucially, scouting does not *become* religious (or need to reconceive its own status or identity as a religious organization) just because a typology has been established to which the ingredients of the Boy Scout movement concur. It is more the case that the movement has always had this predilection but it has simply not previously been construed as religious per se. The movement does not need to change its identity in any way now that the epithet of religion has (for good or ill) been applied to it. Indeed, as Campbell avers, 'one can do Scouting without necessarily ever seeing it as religious, and I am sure that many former scouts would testify to this' (Campbell 2001: 23). In the same way, *Junior Choice* has not changed in any way so that it is now seen to be a religious, as opposed to a 'merely' secular, annual event in the radio calendar. Its status is in no way different now to what it was before being analysed through the lens of Implicit Religion. It is religion that is malleable in this sense, not the phenomena under discussion. Kees de Groot is thus right to exercise caution when he writes that 'What might hamper the study of implicit religion is an on-going discussion of the definition of implicit religion as if it were a phenomenon itself' (de Groot 2012: 458).

To this end it would not make sense for adherents to *Christmas Junior Choice* to argue that listening to or participating in the programme makes the experience part of some sort of wider religious belief system (the programme does not, and nor would it be expected to, correspond to all seven of Ninian Smart's dimensions of religion, for example) and nor could or should a case be made for providing what, if this were in the United States, would be a natural corollary of identifying a movement or organization as religious—namely, giving the believer concerned legal protections under the First Amendment. *Junior Choice* may contain a number of implicitly religious elements which warrant seeing it through a different lens, but it does not suddenly become akin to established belief systems which have their own doctrinal, mythological, ethical, ritual, experiential, institutional, or material components.[2] Bailey is adamant to this end that a definition of Implicit Religion will not be prescriptive along the lines of saying that, for instance, '"Religion" consists of beliefs and rituals and fellowships, and therefore we are simply searching for their secular parallels' (Bailey 1998a: 21), not least because 'we may miss the heart of what we are seeking, if we only use the existing lenses in order to find parallels' (Bailey 1998a: 22).

What stands out here is that, as Pärna indicates, religion can find expression in 'profane' areas of life and the 'study of implicit religiosity looks for frames of reference in new or unfamiliar contexts, in situations where established (religious) grand narratives are not applicable' (Pärna 2004: 105). It should not be viewed as tantamount, equivalent, or even as analogous to institutional belief structures or systems. Rather, the goal of Implicit Religion is best encapsulated by de Groot's talk of highlighting 'parallels, connections, and shifting distinctions, between the religious and the secular . . . , and to show how religious experience, beliefs, ritual and ethics appear, decontextualized, in other fields' (de Groot 2012: 458). *Christmas Junior Choice* will not suddenly become something it has never set out to be—Bailey is thus right when he argues that 'there is no desire to impose the use of "religion" upon any who do not wish it' (Bailey 1998a: 17)—but the insight it elicits, at least for the scholar, into the meaning and definition of religion is immense, exposing as it does what de Groot refers to as 'the sheer contingency of our scholarly and societal concepts of

---

[2] It is worth pointing out, though, that for Ninian Smart there is a functional analogy between implicit and explicit religion along the lines of his seven dimensions of religion. He sees Implicit Religion as containing the same 'ethics, doctrine, myth, ritual, material manifestation, experience and social organisation' (Smart 1998b: 23) that characterize and define explicit religions. For example, he refers to nationalism as being implicitly religious and looks at how his dimensions of religion fit nationalism, e.g. the mythic dimension is seen in the great stories of the nation and the material dimension is found in the Cenotaph, Cardiff Arms Park, etc. (Smart 1998b: 23).

what counts as religion' (de Groot 2012: 458). The possibility is then opened up for what Bailey refers to as 'a wider public understanding and dialogue' (Bailey 1998a: 17) which can foster questions about the various ways in which it might be possible to practise, encounter, experience, or understand religion in the modern world, which may (or may not) entail a reconception of the primacy or exclusivity of traditional definitions of religion vis-à-vis their 'implicit' counterparts in a culture where the 'line between what is sacred and secular is often blurred, and the Western notion that dogmatic religion is primary and civil or implicit religion is secondary, has to be reconsidered' (Riis 2012: 425). The division need no longer be between, as Dawkins would see it, the explicitly religious and the explicitly antireligious (or atheistic) but attention can be accorded instead to what Bailey designates 'that "secular" area between these two ends of the spectrum' where, as he sees it, 'lies an implicit religiosity' (Bailey 1998a: 73).

What Bailey is thus saying is that in identifying a phenomenon as implicitly religious there need not be any causal relationship between the phenomenon concerned and explicit religion (see Bailey 1998a: 70). Rather, a particular advantage with the term Implicit Religion is that 'it keeps its options open with regard to its referent's structural and historical origins, its social and cultural location, its mode of religiosity, and its relationship with other forms of religion' (Bailey 2006: 41). A good analogy is with Harry Williams' secular use of the term 'resurrection' in his 1972 publication *True Resurrection*, which is replete with illustrations of how a discernibly Christian term can be appropriated to seemingly banal and prosaic contexts. Williams gives the example of how an artist who at first experiences only emptiness and then finds his or her imagination 'stirred into life' might be said to be undergoing 'resurrection' (Williams 1972: 10). Similarly, when a married couple's dormant relationship suddenly blossoms and finds new depth that, too, for Williams might be deemed to be an experience of resurrection (Williams 1972: 10–11). Williams also uses the term 'resurrection' to categorize the scenario whereby what he calls 'the prisoner of irritating or confining circumstances, the man who slips on one of the many kinds of banana skin, the man whose great expectations are belied, the man who is tied to triviality' suddenly 'realizes the humour of his situation, and by his laughter shows that he has risen above what cabins and confines him because he can relish the joke at his expense' (Williams 1972: 11). Admittedly, not everyone

is enamoured with Williams' rather too malleable use of the word.
According to Badham and Badham, 'Frankly I believe most people
would regard the use of the term "resurrection"' in such contexts 'as a
crude joke', and, referring to Williams' status as an Anglican clergyman,
they add that 'It is hard to believe that a member of the Community of
the Resurrection could give so banal an interpretation of the term'
(Badham and Badham 1984: 20). But, where the analogy does work is
in the attempt to broaden the basis and scope of traditional religious
activity from one which is deemed to function exclusively within the
constraints of a particular tradition or world-view to one which goes
beyond conventional boundaries. To Bailey's credit, where his work
does genuinely make a solid contribution to contemporary religious
debate is in his inclination to focus on the role of *secular* dispositions
and commitments. After all, as Bailey sees it, 'The sacred may be special
and set-apart, but it can only be either of those, in *relation* to that which
is not so special, and from which it is set apart' (Bailey 1998a: 79).

Ironically, in his mission to find new locations of contemporary
religiosity one thing that Bailey tends to do is take it as a given that
traditional, explicit forms of religion are fixed and clearly demarcated.
As Ménard writes to this end, work in the field of Implicit Religion
'might seem to suggest that explicit religion "goes by itself", is taken
for granted', whereas Implicit Religion 'somehow always has to
"prove itself", constantly having to present its credentials' (Ménard
2001: 87). This is quite similar to Williams who is trying to move the
discussion away from seeing 'resurrection' as a term that is rooted
exclusively either in the past (vis-à-vis what happened to Jesus after
his crucifixion on Calvary some 2,000 years ago) or the future (in
terms of an afterlife that may be in store for us after the cessation of
our physical lives) but to reframe the contours of the debate so that
present resurrection lies at the centre, rather than on the periphery, of
what we mean when we use the language of 'resurrection'. Just as for
Williams it is key that the 'resurrection' is allowed to function beyond
traditional, parochial boundaries to encompass secular manifestations of the term, so Bailey is keen to emphasize the pivotal role
that secular manifestations of religion have *in their own right*—and
not merely vis-à-vis traditional accounts of religion in relation to
which they will invariably be deemed to 'fall short'. In Hamilton's
words, 'they are what they are and we shall understand more about
them if we treat them as such and not primarily as things which are
like something else but which they are not' (Hamilton 2001: 12).

Although Ménard is correct that Implicit Religion tends, by definition, to elicit comparisons with explicit (and so ostensibly taken for granted and self-evident) forms of religion, where Bailey's model comes into its own is in its preparedness to look at the phenomena first and only then to ascertain its religious provenance. The process is discernibly 'bottom-up' rather than 'top-down'. As Tatjana Schnell sees it, 'Instead of defining certain features of religion and setting out to reveal them in secular contexts, implicit religion searches the context empirically and only then, in a bottom-up process, formulates emerging contents and world-views' (Schnell 2000: 115). To return to the analogy with resurrection, Badham and Badham's critique that Williams' use of the term resurrection to refer to, for example, a mediocre tennis player who suddenly plays 'a really good game' (Badham and Badham 1984: 19) is 'banal', or even, as the authors say in relation to another of Williams' illustrations, 'a crude joke' (Badham and Badham 1984: 20), is spot on when judged from the vantage point of historical tradition. But, even if Badham and Badham are right when they profess that they 'have never heard a Wimbledon commentator talk of a player's "resurrection"' (Badham and Badham 1984: 19), the crucial matter both for Williams and Bailey is that the religious provenance or essence of any phenomena should not be rejected out of hand simply because it fails to conform to pre-established serious or purportedly 'objective' accounts of what is religion.

Indeed, Hills and Argyle have written about how there is a range of phenomena, which they categorize as 'para-religions', where, as with Implicit Religion, the foundation is 'a secular/materialistic framework with no reference to any supernatural power' (Hills and Argyle 2002: 74) yet which exhibit functionally similar characteristics to their formal counterparts. The examples they give here include the important role played in Weight Watchers, Alcoholics Anonymous, and Tupperware parties of 'testimony and a "revivalist" spirit' (Hills and Argyle 2002: 74). Viewed through the lens of Implicit Religion, such phenomena may seem prosaic, even facile, when compared to the formal structures and substantive beliefs of established religions, but they may be no less intense and invigorating—salvific, even—for the participants concerned. Popular psychology or self-development may similarly be felt to comprise forms of religiosity, along the lines of self-help books by the hypnotist Paul McKenna which contain titles such as *I Can Make You Thin, I Can Make You Smarter, I Can Mend*

*Your Broken Heart, I Can Make You Rich, I Can Make You Happy,
I Can Make You Sleep* as well as pledges to *Quit Smoking Today
Without Gaining Weight, Change Your Life in Seven Days, Control
Stress,* and *Instant Confidence* which employ religious, or quasi-
religious, vocabulary. As Hills and Argyle say about such writings
more generally, they 'similarly emphasize the value of absolute faith
and belief in the possibility of (self) improvement and also rely on
accounts of near-miraculous changes in the circumstances of those
who have followed the prescribed path' (Hills and Argyle 2002: 75).

In promising virtually immediate gratification they are somewhat
reminiscent of the way in which Hollywood films about the afterlife,
such as *Flatliners* (1990), are interested in expediting the process of
salvation so that rather than having to wait until after we have died
until the possibility of new life may be countenanced, salvation
becomes a present, this-worldly, and realistically attainable goal
which can begin straight away (see Deacy 2012a: 49). *Flatliners* is a
prime example, indeed, of how ultimate questions as traditionally
conceived through the language of heaven and hell become trans-
planted into the everyday, prosaic, secular realm where the goal is not
so much whether we will be judged by a Deity for our actions and
behaviour on earth as whether we can confront, now, our 'failings
and past traumas, so that flatlining becomes a kind of extreme
therapy' (Ruffles 2004: 129; see also Deacy 2012a: 51). As I have
written elsewhere, it is this present life rather than a life after death
that is being sanctioned in *Flatliners* in which ethical lessons about
how we behave on earth towards other people are more pressing for
the filmmakers than any attempt to delineate the afterlife per se (see
Deacy 2012a: 51). Similarly, if one follows the path outlined by
McKenna then one can purportedly change one's life in seven
days rather than have to wait until the afterlife before the attainment of bliss.

François Gauthier is thus right in his understanding that 'The
concept of implicit religion was devised precisely to help emancipate
our perspectives and acknowledge the workings of religion outside its
traditional forms' (Gauthier 2005: 253). Compared to Augustine's
fixed understanding of the afterlife in which he saw hell, for example,
as a bottomless pit containing a lake of fire and brimstone where the
bodies of sinners would be tormented forever (see Augustine 1998:
1068), the notion that salvation can be short-circuited by following
the precepts outlined in popular psychology and self-help manuals

would be unintelligible and distorting (and certainly when viewed from Augustine's theistic framework an anathema). Seen in this light there is something deficient about Implicit Religion as it could be construed as expressing 'the idea of something which is . . . rather like but not quite religion' (Hamilton 2001: 5) and, were the 'religion' concerned not to be 'implicit' then the term 'religion' might be prefixed, almost apologetically, with words like 'quasi', 'surrogate', or 'pseudo' to categorize the form of religion being referred to as a pale imitation of the 'real' thing.

Despite Bailey's protestation that there is nothing arbitrary in his typology—as we have already seen, he agrees that though *anything* can potentially be religious it is not the case that *everything* is religious—this is belied by the looseness of the language he uses, as when he writes that the 'concept is innocent of theory, as well as neutral in value' (Bailey 1998a: 18). This does a disservice to what is otherwise a well thought-out and cogent typology as it suggests that Implicit Religion is devoid of strict definitional or theoretical contours and as such is academically lightweight. This concern that it is a somewhat vague and nebulous construct is reinforced by William Dupré's point that 'One of the problems of implicit religion concerns the observation that it seems to occur everywhere once we have formed this concept and use the perspectives it provides' (Dupré 2007: 146). Nothing, as was suggested in chapter 3, exists in a vacuum and whenever religious typologies or definitions are coined in the West Karen Lord's point that 'it is safe to assume that a Western bias exists at all levels of the available literature' (Lord 2006: 214) has a particular saliency. Lord is quite categorical in her assessment that Implicit Religion is simply 'another Western construct which carries with it a particular bias', comprising as it does 'a construct shaped in the context of the secularization debate' which 'assumes a particular understanding of "religion" and then qualifies that understanding with the term "implicit" to indicate behaviours that resemble religious behaviours although they take place in "non-religious" settings' (Lord 2006: 214).

There is thus a certain naïveté in the assumption that Implicit Religion does not come with the sort of baggage that necessarily pertains to all (other) models and typologies. Ultimately, its status as a religion is relative to how flexible one is in their definition of religion more generally. As Hamilton sees it, for example, 'for those who define it very broadly, implicit religion probably is indeed religion'

(Hamilton 2001: 10), whereas for those who would define religion more strictly then it could not be defined in such terms, in line with John Badertscher's consideration that 'Implicit religion is by definition in hiding... because the culture has reserved the use of the term "religion" for the explicit traditions' (Badertscher 2001: 72). Where Bailey's work is innovative is precisely in its readiness to toy with our preconceptions of what religion is and where it may be found. While he is keen to differentiate between saying that *anything may be* and *everything is religious*, he also makes the vital point that 'a religion that was not... relevant to the whole of life would hardly qualify as such, in the opinion of most adherents (or, indeed, critics)' (Bailey 2006: 45).

HOW MIGHT CHRISTMAS FUNCTION AS A SITE OF IMPLICIT RELIGION?

So, while acknowledging that religion needs to have some definitional contours, Bailey is against any attempts to compartmentalize religion in such a way that it can only be thought to operate in specific spheres of life, as if one is either doing something 'religious' or 'profane' at any one moment. Where Bailey's influence is crucial is in his readiness not to bracket out the extent to which religion may impact on a person's, or a community's, or a nation's, life. He is aware, for example, that it has long been recognized by sociologists that 'there seems to be no *a priori* limit to what can be religious. One society's sacred is another society's profane; or, perhaps more tellingly, a third society's insignificant secular' (Bailey 2006: 46). On this basis, there is no reason why *Christmas Junior Choice* should not be interpreted through the lens of Implicit Religion *because of*, rather than in spite of, the fact that, to paraphrase what Karen Pärna writes about the Internet as a site of religious activity, it is 'not embedded in religious traditions', nor does it 'serve the purposes of clearly defined religious groups' (Pärna 2006: 200). Indeed, for Pärna, the 'veneration of the Internet as sacred originates from the mundane domain of journalism, the business and financial world, and futurist bestsellers' (Pärna 2006: 200) rather than from any causal relationship to, or dependence on, traditional, explicit forms of religion. The fact that the Internet 'is a product of scientific endeavour, linked to commercial enterprise' (Pärna 2006: 200) would negate its ability to be religious from a traditional point of view, but, as I am contending here with respect to *Junior Choice*, 'This sort of religiosity nestles in ostensibly secular discourses' (Pärna 2006: 200) and contexts.

Implicit Religion is, however, about more than simply the purported presence of religiosity but in a non-traditional context or where there is the absence of an explicit religious framework. For Bailey, there are firmer contours than this—specifically that for any phenomena to count as implicit religion there needs to be 'the presence of commitment, *of any kind*' (Bailey 1998a: 18). This is what makes Bailey's typology distinctive. His is a reductionist framework for understanding religion, in which the bottom line is what he calls 'understanding people, from the point of view of their intentionality, at any and every level of consciousness' (Bailey 1998a: 78).[3] Seeking as his goal 'understanding what being human can mean' (Bailey 2006: 9), Bailey puts forward a conceptualization of religion which 'makes "common sense" with the man in the street' (Bailey 2006: 48) and in which he takes the line that the study of Implicit Religion 'takes the whole of a human context as its agenda, rather than any pre-determined segment of it' (Bailey 2006: 49). It is this absence of a pre-set agenda or delineation of religion which for Bailey is pivotal and is closer to how religion is *lived* for most people anyway. Rather than bracketed out from the rest of life he correlates 'being religious' with 'being human' and attests that 'Being human, for the vast majority of human beings, seems to involve both being religious, in a secular sort of way, and being secular, in a religious sort of way' (Bailey 2006: 48).

While indubitably vague, this for Bailey is precisely what religion is essentially about. Rather than focusing on such factors as affiliation to a religious group or whether or not one believes in God—or, as James Gollnick also identifies, 'frequency of prayer and attendance at religious services, or financial contributions to religious organizations' which 'can be more easily observed and quantified' (Gollnick 2002:

---

[3] This is also quite a serious problem with Implicit Religion, as typified by Douglas Davies' critique that 'Implicit religion has, essentially, nothing to do with religion, but everything to do with being human as a member of a particular society. Thus understood, it is one way of talking about the data of social anthropology and not of theology' (Davies 1999: 17).

83)—'the criterion of religiosity must be primarily subjective' (Bailey 2006: 3) and comprise what ultimately reflects 'the strongest motivations and commitments around which people organize their mental and spiritual lives' (Gollnick 2002: 83). Anything, in other words, which gets to the hub of 'the less obvious and less conventional aspects of religion' (Gollnick 2002: 83) comes under Implicit Religion's auspices and remit. Bailey acknowledges that this may make Implicit Religion appear only to be a 'quasi-religion' (Bailey 2006: 49), or, as Grainger puts it, 'an ersatz form of "the real thing"' (Grainger 1999: 52). But, crucially, Bailey takes the line that 'it could be that the unofficial religion is, for a certain (individual or social) unit of personal life, at a particular moment, perhaps only in specific ways, their real religion' (Bailey 2006: 49) while they may merely pay only lip service to formal, explicit forms of religion. On this basis, *Christmas Junior Choice* may have more impact and comprise more of a *commitment* on the part of the adherent than allegiance or devotion to mainstream, explicit religion, and it is no less profound or efficacious for that.

Ultimately, as Grainger attests, 'For Bailey, implicitness and profundity go together' (Grainger 1999: 52), and the 'implicit' should not be conceived of as subordinate to or a substitute for explicit religion. Just because someone's religion is not explicit does not mean that they don't have one: 'All it may mean is that the main force of their commitment is directed elsewhere' (Grainger 2003: 56). It is not the location—such as a church, synagogue, temple, or mosque—but the force or the power of one's commitment that characterizes and determines religion's implicit ethos, even if much of the language that we associate with explicit religion is being utilized in this new context. None of this is especially new, of course, as when for John A.T. Robinson in *Honest to God* back in 1963 the language of transcendence was integral to his theology, but the context was very much that of *human* rather than metaphysical transcendence. In Robinson's words, 'Statements about God are acknowledgements of the transcendent, unconditional element in all our relationships, and supremely in our relationships with other persons' (Robinson 1963: 52; see also Deacy 2012a: 85). For Don Cupitt, similarly, 'the progressive weakening of religious institutions and religious thought does not alter the fact that at the deepest level religious needs and impulses are as great as ever', with the corollary that 'Some of the traditional functions of religion have now been taken over by other agencies' (Cupitt 2003: 33).

In *Screen Christologies* I made a case for seeing popular media, specifically film, as one such new site of religiosity on the grounds that 'redemption has the capacity to be apprehended and encountered in the secular sphere, and, in particular, for seeing in the medium of film robust indications and manifestations of religious activity' (Deacy 2001: 10). Re-reading this passage, it is clear that this focus on what is happening in the 'secular sphere' ties in well with the remit of Implicit Religion. Just as I proposed that it is the inherently *human* experience that a film character undergoes 'and which has the capacity to resonate with the lives and experiences of the *audience members*' that enables certain films 'to be read in theological terms' (Deacy 2001: 10), so Bailey's focus on the human and the secular has quite far-reaching theological ramifications. Bailey thinks that 'we may gain in our understanding of people if we were to try and apply something of what we now know about religious life, to ordinary secular life' and that, crucially, 'we may look to the study of religion to throw additional light on what is happening in secular life' (Bailey 2012: 196) rather than exclusively on any perceived demarcated sacred sphere. Seen as coterminous as opposed to discrete, Bailey thinks that we can learn about people's commitments and values better through religious categories and lenses than by simply restricting ourselves to what he calls 'unrelievedly *secular* understandings of the secular' (Bailey 2012: 196). Akin to Robinson's proposition that theological statements are really 'affirmations about human existence' (Robinson 1963: 52), Bailey's starting-point in the field of Implicit Religion is that we need to move away from those binary models, where the separation between the religious and the secular, the sacred and the profane, is assumed, towards approaches which do not 'hinder the overall understanding of human being' (Bailey 2006: 8) and which acknowledge that it is quite customary for an individual to have more than one area or focus of commitment in their lives, which traditional binary models are not quite able to accomplish. Such breadth and subtlety is necessary for Bailey in order, paradoxically, for a more realistic and precise understanding of what it means to be human to be fully appreciated.

While unquestionably reductionistic in its focus on the human rather than the superhuman, the terrestrial rather than the celestial, Implicit Religion is tapping into a legitimate field of religious and theological enquiry. It is consistent, for example, with how for Don Cupitt 'In the modern period we have come more and more to explain events in this world in this-worldly terms', with the result that 'This great cultural change does not mean the end of religion, but it does mean giving up some obsolete religious ideas' (Cupitt 2003: 36). When Cupitt then writes that since the Enlightenment 'Laws of historical development made the progressive, and ultimately the complete, secularization of culture unstoppable' and that 'To survive, it seemed that religion must change' (Cupitt 1995: 247), Bailey's focus on our attachments, predilections, and commitments does not seem all that unusual. If, as Cupitt outlines, 'In place of the old passive supernaturalism which saw God as having already fully prescribed the whole framework within which human life must be lived, so that nobody but God could bring about any major change in the human condition, it now came to be held that we human beings are historical agents, called upon ourselves to change the world' (Cupitt 1995: 247), then the concerns of Implicit Religion are an inevitable outworking of this post-Enlightenment position.[4] Bailey builds on this 'tendency towards *anthropocentrism*' (Deacy 2001: 75) with a threefold typology which specifically encompasses 'what a person is committed to; when one uncovers the integrating foci of their individual and communal experience; and when one reveals the ways in which commitments and integrating foci transcend the narrow confines of specific experiences to affect the entirety of a person's life' (Porter 2009: 277).

In looking at each of these in turn, it is clear that 'commitment' (or indeed 'commitments') is integral to Bailey's schema and supplies the scaffolding around which the second and third components of his typology are able to operate. As we have already identified, 'commitment' can operate on a multiplicity of levels—it is commitments '*of any kind*' (Bailey 1998a: 18) that he specifically refers to—and, with respect to the first part of his typology, any activity or predilection that exhibits '[b]inding behavior' and which 'involves a certain exercise of freedom' (Schnell 2000: 116), whether on a conscious or unconscious level, and whether they are 'inherited or chosen' (Jespers

---

[4] This ties in with broader theological developments post-Enlightenment, as when a shift has been evinced away from seeing redemption as bound up with how each individual human being has the capacity to undergo redemption within themselves. For Methodists, Quakers, and Pentecostalists, for example, attention was directed more on to the nature and character of the human individual in the redemptive process (see Deacy 2001: 72). As I have argued elsewhere, 'the modern interpretation of redemption has a substantially human-centred, and even subjective, orientation, its tendency being towards *anthropocentrism*' (Deacy 2001: 75).

et al. 2012: 536), can be included here. Bailey is not interested in simply pinpointing a single or singular commitment that might be said to be the pivot around which a person's whole life might be thought to function, as 'Multiple commitments can exist, which are either unrelated or competitive, or united as an expression of one underlying commitment' (Jespers et al. 2012: 536). These might range from belonging to a fan club or film society (with the concomitant tendency to buy or download books, movies, or other paraphernalia relating to such interests) to membership of a political party or local amateur dramatics group. Gauthier writes, for example, about how people committed to rave culture may 'structure worldviews and therefore fill out the function of (implicit) religion as the ground or foundation from which (at least certain paramount areas of) life proceeds' (Gauthier 2005: 236), in a way that ties in with Rupert Till's claim that Electronic Dance Music Culture provides a focus of community for the homeless self (Till 2009: 181) and enables feelings of empathy and connection (Till 2009: 178) and 'the creation of sacred spaces' (Till 2009: 184).

Bailey's second term, 'integrating foci', is additional to, rather than independent of, what he understands as that to which a person is committed, and can pertain either to individuals or groups. Acknowledging that there is a certain 'ambiguity of reference' here, Bailey takes the line that this is deliberate as he sees Implicit Religion, like 'religion' more generally, as spanning 'the whole gamut of the area in which the human operates' (Bailey 1998a: 23). It encompasses 'every width and depth of human interaction, from the individual and personal, through the familial and face-to-face, to the social, societal, corporate, and species' (Bailey 1998a: 23). Indeed, as Jespers, Kleijbeuker, and Schattevoet see it, integrating foci operate in a lateral manner and include both 'inner personal life and inter-personal life' (Jespers et al. 2012: 536), such as the family, community, and society more widely. Wherever, then, there is believed to be the presence of 'focal points that integrate wider areas of life' (Schnell 2000: 116) this second element of Bailey's typology comes into play. Gauthier supplies more specific detail here in his assertion that 'An integrating focus is that which conciliates, solves, amalgamates and unites differences', and 'which integrates into a whole that is larger than the sum of its elements' (Gauthier 2005: 236). His work on rave culture fits well with this definition as, for Gauthier, 'Part of the myth of rave is its claim to be the re-connection with more tribal, primitive, simpler, fuller, truer, more powerful and "more real" times and experiences' (Gauthier 2005: 237) and in which 'The large space fitted out for dancing makes it a morphing, organic integrating focus which places emphasis on participation, corporality and community' (Gauthier 2005: 240).

Finally, Bailey's third model, 'intensive concerns with extensive effects', again quite an amorphous term, specifically pertains to the category of 'religion' itself. Indeed, according to Bailey, 'It does for "religion" what the other two definitions did for the individual and society, and for the conscious and unconscious: it spans a spectrum' (Bailey 1998a: 24). It is disappointing, therefore, that Bailey is not able to supply any specific contours or to flesh out with specific examples precisely what he has in mind. He sees this definition as ensuring that the 'distinction between the sacred and the secular, the holy and the profane, the special and the ordinary, between religion and the rest of life, are both acknowledged as necessary and accurate and helpful, and yet simultaneously restored to reciprocal relationship' (Bailey 1998a: 24), which lacks sufficient precision. Indeed, Bailey seems to be saying here that there needs to be a separation between religion and non-religion while simultaneously looking to see the collapse of this binary model. What is not then clear from this definition is whether Bailey wants to see 'religion' as in some sense a special, set-apart category or whether the religious and the secular should be conjoined in such a way as to cancel out any such differentiation. In terms of our discussion up to this point it would appear that Bailey favours the latter, but having a model which as Bailey sees it 'has the merit of excluding a potential restriction of reference' (Bailey 1998a: 24) also ensures that it lacks definitional clarity and specificity.

Where the model does work, however, is in its attempt to equate Implicit Religion with depth. A 'brief experience of ecstasy', for example, would not qualify, even if it occurred frequently, 'so long as it appears isolated from the remainder of experience' (Bailey 1998a: 24). A concern that is 'intensive' to us and which has profound ('extensive') consequences either for us or for wider society would thus qualify, whereas simply finding something interesting, helpful, or stimulating would not by itself meet the requirements. As William H. Swatos Jr puts it, 'Simply because a person says, "I found reading *The Hobbit* very meaningful," *The Hobbit* does not thereby become an implicit religion . . . Even if *The Hobbit* is "the most meaningful thing" I have ever read, it does not thereby become a religion' (Swatos Jr 2001: 102–3). Whether we are talking about the rave ethos as delineated by Till and Gauthier—in view of the extent to which it might be said to have 'transformed and shaped the lives of those involved' (Gauthier 2005: 245)—or a programme such as *Christmas Junior Choice* with its extensive impact upon the lives of generations of radio listeners, as outlined in chapter 3, Implicit Religion readily supplies a framework and a remit within which such phenomena may be tabulated, apprehended, and understood.

While Bailey is at times unhelpfully elusive in his definitions, he deserves credit for proposing a method of categorizing religion which takes as its focus those occasions when, often outside traditionally configured or demarcated boundaries of where 'religion' is expected to lie, a person's or group's basic beliefs about the way the world is or should be are affirmed or changed (see Porter 2009: 277) can be taken as being of intrinsic religious significance. Bailey sees 'transcendent' experiences as no less 'to be found in times of ordinary consciousness' as 'in those unexpected and infrequent "transcendent" experiences of the numinous that come upon individuals unexpectedly' (Porter 2009: 277). Provided that what we are dealing with is 'what truly matters' (Porter 2009: 271), there is no reason why it cannot be in something as ostensibly trivial a medium as popular culture, as when Jennifer Porter argues that 'Fan communities are, or at least can be, places that embody a person's and/ or a community's expression of what it means to be human, to be in community, to be in space and time, to be moral or immoral, to be finite or eternal, to simply be' (Porter 2009: 271). In place of a hierarchical division between the sacred and the profane, Porter affirms that 'Implicit religion underpins ardent pop culture fandom, just as it underpins ardent explicit religion' (Porter 2009: 271), so that, for instance, 'Uncovering what a person stands for, what they feel they must or must not do, who they feel they are, who they belong with, and how they ultimately situate themselves in their own personal history, their community, the world, and the cosmos' (Porter 2009: 277) should no longer be seen as simply the prerogative of explicit religion. A person who belongs to a *Star Trek* fan community, for example, may find that 'Multiculturalism, tolerance for diversity, evolutionary progress, human potential, political non-interference, sexual equality, free will, scientific and technological progress, and a triumphant destiny that transcends biological limits' are just some of the main ideological commitments which bring such devotees together, and that

> Support for the United Nations, volunteering at food banks and soup kitchens, giving blood to the Red Cross, donating time and money to children's charities, and supporting political candidates who embody the ideals that fans associate with Star Trek, are a few of the ways in which fans reveal the extensive effects of these ideals on their everyday lives (Porter 2009: 278).

If through such ventures adherents obtain a sense of 'hope for the future', 'solace in times of grief or fear', the incentive 'to keep going when life seems darkest', and that 'life has a purpose', as well as defining that which it means to be human (or for that matter inhuman), then Porter is not wide of the mark when she concludes that this is all, ultimately, 'the vehicle for expressing the implicit religion of fans' (Porter 2009: 278).

The net result of all this is to disclose how Implicit Religion can change the face of how religion in general, and Christmas in particular, may be perceived. Despite using a generic and even anodyne term like 'commitments' to underscore his typology, Bailey has demonstrated that it is not sufficient to pay lip service to something for that to count as an authentically religious commitment. *Christmas Junior Choice* may not conform to most people's perceptions of what counts as religious, but, as Lord has highlighted, some of the commitments that we would equate with traditional religion are found wanting on closer inspection. For instance, people who join a particular religious community in order to ensure that their children stand a better chance of going to a good school, who take part in a youth group for purely social reasons, or who baptize their son or daughter 'out of a sense of superstition or tradition without any real intention of keeping the baptismal vows' (Lord 2006: 209), may be demonstrating *commitment*, but the commitment is not grounded in or predicated on the religious tradition or community per se. They may not believe in God, for example, but nominally and superficially are more religiously committed (if only because they 'go to church') than their 'secular' counterparts. 'Non-religious' people may also often choose to give their children 'religious' names. A brief perusal at the Office for National Statistics list of the top hundred names of boys born in England and Wales in 2012 shows that the list is replete with biblical names, with Elijah at number 82, Reuben at 68, Benjamin at 32, Isaac at 30, Joseph at 22, Daniel at 16, Samuel at 15, Noah at 14, Joshua at 11, and Jacob at number 5 (Office for National Statistics 2013: www.ons.gov.uk/ons/rel/vsob1/baby-names–england-and-wales/2012/stb-baby-names-2012.html#tab-Top-100-baby-names-in-England-and-Wales-in-2012). While there is no doubt that some of these children will have been named deliberately after their Old Testament forebears, not every parent who decides to call their child Jacob or Joshua will do so due to any association with Judaism. By the same token, when a person recites the English national anthem there are quite explicit references to God which are allied to patriotism but not everyone who sings 'God Save Our Gracious Queen' or 'Land of Hope and Glory', with its chorus line 'God, who made thee mighty, make thee mightier yet', will be a committed theist. Indeed, even Richard Dawkins, who has referred to himself as a 'cultural Christian' explained in a BBC interview in 2007 that he enjoyed 'singing [Christmas] Carols along with everybody else' (in BBC News 2007: http://news.bbc.co.uk/1/hi/uk_politics/7136682.stm). Dawkins was also cited the following year as stating that

> I am perfectly happy on Christmas day to say Merry Christmas to everybody . . . I might sing Christmas carols—once I was privileged to be invited to Kings College, Cambridge, for their Christmas carols and loved it. . . . I actually love most of the genuine Christmas carols. I can't bear Jingle Bells and Rudolph the Red Nosed Reindeer and you might think from that that I was religious, that I can't bear the ones that make no mention of religion. But I just think they are dreadful tunes and even more dreadful words. I like the traditional Christmas carols (in Todd 2008: www.dailymail.co.uk/debate/article-1100842/Why-I-celebrate-Christmas-worlds-famous-atheist.html).

John Badertscher is thus right in his declaration that 'In our now nearly global culture, there are many expressions of loosely shared faith that can convincingly be identified as religious, and that belong to the culture without belonging to any of the explicit religions' (Badertscher 2010: 203). Explicit religious terminology is being appropriated in an entirely 'secular', and implicit, fashion, to the point that explicit and implicit religiosity seem curiously, and often indiscernibly even by many of those who use the terminology concerned, intertwined. When Lord speaks of 'the arbitrary, shifting boundaries of the set defined as "religion" within the larger set of human commitments called "implicit religion"' (Lord 2006: 218) we can begin to see how the traditional sacred–profane binary is no longer applicable and that implicit forms of religion are a significant marker of the way in which the category of religion debate has moved, and needs to move further. Maybe, then, Swatos Jr is not exactly wide of the mark when he goes so far as to label Implicit Religion 'a categorically different kind of thing from other kinds of religion' (Swatos Jr 2001: 102) precisely because of the way in which it is able to bring to the fore, and to disclose, phenomena which would otherwise remain camouflaged in a culture where 'religion' is still associated with its explicit and institutional counterparts. It is in seeing religion in, rather than in contradistinction to, the everyday— Gollnick, to this end, paraphrases Abraham Maslow's observation that 'the sacred is in the ordinary, that it is to be found in one's daily life, in one's neighbors, friends, and family, in one's back yard' (in Gollnick 2002: 87) in the light of Bailey's schema—that makes Implicit Religion simultaneously an aberration and the quintessence of both what religion is and where it can be found in the contemporary world.

5

Christmas Films and the Persistence of the Supernatural

CHRISTMAS MOVIES AS VESSELS OF TRANSFORMATION AND RENEWAL

Although Christmas radio has been a focus of this book up to this point, this chapter will critically explore the relationship between Christmas and a particular genre of movies—Christmas-themed films—which are not only exclusive to the Christmas season but, as was discussed earlier with reference to Christmas music, are not readily transferable to any other point in the calendar. As Connelly informs us, 'From film's earliest days British and American film-makers had shown a keen interest in Christmas' (Connelly 2012: 159), and so integral are Christmas movies to the Christmas season that he even goes so far as to attest that cinema is the reason why 'Christmas is known everywhere.... Cinema and Christmas are intertwined' (Connelly 2000a: 1).[1] This is further borne out by Mundy's claim that 'Quite apart from the commercial importance of Christmas as a major release period for new films, representations of Christmas have become increasingly pervasive in contemporary Hollywood' (Mundy 2008: 165). Connelly's premise is that cinema, more than any other medium, 'has shown people what the festival of Christmas is like', and that 'Most people know of at least one Christmas movie and

---

[1] This is evidenced, for example, by Golby and Purdue's assertion that 'Whereas we have little idea of how the majority of people in Britain were spending their time at 8 p.m. on Christmas Day in 1884, we do know that at the same time one hundred years later, over 70% of the population were watching television and that of these nearly 20 million, or 37.5% of the population, were watching one film, *Raiders of the Lost Ark*' (Golby and Purdue 2000: 105).

most people can recall a childhood visit to the cinema at Christmas' (Connelly 2000a: 1). What is especially pertinent, however, is that, as with the focus in the lyrics of Christmas pop songs on Santa and Frosty rather than the baby Jesus in a manger, which we discussed in chapter 3, so there is a clear disjuncture between Christmas movies and the Christian religion. In *It's a Wonderful Life* (1946), for example, Myers makes the instructive observation that 'organized religion plays almost no part in the plot' and that George Bailey and his family 'not only never go to church, they never mention religion, and, in fact, they seem to be the perfect secular, civic-minded family' (Myers 2001a: 50). Haire and Nelson similarly note in relation to *A Christmas Story* (1983), a movie predicated on nostalgia for the Christmas of a previous generation of children growing up in the 1940s, that 'the film itself only dares for a split second to enter into the religious history associated with Christmas' and in which 'There are no crosses and no Bibles or other religious symbols often associated with Christmas' (Haire and Nelson 2010: 83).

These are not isolated examples, and, with the very *absence* of religion (as traditionally configured) one of the most discernible characteristics of the genre of Christmas films, what we have in its place is an implicit emphasis on the importance of consumerism. As Haire and Nelson identify with specific reference to *A Christmas Story*,

> It seems as if the Parkers' Christmas is motivated almost entirely by the pile of presents they will open. We see in the Parkers' *Christmas Story* the replacement of the religiously significant Christmas with the notion that happiness on Christmas morning will be had only if the right presents are received, the perfect tree is in the living room, and a wonderful Christmas feast is on the table (Haire and Nelson 2010: 86).

This matches Restad's assessment that in the course of the twentieth century 'the cliché of Christmas's rampant materialism threaded its way unexamined through nearly every story line' (Restad 1995: 171). Even in films where characterization and depth may be in short supply, as betokened by the poor (invariably) one-star reviews that attended the release of such Christmas fare in recent decades as *Jingle All The Way* (1996), *Christmas with the Kranks* (2004), *Surviving Christmas* (2004), and *Deck the Halls* (2006), one constant dynamic that suffuses such releases has been the notion that Christmas is a demonstrably consumerist celebration per se.

This sort of assessment is certainly one that is engrained in the discourse about Christmas. Myers writes, for example, about how 1940s films about Christmas 'had the effect of making Christmas, and specifically the American consumer Christmas, an integral part of the normal social world of Americans' (Myers 2001a: 39). It is, however, too simplistic a way of categorizing the essence of Christmas movies, reducing and caricaturing the genre as it does to an uncomplicated discussion about the importance of spending money. The aforementioned four films are all fairly one-dimensional for the way in which they equate success with capital, as highlighted by the premises of *Jingle All The Way*, in which Arnold Schwarzenegger's character feels the need to prove how much he loves his son by purchasing the latest 'Turbo Man' action figure on Christmas Eve, and *Surviving Christmas* in which a millionaire, played by Ben Affleck, resorts to paying a family the sum of $250,000 in order to let them allow him to spend Christmas in their house. In *Christmas with the Kranks* and *Deck the Halls*, also, the 'spirit' of Christmas is invoked by the need to erect the biggest, brashiest, most ostentatious and expensive adornment of Christmas lights and figurines on the rooftop of the family home.[2]

But, even if consumerism is rightly deemed integral to these pictures, Christmas films are also preoccupied with exploring the magical, transformative, and even supernatural *telos* of Christmas whereby characters are shown, Scrooge-like, to have the capacity to change, albeit against the backdrop of a materialist or consumerist world-view which is shown to be wanting. During the Second World War Christmas-themed films, such as *Holiday Inn* (1942), *I'll Be Seeing You* (1944), and *Christmas in Connecticut* (1945) all have narratives which, as Glancy observes, hinge 'upon the impact that Christmas has upon the characters' in the respect that 'Their lives are found to be lacking and dominated by selfish ambitions and cold

---

[2] To this end, the following from Dell deChant in the context of Christmas house displays perfectly encapsulates the world of *Christmas with the Kranks* and *Deck the Halls*: 'for these houses the owners have gone quite a bit "over the top" in their observance of the season, sparing no expense in transforming their residences into public spectacles. There are so many lights on these houses that adjacent residential streets look dim by comparison; their lawns are covered with a cornucopia of seasonal blow-mold objects; every available bit of residential foliage is festooned with even more lights; Christmas music may be blasting out of loudspeakers; reindeer-pulled sleighs can be spotted on their roofs; and as often as not, actual Santas are seen waving to gasping motorists stopping to gawk' (deChant 2002: 180).

materialism', with Christmas then serving 'as the occasion and the solution for these ills, as humanism overcomes materialism, disunity gives way to unity and nearly miraculous reunions are granted to separated families or lovers' (Glancy 2000: 60; see also Deacy 2013: 198). In *Meet Me In St. Louis* (1944), for instance, the lesson learned is that 'home and family come first and the pursuit of money must be put aside to maintain them' (Glancy 2000: 70). In the musical *White Christmas* (1954), similarly, the scenery may cry opulence and it may be, as Marling attests, an 'unabashedly glitzy, image-driven' spectacle—indeed, 'the very picture of a Christmas from a greeting card' in which 'everybody is wearing Technicolor Santa suits and snow is falling softly in the background'—but the expectation is that, ultimately, '[Bing] Crosby will marry [Rosemary] Clooney, settle down, and raise a family' (Marling 2000: 331). Even when a *Sight and Sound* review from 1997 put a different gloss on the film, in its suggestion that 'Beneath the Yuletide coating this is really a story about men sticking together', in which 'Crosby and [Danny] Kaye seem more interested in each other than in Rosemary Clooney or Vera-Ellen' (Anon. 1997: 62), the unmistakable corollary that the filmmakers seem to be conveying is that it is people and relationships that matter first and foremost.

Crucially, therefore, Christmas is synonymous with change and transformation for the human characters in such festive fare, and the fact that it is all happening against the backdrop of a time of year associated with miracles and celestial otherness only serves to underpin the momentousness of the conversions or resolutions on display. As Glancy puts it, 'A key component of the Christmas film is the climactic and joyous scene that occurs as if by magic on Christmas Eve or Christmas Day' (Glancy 2000: 75) as is borne out in 1940s films in which 'Audiences enduring long separations from their families, a loss of community and uncertainty for the future were eager to see these threats banished, and found the resolutions all the more convincing and fulfilling for arriving at Christmastime' (Glancy 2000: 75). We also see this same dynamic in more recent action and slapstick festive movies such as *Die Hard* (1988) or *Home Alone* (1990) where, as Mundy explains, 'the transformative power of Christmas is co-opted to resolve tension and conflict in ways that are ideally suited for Hollywood's formal requirement for narrative resolution' (Mundy 2008: 165). In many cases the transformation concerned is quite modest—bringing families together during times of crisis and upheaval, whether we are talking about wartime or the tumult caused in the latter films where the dysfunctional family unit is brought together after a major terrorist incident at the Nakatomi Plaza in *Die Hard* or when in *Home Alone* Macaulay Culken's character is left to fend for himself and to defend the family home after his parents and siblings managed to go on holiday for Christmas without him. Whether supernatural agencies such as angels, elves or Santa are involved or not (in the case of *Home Alone* it is notable that young Kevin offers a prayer to Santa in the hope that he will be reunited for Christmas with his estranged family), the bottom line is that Christmas could not be more concerned with questions of human agency and pertain to this world. Celestial emissaries may be involved, as when in *It's a Wonderful Life* a heavenly angel, Clarence (Henry Travers), is sent to intervene in the life of a suicidal George Bailey, but the denouement—and indeed the *raison d'être* of the miraculous intervention in the first place—is to bring about the restoration and re-establishment of the ruptured family unit.

THE PARADOX OF ESCAPISM

It is all the more ironic, then, that such dynamics take place within a body of films which are characteristically escapist and fantastic in their orientation. Since, as Jobling points out, fantasy tends to be 'associated with a number of undesirable features', such as that it is 'presumed to be childish' in a 'derogatory' sense and to 'represent the "non-rational"' (Jobling 2010: 7), there is a certain paradox involved. Despite being so tied to questions of familial identity and security and to the bringing together of estranged spouses or fathers at Christmas-time, festive films are laden with scenarios and characters which belong to the world of the illusory. There may be, as we discussed in chapter 1, characters who make the case for rationality over illusion—we see this for instance by the role played by psychologists in *The Santa Clause* (1994) and *Miracle on 34th Street* (1947, 1994)— but in such instances such characters are merely patsies who end up affirming the reality and splendour of the world of magic without equivocation despite hitherto doubting the mental health of anyone who would deign to profess belief in the existence of Santa Claus. It is all the more remarkable, therefore, that such predilections are a mainstay of popular, Christmas films when for sociologists such as Steve Bruce the United Kingdom is, as Abby Day construes such a position, 'now a secular culture with traces of a Christian identity, where secular means a rational worldview without beliefs in super-natural powers' (Day 2012: 442). Bruce and others may of course be correct that belief in the supernatural is infantile and out of step with trends in secularization, but it still begs the question of why fantasy and magic is so popular. Might it be the case, for instance, that, as Jobling asserts with reference to fantasy material in popular culture more generally, Christmas movies 'tap into' or even 'promote, illu-minate or subvert' a number of cultural fashions and currents such that 'the charges of escapism and irrelevance on the part of some critics seem distinctly short-sighted' (Jobling 2010: 7)?

One hypothesis which Jobling is keen to propound is that 'fantasies offer a sense of meaning, purpose and value which accords with spiritual concerns, anxieties and desires' (Jobling 2010: 8). Applied to Christmas movies, we can also cite Ole Riis's observation that 'At Christmas, all adults know that the added myths and symbols and rituals are fiction', but, crucially, 'That does not make them irrelevant, superficial or meaningless' (Riis 2012: 430). In a Durkheimian sense, indeed, it could be argued that the ritual of watching and participat-ing in a Christmas movie engenders a sense of social solidarity and becomes a site for families to come together and share in a collective experience. This would certainly account for the popularity at cin-emas each December of re-runs of festive favourites. In recent years, for example, my nearest cinema in Kent has put on special screenings of *It's a Wonderful Life* and *White Christmas* while Saturday morning children's screenings customarily include in their schedules the likes of *The Muppet Christmas Carol* (1992) and *How the Grinch Stole Christmas* (2000)—perennial Christmas favourites which comprise communal sites of collective emotions and memories. To paraphrase Riis, 'We do not believe in myths about Santa Claus or pixies, but we participate in the game anyway' (Riis 2012: 437). Claims that Christ-mas movies are trivial or merely diversionary thus tie in with Jobling's assessment at the heart of *Fantastic Spiritualities* that 'the fantastic has often been neglected as subject for critical study, or marginalized as literature' (Jobling 2010: 5). In lieu of seeing fantasy and reality to be distinct from, and even antithetical to, one another, in keeping with the separation in accounts of secularization between the sacred and the profane, the religious and the secular, Jobling's thesis that

'Fantasy negotiates a boundary between the actual and the incredible, the real and the illusory'—and, indeed, that fantasy 'is inevitably a commentary on or counterpart to reality'—is quite in keeping with the popularity of Christmas movies which may also be construed as 'expressions of deep human drives' (Jobling 2010: 5).

This is not to say, of course, that Christmas movies have special or privileged access to such contemporary sites of religious activity. But, it does not automatically follow that by virtue of being an entertainment medium religion is any less manifest in film (of whatever genre) than, say, news media or documentaries. According to Gordon Lynch, 'The genocidal killing of six million Jews in the Holocaust, or a million Rwandans, simply matters much more as the destruction of historical lives than the fictionalized representation of genocidal violence in *Star Wars* or *Lord of the Rings*' (Lynch 2012: 92). Lynch's is certainly not an isolated position. Writing with specific reference to computer technology, William A. Stahl wrote in 2002 of the dangers concomitant with finding in cyberspace and virtual reality merely a pale imitation or simulacrum of spiritual longing. In his words, 'In cyberspace we find spirituality without transcendence' (Stahl 2002: 98). Stahl's prognosis is not dissimilar to accounts of how film, too, may encourage a merely passive response from participants especially when he cites studies which show that, as he puts it, 'as the amount of time spent on-line increases, interaction with flesh-and-blood people drops dramatically' and that 'the more we dream of a magical future, the less likely we are to actively participate in building the real one' (Stahl 2002: 99).[3]

Yet, the fact remains that there are always going to be people whose lives revolve around, say, *Twilight* or *The Lord of the Rings* who never watch the news or care about what happens overseas. To that end, it is difficult to make the definitive adjudication that fantasy matters little. There are always going to be claims made about how, for example, celebrities lack the authority or legitimacy of religious leaders, as when Karen Pärna refers to arguments that present-day charismatics, which also include politicians, lack the authority and legitimacy that may in the past have been held by

---

[3] This position was refuted in chapter 1 with reference to the work of John Lyden where I argued that escapist films may be capable of enriching our apprehension of the empirical world rather than distancing us from them.

'sacred individuals' (Pärna 2004: 103).[4] However, as Pärna proceeds to assert, 'no reliable, scientific means have been developed for determining whether the implicitly religious in—for example—today's cult of the celebrity or devotion to certain (commercially propagated) "life styles" is more or less meaningful, profound or sincere than what one might encounter in a church environment' (Pärna 2004: 103). Although, she attests, 'We may claim that *Dallas*, the Texan soap opera, is somehow less meaningful and less profound than Dante's *Divine Comedy*' this is not based on any 'reliable' or 'objective' criteria but is nothing more than 'a precariously one-sided statement' (Pärna 2004: 103). The same could, of course, be said about *Junior Choice*. Tony Blackburn may be right when he believed that his career was in decline when he was consigned to playing 'Nellie the Elephant' to children under eight, but this is not to say that *Junior Choice* was not of ultimate importance to those young children, and still may be as they go on to have children and grandchildren of their own and look back on the music of their childhood with affection and longing for those halcyon days. As Pärna tells us, 'many seemingly flimsy popular images do in fact function as legitimate and powerful sources of meaning' (Pärna 2004: 103), to the point of asking, 'Who would dare claim that, in a particular niche, the charismatic authority of Britney Spears is not strong enough or her myth not significant enough' (Pärna 2004: 103–4)?

It does not therefore follow that Christmas films are per se inauthentic or defective sources of religious activity or expression. They may not have been conceived as theologically or spiritually profound pieces of work, but, as Jennifer Porter has argued in an article on the religious dimensions of fan communities, 'It is in the impact of [a] text on its audiences that the religious import is to be

---

[4] Pärna is here referring to a paper given by Timothy Jenkins entitled 'Sacred Persons in Contemporary Culture' at the 2004 *Implicit Religion* conference. In the published version, however, in the July 2005 edition of the *Implicit Religion* journal ('Sacred Persons in Contemporary Culture', *Implicit Religion*, 8/2: 133–46), Jenkins is far less specific. He writes that 'In the past, all sorts of things, institutions, places and people were marked as "special", in the sense that they possessed exceptional value or legitimacy, worth or authority. They were what we may call "sacred". In the modern period, however, this characteristic force or quality has departed from these different locations. This loss, which may be celebrated or regretted according to taste, is a way of describing both the character of modernity and the transition to it: we have become secularized' (Jenkins 2005: 133). In other words, Jenkins does not pass judgement on whether or not these modern counterparts are of lesser worth.

found, and this is true for mainstream religious contexts, as well as those contexts informed by popular culture' (Porter 2009: 275). None of this need be construed as especially wide of the mark or innovative. After all, as Jonathan Brant writes with respect to the work of Paul Tillich, 'an art object that is not highly regarded with regard to "quality" can still have a profound, and by implication revelatory, effect at the point of "involved encounter"' (Brant 2012: 223). It may be the case, for instance, that Christmas films and religion perform an analogous function to what Rachel Wagner writes about virtual reality, namely, that they 'can be viewed as manifestations of the desire for transcendence, the wish for some mode of imagination or being that lies just beyond the reach of our ordinary lives' (Wagner 2012a: 4; see also Deacy 2013: 198). This could certainly be the case if, say, Christmas movies are able to provide us with what Wagner sees in virtual reality—'secular forms of ritual that offer us meaning, imaginative engagement, enchantment, desire and temporary escape from our ordinary routines' (Wagner 2012a: 7; see also Deacy 2013: 198), not least as they could be said to be about (again to paraphrase Wagner) 'stories that animate our lives, rituals that shape our consciousness, and modes of interacting that define who we are' (Wagner 2012a: 234–5).

Contrary to claims that religion is on the wane, Wagner is emphatic that 'human beings are notoriously creative, imaginative creatures and will find ways to craft meaningful experiences whether or not we feel comfortable labeling them as explicitly "religious"' (Wagner 2012a: 7; see also Deacy 2013: 198), and it is here that Christmas movies do seem to supply just such a religious ethos or temperament. For, they are grounded in a vision of a utopian time and space, akin to our discussion in chapter 1 of the New Jerusalem, where dysfunctional family relationships often give way to opportunities for children to bond more with their parents especially when, as happens in *The Santa Clause*, the father finds his real vocation in life as the champion of children and bestower of gifts to all households around the world as Tim Allen's hapless and non-committal Scott Calvin learns the value of fatherhood when an unexpected turn of events leads him to metamorphose into Santa Claus. He even gets to employ his son, Charlie (Eric Lloyd), as one of his helpers at the North Pole as they work on the delivery of that year's Christmas toys and his ex-wife Laura (Wendy Crewson) is now not only convinced that Scott really is the real Santa Claus but she sets fire to the legal papers which would have awarded her sole custody of Charlie. As when Mazur and Koda write of how 'Disney's parks and films exploit the desire to live in a world of peace and beauty, to hope for a better time, and to leave troubles... behind' (Mazur and Koda 2011: 319), so *The Santa Clause*, which was made by Walt Disney Pictures, concludes on the most optimistic, even beatific, note imaginable as a reformed Calvin turns dreams into reality, dispensing not only tangible gifts but managing also to overcome the scepticism of the most hardened and uncompromising adults about the veracity of subscribing to a belief in a magical and seemingly irrational figure before whisking Charlie up in his sleigh for one final spin around the earth in his elaborate reindeer-pulled sleigh.

As Scott Calvin/Santa Claus discloses the reason why his ex-wife and her new partner, Neal (Judge Reinhold), a psychologist, are so impervious to believing in Santa—he has learned that as children Santa failed to give them the toys, an Oscar Mayer Wiener Whistle and a 'Mystery Date' board game, they had respectively pined for from their own childhoods in the mid-1960s, leading to a life-long grudge against him for engendering such disappointment—so Mazur and Koda's claim that Disney films (as well as its parks) 'provide a utopian time and space that allows people, if only for a moment, to re-create time and space as they could be, and as they might have been in some mythic (personal or national) past' (Mazur and Koda 2011: 319; see also Deacy 2013: 198) seems especially suitable to the genre of Christmas films (and *The Santa Clause* in particular). Indeed, at the end of *The Santa Clause*, Scott/Santa finally gives them the presents they had been deprived of all these years, to much emotion, release, and relief on the part of Laura and Neal (the latter apologizes to Charlie for disbelieving his story). When they then affirm for the first time since their own childhoods that they really do believe in Santa Claus, and in so doing they become more enlightened, tolerant, and open to the world of the imagination more than they (and we) had hitherto thought possible, so it is difficult to see what is happening in the movie as a merely throwaway, hollow, and unedifying escapist spectacle. As Mazur and Koda see it, 'Through the production and maintenance of meaning and symbol systems, Disney plays the same role of orientation that traditional religion once did exclusively', to the point that 'Americans (and others) can find in Disney many of the elements they once found exclusively in traditional religion' (Mazur and Koda 2011: 319; see also Deacy 2013: 198). Indeed, it does not seem too far-fetched, on such a reading, to see in Christmas films a crystallization of what for audiences amounts to the existence or presence of the sacred. Certainly, the conversion and transformative message that is intrinsic to every Christmas film (and which, as we have previously discussed, itself derives from Dickens) have long been a staple of the celebration and ritual of Christmas. They are, in other words, an extension of what Christmas has meant for centuries.

To this end, Christmas movies may well be escapist, but that escapism needs to be understood as a means to an end rather than an as an end in itself. Films like *The Santa Clause* may well celebrate the power of imagination and magic but they also seem to be about something more grounded and terrestrial in their frame of reference. Sara Vaux encapsulates this well when, in a discussion of the ethical vision of the cinema of Clint Eastwood, she makes a passing, but highly pertinent in terms of our present discussion, reference to how in *Mystic River* (2003) 'In one key sequence, a Christmas tree twinkles in the background, shorthand in Hollywood mainstream movies for the possibility of renewal' (Vaux 2012: 86). Yet, what stands out in so much of the literature, and critics' reviews, of Christmas films is the sense that Christmas movies are lacking in depth and follow limited, pre-set, and predictable paths towards an ultimately cheap and inauthentic pay-off. In this regard, the situation is not wholly distinct from what Rachel Wagner says about video games, which, she argues, 'lead us through predictable scripted experiences, give us limited choices and urge us to act in certain ways' (Wagner 2012b: 125). This, indeed, is one of the most peculiar and ironic facets of Christmas films. Popular though they may be in terms of box office receipts, they are derided and ignored within the academy in much the same way that, as I argued in a previous book, films about the afterlife have never been accorded serious treatment as they are 'not fruitful academic material and should be broached at the scholar's own peril' (Deacy 2012a: 2).

CRITICAL VS. POPULAR INTERPRETATIONS OF CHRISTMAS FILMS

Beginning in December 2012 I revisited every edition of the *Monthly Film Bulletin* and *Sight and Sound* since their inception in the early

1930s,[5] with a view to reading every article and review that discussed Christmas, no matter how obliquely. After subscribing to their digital repository I worked my way through each edition, starting with the earliest, and using their search engine looked for any references to 'Christmas', 'Xmas', and 'Santa', on the grounds that any specific Christmas-themed film would contain at least one of these words (while 'Father Christmas' would be covered by the word 'Christmas' itself). Inevitably there were some journals where the terms did not appear at all, or if they did they were not germane to the discussion at hand, as when the search for 'Santa' yielded results pertaining to the locations Santa Barbara or Santa Fe, or when 'Christmas' merely referred to issues around the publication or release dates of some of the editions or films being reviewed. What was left were fifty-one articles and reviews in *Sight and Sound* and twenty-one reviews in the *Monthly Film Bulletin* which contained substantive references to Christmas. These ranged chronologically from an article published in the Summer 1938 edition of *Sight and Sound* by Alberto Cavalcanti which refers to the 1912 film *Santa Claus* in which 'there was a scene showing the world travelling through space with Santa Claus driving his sledge in pursuit', and which focused on the technical elements to that colour film ('It was an entirely mechanical model of terrific dimensions' [Cavalcanti 1938: 56]) to Matthew Sweet's article on the legacy of Charles Dickens in cinema, 'Charlie's Ghost', in the February 2012 edition of *Sight and Sound* where the argument is advanced that '*The Muppet Christmas Carol* (1992) is unquestionably one of the great literary adaptations—anyone who remains unmoved by the sight of Michael Caine accepting the gift of Beaker's scarf is surely some species of psychopath' (Sweet 2012: 51).

On the whole there is no suggestion that any durable or fulfilling quality pervades this body of films. Even those without a supernatural or escapist element tend to be given short shrift, as when the *MFB*'s review published in September 1944 of *Christmas Holiday* (1944), a *film noir* set at Christmas-time in which a man escapes from prison 'filled with murderous jealousy of his wife' who he thinks has been

---

[5] In 1991 the two British Film Institute publications merged. Previously the *Monthly Film Bulletin* which was first published in 1934 contained reviews of all motion pictures released in the UK while *Sight and Sound*, which was first published in 1932, was predominantly focused on articles, though short reviews of releases did appear.

unfaithful, refers to the dignity and beauty of the scenes in a cathedral but which makes 'the rest of the story artificial and unconvincing' (Anon. 1944: 101). Similar language is employed in the *MFB* review of *The Cheaters* (1945)—'This highly unlikely story, though well acted and directed, certainly does not convince' (Anon. 1945a: 96)—while in the case of *I'll Be Seeing You* (1945), where two lost souls—a soldier suffering from severe panic attacks caused by his time in combat and a woman in prison for manslaughter—tentatively embark on a relationship, the *MFB*'s verdict was that apart from what it calls the 'psychiatric sequences' the film is dismissed as 'artificial mush' (Anon. 1945b: 135). Even in films not set during the festive period, it is significant that their deficiencies may be identified by drawing unfavourable comparisons with the shortcomings of their Christmas counterparts. In the Doris Day romantic comedy *It Happened to Jane* (1959), for example, in which the eponymous heroine takes up a seemingly unwinnable battle against the railroad company whose carelessness has inconvenienced her small lobster business after a consignment of fish was damaged in transit, the *MFB* review likens the eleventh-hour change of heart on the part of the railroad chairman, after he had pulled out all the stops to wipe out her business following her campaign against him and his company, to that of the dynamics of a Scrooge-like Christmas drama:

> Even the nominal villain, played with ruthless geniality by Ernie Kovacs, eventually throws in his hand and emerges as a Father Christmas figure. This, combined with the overt appeals to sentimentality, gives a slightly sticky quality to a film whose charm and humour might have seemed more genuine if less insistently stressed (Anon. 1959: 56).

The following year, a similar fate was meted out by the reviewer of the 1955 Italian war movie *La Grande Speranza* (1955) upon its release in the UK, who wrote, disparagingly, that 'Unbelievable love interest, the characterisation of the Italian captain as a sort of Father Christmas in oilskins, and lashings of bathos destroy all dramatic conviction in this plea for the humanities' (Anon. 1960: 142).

These criticisms notwithstanding, what the critics do at least seem to concede is that audiences relish the dynamics of Christmas films, as when Nigel Floyd's review of *Home Alone* for the *MFB* in January 1991 expresses some incredulity at how this 'cute family comedy . . . should have provoked such an enthusiastic audience response and gained such a phenomenal word-of-mouth reputation' (Floyd 1991:

20). Notably, in addition to Floyd's clear reservations about how the filmmakers are 'indulging the audience's weakness for cartoon-style slapstick violence', he does make passing reference to 'an ending that stresses a topical Yuletide togetherness' (Floyd 1991: 20) as one of the principal reasons for the film's huge success. The sequel, *Home Alone 2: Lost in New York* (1992), is castigated by Tom Charity in his January 1993 review for *Sight and Sound* (the *MFB* having been incorporated into *Sight and Sound* in the spring of 1991) for being a mere 'slavish imitation of the first film' and for replaying 'the original story with the same structure, the same characters, and most disappointingly, the same box of tricks' (Charity 1993: 47), with Kevin (Macaulay Culkin) now abandoned in the city of New York rather than in his plush suburban home in Illinois. What really stands out in Charity's critique is the fact that the film works from an audience point of view in a way that makes no rational sense at all. Yet, it is the very familiarity and (ironically for a film about a child being lost on the 'mean streets' of America's most populated city) safety offered by the movie that constitutes its very appeal. Charity may think that 'It is as if [the screenwriter John] Hughes was as nonplussed as everyone else by *Home Alone*'s phenomenal box office success, and decided to retain each and every element—flaws and all—when he fed the sequel into his script computer' (Charity 1993: 47), but, as we discussed in chapter 1, even more subversive Christmas offerings like *Bad Santa* (2003) follow the same conventions as their more mainstream counterparts, where no one is allowed to be irredeemable at Christmas and the utopian always supersedes the dystopian (see Mundy 2008: 166). As Xan Brooks puts it in his *Sight and Sound* review of *Bad Santa* in January 2005, 'Despite its misanthropic trimmings, the script . . . turns soft and formulaic in its closing minutes' (Brooks 2005: 43). Christmas films are not therefore successful in *spite* of but *because* of their escapist, diversionary, and trite dispositions.

While nowhere near as successful commercially as *Home Alone*, this spirit is encapsulated in another 1990s Christmas confection, *Trapped in Paradise* (1994), a film which also features a pair of dim-witted petty criminals (here played by Jon Lovitz and Dana Carvey, who play functionally similar roles to the slapstick antics of *Home Alone*'s Joe Pesci and Daniel Stern) who bring chaos to (in this case) the small Pennsylvanian town called Paradise when they attempt, together with their less wayward brother Bill (Nicolas Cage) who finds himself, against his better judgement, dragged into their crackpot scheme, to rob a bank with only limited security provision in place (because this is a town too trusting) one snowy Christmas Eve. As Nick Hasted wrote in his *Sight and Sound* review in April 1995, 'We first see Paradise as a model enclosed in a paperweight, and this image of suspension proves apt. The real Paradise is picture-postcard perfect, its niceness unrelenting, badness beyond its ken' (Hasted 1995: 53). The characters may all be adult, whereas the protagonist in *Home Alone* is a child, but the infantile and imbecilic mayhem engineered by the Firpo brothers follows the same generic template, with the same predictable reconciliation at the end when lessons are learned and all of the robbery money has been returned. When Rachel Wagner thus writes that 'video games lead us through pre-dictable scripted experiences, give us limited choices and urge us to act in certain ways' (Wagner 2012b: 125), this does not seem to be a world wholly different from how in the genre of Christmas films we are presented with a narrow, pre-established story or narrative, with which we are invited to engage, and, to apply Wagner's argument in the context of the ritual of gaming, then to 'use this interaction to shape how we see the world' (Wagner 2012b: 125). Critically, though, *Trapped in Paradise* was mauled by the critics, with Roger Ebert not alone in giving the picture his lowest possible rating (just half a star). Ian Nathan's review in the March 1995 edition of *Empire* magazine was only marginally better (two out of a possible five stars), in which he referred to moments of promise in the film being mere 'ripples in an ocean of overacted slapstick, put together with little attention to detail' (Nathan 1995: www.empireonline.com/reviews/reviewcomplete.asp?FID=3442). Nathan continues that the film gets 'hopelessly farcical by the close', with 'the whole threadbare notion' covered 'with total chaos' (Nathan 1995: www.empireonline.com/reviews/reviewcomplete.asp?FID=3442).

While undoubtedly true, this is also a winning recipe when it comes to Christmas movies. The critically admired (if commercial flop) *Nobody's Fool* (1994), which was on release around the same period, supplies a good point of comparison of how the critical and commercial sensibilities differ so strongly here. *Nobody's Fool* is only tangentially linked to Christmas, set as it is in a wintry small town in upstate New York. It presents us with a sixty-year-old divorcee played by Paul Newman whose life seems to have been one of a lack of commitment and of shirking responsibilities but who comes closer than ever before to making amends for the failures of his past. In his *Sight and Sound* review of the film from April 1995 Ben Thompson wrote that 'It is rare in a modern American film to see a small town setting used as more than just shorthand for nothing much in particular' and that 'there is a real sense here of relationships . . . striding on down through the years, taking both animosity and fondness, success and failure in their stride' (Thompson 1995: 50). Different though the two films are, *Trapped in Paradise* is adept at recycling the trajectory so familiar from Dickens of an individual (the Nicolas Cage character in this case) learning from the goodness of others—in *A Christmas Carol* it is Bob Cratchit; in this film it is the entire townsfolk of Paradise—and seeking to change, beginning with Bill Firpo's decision on Christmas morning to stay behind in Paradise and to embark on a relationship with one of its inhabitants. Both literally and metaphorically it could be said that Paradise—referred to by Hasted as 'a distillation of genuine small town goodness' (Hasted 1995: 53)—might rub off on him just as Ebenezer Scrooge's decision to change his character, again on 25 December, was both instantaneous and (we are to assume) irrevocable. This is very much a trite, simplistic, binary universe where good can only ever prevail. The great irony, of course, is that it takes a film without the nuance or character-driven sophistication of *Nobody's Fool* (or for that matter of *A Christmas Carol*) to make the trajectory so complete. But, as we have learned, Christmas movies are replete with one-dimensional characters attaining redemption against the odds, and the further they are from 'reality', such as with the addition of sleigh-rides, angels, pixies, and Father Christmas—very much a staple of Christmas movies—somehow that redemptive arc impacts on audiences (if not on critics) more than when, as in *Nobody's Fool*, the world delineated is perhaps a little too realistic and close to home.

Ironically, then, it may be the failure of *Trapped in Paradise* to introduce any supernatural or magical elements in a way that is a given in traditional Christmas fare that was the cause of its box office disappointment. The film invokes the spirit of Christmas movies but where it falls short is in its failure to capitalize on the full adornment of magical and celestial otherness that the genre does not seem to be able to do without. Critics' reviews of Christmas films may mourn the fact, as Liese Spencer wrote of the 1990s remake of *The Bishop's Wife* (1947), now known as *The Preacher's Wife* (1996), that they tend to be 'as shiny and weightless as a Christmas bauble'—this particular movie, for instance, is dismissed as 'a snow and schmaltz affair' (Spencer 1997: 61)[6]—but audiences do seem to plump, against all talk of secularization, for fairytales where snowmen come to life, as in *Jack Frost* (1998) when Michael Keaton's Snowman is the reincarnation of the father of the boy, Charlie (Joseph Cross), who builds him and who intervenes once a magical harmonica is used to summon him, or when, as in Disney's *One Magic Christmas* (1985), Father Christmas is even able to raise the dead. If all of this can happen with the aid of what Amanda Lipman writes in her review of *Jack Frost* as 'a picture-postcard setting, featuring row upon row of twinkling Christmas lights and endless snowy vistas' (Lipman 1999: 44)—or in the case of *Christmas with the Kranks* of rooftops full of giant twinkling displays of lights and snowmen together with that film's 'predictable feast of frosted snow, fairy lights and pristine carol-singers' (Jafaar 2005: 45)—then all the better. The supernatural is not an addendum to these family favourites; it is core to them and vital to their appeal.

Cries of 'shamelessly derivative' (Macnab 2001: 41) in relation to *The Family Man* (2000), 'heavy-handed' (Anon. 2002: 71) in the case of *How the Grinch Stole Christmas* (2000), 'cynically formulaic' (Stables 2009: 59) with respect to *Four Christmases* (2008), 'eminently forgettable' (Ivan 2010: 60) as far as *Christmas in Wonderland* (2007) is concerned, or 'a predictably sentimental tale' (Lamacraft 2008: 62) in the case of *Fred Claus* (2007), or that *The Santa Clause 2* (2002) is 'horribly contrived' (Lawrenson 2003: 52) while *Christmas with the Kranks* constitutes 'facile slapstick' (Jafaar 2005: 45) and 'laboured farce' (Fahy 2006: 87) and that *Deck the Halls* (2006) amounts to 'a predictable chain of slapstick episodes' and, for all of that film's obsession with festive rooftop lighting, remains 'stubbornly unilluminating' (Fahy 2007: 50), are certainly familiar refrains when it comes to the critical reaction to Christmas movies. Even when the occasional film, like *Bad Santa*, though fitting into the classic mould, is given critical praise for its willingness to offer something more

---

[6] There is the further irony here, however, that Spencer contends in her review of *The Preacher's Wife* that the film falls short precisely because it does not make full use of the supernatural element that is introduced. She writes that Denzel Washington's 'angelic intervention is strangely attenuated, his powers limited to a glowing handshake and the ability to make piano keys move on their own. [The film] introduces the supernatural and then perversely fails to use really fully it [*sic*] in the storyline' (Spencer 1997: 61).

subversive or imaginative than its counterparts—as when the DVD release of *Bad Santa* was lauded in the January 2006 issue of *Sight and Sound* for being an 'invaluable and dyspeptic antidote to seasonal sicklies such as *Miracle on 34th Street*' (Anon. 2006: 86)—Christmas movies 'buck the trend' when it comes to categorizing and appraising the relationship between the 'secular' and the 'religious' in the contemporary world.

JUXTAPOSING THE TRANSCENDENT AND THE SECULAR

It is all the more ironic, therefore, that Rudolf Bultmann, arguably the greatest New Testament scholar of the twentieth century, took it as a given that to call upon men and women to subscribe to a pre-scientific, mythological world-view was one of the greatest stumbling blocks in Christianity. As he saw it, 'nobody reckons with direct intervention by transcendent powers' because 'modern man acknowledges as reality only such phenomena or events as are comprehensible within the framework of the rational order of the universe' (Bultmann 1964: 37). It was precisely because, for Bultmann, there was an ontological distinction between the mythological cosmology of the New Testament on the one hand and our daily experience of life on the other that the Christian message required an urgent reconfiguration, which resulted in his radical programme of 'de-mythologization'. Bultmann could not have been more emphatic: 'It is impossible to use electric light and the wireless and to avail ourselves of modern medical and surgical discoveries, and at the same time to believe in the New Testament world of spirits and miracles' (Bultmann 1972: 5). According to Bultmann, when we are ill we go to the doctor and depend upon science, technology, and medicine to cure us rather than on supernatural or miraculous intervention, and so the New Testament picture of the universe was no longer intelligible or relevant to modern men and women.

Similar language is employed by Don Cupitt who wrote in *The Sea of Faith* that instead of explaining things in relation to spiritual powers we explain them with reference to 'mathematical frameworks and structural regularities' (Cupitt 2003: 31). As he sees it:

In the modern period we have come more and more to explain events in this world in this-worldly terms. We no longer seem to require the old idea that there is an invisible world of supernatural beings lying behind this world. By and large, people have found that scientific explanations are better explanations than the old explanations in terms of spirit-agencies (Cupitt 2003: 35–6).

Paul Fiddes encapsulates Cupitt effectively when he writes about how, in terms of such a position, there is no 'outside' to our existence and we must thus embrace the material world of signs as the only truth that we have, and that there is no other space of transcendent reality which interacts with the here and now (Fiddes 2000: 244). Moreover, according to Cupitt, most Christians are embarrassed at the notion that God would intervene in history, in the form, for instance, of the 'myth of a supernatural redeemer' (Cupitt 2003: 7). Christmas carols make tacit mention of this myth, as when *Once In Royal David's City* contains the line 'He came down to earth from Heaven' (Alexander 1852: 30) and *Away in a Manger* concludes with the words 'Bless all the dear children in thy tender care / And take us to heaven, to live with thee there' (Anon. 1992a: 3). But, for Cupitt, 'the authority of the myth has been visibly deteriorating' (Cupitt 2003: 8; see also Deacy 2007: 242) and is no longer taken literally.

This is borne out in *Christmas with the Kranks* where, as Roger Ebert pointed out, the film merely pays lip service to Christmas as being a Christian festival, inasmuch as the film celebrates the ceremonial allure of Christmas but without 'a single crucifix . . . , a single crèche . . . , a single mention of the J-name' (Ebert 2004: www. rogerebert.com/reviews/christmas-with-the-kranks-2004; see also Deacy 2007: 242–3). Indeed, even though the film does include the presence of a Roman Catholic priest, his role is not to preside over Midnight Mass on the busiest night in the Christian calendar but as a guest at the Kranks' annual Christmas Eve house party. As I have written previously, when it comes to this film, 'Commercialism is given more status than Christology, and the kerygma has been supplanted by kitsch' (Deacy 2007: 243). Yet, while this film does somewhat corroborate Cupitt's notion that the traditional functions of religion have been displaced (and replaced) by secular agencies, *Christmas with the Kranks* is entirely representative of Christmas films for the way in which it is predicated on the existence of a supernatural world view. Although in his *Sight and Sound* review Ali Jafaar writes that 'The final scene shows Luther and Nora standing outside their house as revellers sing merrily within' (Jafaar 2005: 45), the film actually concludes with a distance shot of Luther (Tim Allen) and Nora (Jamie Lee Curtis) Krank while, upon their rooftop, a CGI snowman takes off his hat and bows his head and Santa (Austin Pendleton) and his reindeer fly across the skyline en route to delivering presents to all the children of the world. Ironically, therefore, this is a film which both seems to encapsulate Cupitt's understanding that traditional forms of religion are increasingly peripheral to modern life and have been displaced by secular agencies *while at the same time* it cannot do without the supernatural.

Christianity may be paid mere lip service in this film but this is by no means a 'secular' film if, by 'secular', we mean that, as Cupitt sees it, 'we cannot help recognising infantile fantasies of omnipotence for what they are' (Cupitt 2003: 7) and that, in our post-Enlightenment age, we no longer subscribe to myths about supernatural redeemers. *Christmas with the Kranks* does not signify that this-worldly explanations have triumphed over what Cupitt refers to as 'obsolete religious ideas' (Cupitt 2003: 36). I may have once written that this film comprises the quintessence of the idea that traditional forms of religion are being relegated to the margins of life with no more than a veneer remaining (Deacy 2007: 242), but the supernatural, mythological veneer is integral to *Christmas with the Kranks* even if the Christian religion which once supported such teachings and worldviews is not. Whereas Bultmann once attested that Christianity needed to be divested of its pre-scientific, obsolete cosmology, the irony is that it is the 'secular' film industry which is so brazenly beholden to it. Rather than dismissing Christmas movies for their fantastic or escapist predilections, Christmas films might thus be seen to offer one of the most direct challenges to the secularization thesis in the contemporary world. Despite Dell deChant's premise in *The Sacred Santa* that Christmas is a religious festival due to its cosmological and naturalistic ingredients, where emphasis is on the Ultimate Power of the economy rather than on the supernatural or the transcendental, Christmas films do suggest that the transcendentalism that deChant is so keen to move away from is central to the modern Christmas celebration.

Of course, this does not mean that Christmas films are all formula-laden, lightweight products which seek to perpetuate archaic fantasy and escapist world-views. Jenny Diski has written, for example, about how *It's a Wonderful Life* is 'one of the darkest films I know' as the protagonist comes to the realization that 'it would have been better if he'd never been born' (Diski 1992: 39). Connelly similarly labels Capra's Christmas classic as 'a parable of malaise and a warning that America is not all it might be' (Connelly 2000a: 4), a point further developed by Mundy for whom 'In the immediate aftermath of the war, *It's a Wonderful Life* addressed the starker realities of a culture transformed and uncertain about its future' (Munby 2000: 46).[7] In stark contrast to the platitudes of a festive drama such as *Trapped in Paradise* or *The Santa Clause*, Munby hails the fact that 'A dark (*noir*-like) shadow haunts the affirmative (small-town) story in what amounts to an interrogation of Hollywood conventions' (Munby 2000: 47). Christmas films do, then, have the capacity to be multifaceted and subversive and, as John Mundy attests, they 'have always acknowledged the ambiguities enshrined in our experience of the festive season' (Mundy 2008: 165). They may ostensibly be made for entertainment and commercial purposes but Rowana Agajanian has likewise categorized Christmas movies as 'a remarkably sophisticated sub-genre that utilizes visual and musical iconography to great effect' (Agajanian 2000: 162). Whether such films foreground the supernatural and miraculous or if, like *It's a Wonderful Life* or a black comedy like *Gremlins* (1984), they are inclined to flag up the more destructive and dystopian facets of the festival, Christmas films encapsulate the difficulty of squaring our dreams, hopes, ambitions, and desires with the reality that we experience day to day.

Christmas films act as a barometer of how we might want to live and how we see and measure ourselves, thereby functioning as 'a potent, highly condensed expression' and crystallization of our most basic 'faith and values' (Restad 1995: 178). To an extent, these dynamics are on display in the films themselves: the idyllic-sounding Bedford Falls of *It's a Wonderful Life* or Paradise in *Trapped in*

---

[7] There is no consensus, however, over whether *It's a Wonderful Life* is escapist or *noir*-like in its sensibilities. Jonathan Munby refers to how film reviews at the time tended to see the film as rather trite (Munby 2000: 46), whereas Max A. Myers writes that 'the critics' complaint, at the time of its release, [was] that *It's a Wonderful Life* was too gloomy and dark' (Myers 2001a: 48). Munby sums up this disjuncture when he contends that 'Ostensibly, *It's a Wonderful Life* resolves the struggle between doubt and optimism in favour of the latter. To an audience in 1946, however, the candid treatment of George Bailey's doubts and the fantastic recourse to miracle would have provided an interpretation at odds with the movie's triumphant conclusion' (Munby 2000: 54).

Paradise comprise sites of conflict and corruption rather than unadulterated perfection, and although young Charlie is privileged to have Santa for his father in *The Santa Clause*, the film never shirks the reality that Charlie's parents are divorced and he is caught up in acrimonious custody proceedings. Kim Newman thus hits the nail on the head when he writes that *Die Hard* (1988) 'would hardly be as suspenseful if Bruce Willis were trapped in a skyscraper with a gang of ruthless terrorists during a Thanksgiving party' (Newman 2000: 136). In the same way Restad makes the key observation that Christmas sheds light on the sordidness of the settings in *Havana* and *Goodfellas* (see Restad 1995: 178)—films about gambling and the Mafia, respectively, where the celebration of Christmas serves to exacerbate the corruption or venality on display. In the latter film one of the most brutal murders is carried out over a supposedly quiet Christmas vacation and Jimmy Conway (Robert De Niro) loses his cool after a successful heist has started to go awry to the dissonant music on the soundtrack of 'Frosty the Snowman' by The Ronettes. Christmas serves in such instances as a dramatic device for drawing attention to the diseased and the dysfunctional. Christmas movies may ostensibly be about escapist flights of fancy but in reality they operate within a contested and ambiguous terrain where dreams are soured, crime is endemic—in *It's a Wonderful Life* we must not forget that Potter (Lionel Barrymore) gets away with stealing $8,000 from George Bailey's Building and Loan Association—and even Santa Claus cannot quite perform the miracle of bringing back together families torn asunder.

6

Reframing Christmas and the Religion of Materialism

RELIGION AND CONSUMER CAPITALISM

As the discussion of Christmas-themed movies has shown us, Christmas is a far more complicated and eclectic festival than most critics and commentators seem prepared to acknowledge. It may be the case that traditional manifestations of religion are often peripheral to the Christmas celebration, but it is not entirely clear that what we are left with is a 'secular' construct as the supernatural and transcendental comprise essential fixtures of the modern (or as Dell deChant would see it, the postmodern) Christmas landscape as typified by its cinematic renderings. Even when these films appear to offer uncritical celebrations of consumerism, as when in *Jingle All The Way* (1996) there is an implicit conflation of present-buying and happiness, it is difficult to argue that this is somehow a religion-free zone. As Margaret Miles is cited as saying in the publicity for Horsley and Tracy's *Christmas Unwrapped*, 'the most popular holiday of the year is no longer, if it ever was, a religious holiday. It is, rather, a celebration of consumer capitalism as a religion' (cited on the rear cover of Horsley and Tracy 2001). Even here, however, there is an all-too-familiar attempt, as discussed previously in relation to Flynn and others, to circumscribe the contours of what religion is (or is not), although in this particular instance there is the additional confusion that, taken at face value, Miles appears to be saying both that Christmas is not a religious celebration while at the same time that this non-religious event can best be categorized by drawing an analogy with that which *is* religious.

To complicate matters still further, plenty of the literature on Christmas is emphatic that capitalism and religion are antithetical to one another, as when Marling refers to those people who speak of the modern Christmas having 'devolved into an orgy of capitalist greed, to which the birth of Christ is largely irrelevant' (Marling 2000: 43). For David Parker, there is an ontological difference between what Christmas and Christianity represent, as when he writes that in the early Church 'Christianity was recommended to those without wealth or influence by representing the Holy Family as long-suffering plebeians, the Nativity as a revelation first made to the poor and the powerless' (Parker 2005: 23). James G. Carrier expresses the similar reservation that 'the majority of Americans are practising Christians, and the materialistic, commercial air of Christmas conflicts with important religious values bearing on the birth of Christ in particular and the glorification of material wealth more generally' (Carrier 2001: 62; see also Deacy 2013: 196). Likewise, for Bill McKibben, 'Market capitalism, if it is as rational as its proponents always insist, cannot actually depend for its strength on the absurdly lavish celebration of the birth of a man who told us to give away everything that we have' (McKibben 1998: 84–5). When we add to this Libanius' fourth-century CE objection that (as Miller paraphrases it) 'Christmas was once indeed the pure festival of close family togetherness, but its heart has been lost in the relentless exploitation of its possibilities by a combination of individual materialism and capitalist profit-taking' (Miller 2001: 18; see also Deacy 2013: 196), we can see that there is much work to be done before a straightforward juxtaposition or alliance between religion and capitalism can be undertaken.

Although Connelly may be right that 'The links between Christmas and capitalism are clichés' (Connelly 2012: 186) and Myers offers the telling observation that in *Holiday Inn* (1942) 'the version of Christmas that [is being celebrated] has little to do with anything specifically Christian but [is about] celebrating American life within the context of consumer capitalism' (Myers 2001a: 43), the issue is complicated by the failure of authors to agree on whether any of this is congruous with or diametrically opposite to religion. Whereas the authors cited above are inclined to see Christianity and capitalism as antithetical to one another, this chapter will ask whether retail spending (and as a corollary Christmas) is itself a religious phenomenon. This will be outlined with reference to Dell deChant's work in *The Sacred Santa* on how precisely because of its consecration of a consumerist teleology Christmas comprises 'the best example of religiosity in our culture' (deChant 2002: 3; see also Deacy 2013: 196). However, while deChant offers a more sophisticated understanding of religion than many other theorists precisely because he is able to move away from the conventional binary approach whereby Christmas differs or deviates from traditional forms of religious agency and for seeking to reconfigure the way in which we understand the source and location of religion in the postmodern world, this chapter will query whether his thesis is completely convincing.

Correct though deChant may be that the economy is to the modern world what nature was to the ancient world, such that Christmas and the economy are indissoluble, his argument does not wholly work with respect either to the aforementioned work on the supernatural nature of Christmas films which bring to the fore the very focus on supernaturalism that for deChant is no longer tenable in the modern world or to the success of *Christmas Junior Choice*. The latter is transmitted not on commercial radio but on the BBC and there is no transaction of money involved in the programme which is characterized by listeners sending in requests for records which are played in the course of the two-hour programme. deChant may merely see Christmas as a festival of consumption in which 'we reaffirm our harmony with the economy by shopping' (deChant 2002: 113; see also Deacy 2013: 203), but *Junior Choice* suggests that other authentic models or perspectives which do not entail the exchange of capital can still function. Notwithstanding that there is some truth that as deChant sees it 'In today's postmodern America, under the watchful gaze of the sacred Santa' (deChant 2002: 183), many of us are 'queuing up before the sacrificial altar of the cash register' and 'strolling through shrines of consumption' (deChant 2002: 114; see also Deacy 2013: 203), these are not the only forms of ritual activity that can be evidenced. It is thus my aim to qualify deChant's thesis in the light of this over-emphasis on the sanctity of the economy per se.

CHRISTMAS'S INDISSOLUBLE ASSOCIATION WITH THE ECONOMY

From the outset, it is clear that much of the literature uncritically takes it as a given that Christmas is an indissolubly commercial festival. Storey writes that 'Christmas was invented first and foremost as a commercial event' in which 'Everything that was revived or invented—decorations, cards, crackers, collections of carols, going to a pantomime, visiting Santa Claus and buying presents—all had one thing in common: they could be sold for profit' (Storey 2008: 20). Accordingly, for Storey, there is little point in going down the condemnatory path—quite simply, 'it was invented as a commercial festival' (Storey 2008: 20) in a market economy that developed within a context of industrial capitalism where 'If a nativity was being celebrated, it was the birth of a market economy underpinned by the new power of industrialisation' (Storey 2008: 22). On such a reading, there is a conjunction of the market and the realm of the secular; there is nothing discernibly Christian or (conventionally) 'sacred' about Christmas, as demonstrated by the fact that 'Even an officially atheist society like the People's Republic of China has no difficulty in embracing the festival' (Storey 2008: 22). Similar convictions underpin Stephen Nissenbaum's highly regarded historical survey of the development of Christmas in America since the Puritan background of the seventeenth century, *The Battle for Christmas*, where the claim is adduced that 'there never was a time when Christmas existed as an unsullied domestic idyll, immune to the taint of commercialism' (Nissenbaum 1996: loc. no. 6448). Rather, 'the domestic Christmas was the commercial Christmas—commercial from its earliest stages, commercial at its very core' (Nissenbaum 1996: loc. no. 6448).

Horsley and Tracy's *Christmas Unwrapped* effectively picks up where Nissenbaum left off in the nineteenth century, with Tracy making the case in the first chapter of that book that 'What a century ago was a season of relatively minor indulgence encouraged by enterprising manufacturers is now so gargantuan a retail orgy that it is fervently monitored by Wall Street as a fundamental index and determinant of the nation's economic soundness' (Tracy 2001b: 9). Indeed, according to Tracy, 'It is no exaggeration to predict that the American economy would lapse into recession if no one bought Christmas presents this year' (Tracy 2001b: 9). Horsley, writing in a later chapter, makes the corresponding claim that 'Christmas now entails a dazzling and pervasive display of abundance . . . , inducing us into consumption of luxurious goods and overindulgence of every kind', all of which 'is absolutely integral to and necessary for the economy, for the holidays have become the climax of the society's annual economic cycle without which the economy would quickly and catastrophically collapse' (Horsley 2001a: 173).[1]

Whereas at the beginning of the nineteenth century the emphasis at Christmas was on food, drink, and revelry, Golby and Purdue have documented how as the custom of giving presents to children, family members and friends developed shopping became an intrinsic part of the Christmas ritual (Golby and Purdue 2000: 78). When adults exchanged presents they tended to be handmade (see Waits 1993: 1) and to be modest ones such as (to give the examples cited by Robinson and Staeheli) fountain pens and handkerchiefs, but after the First World War when 'there were fears that the boom times of the war years were going to be followed by a stagnant economy, so advertisers did their best to stimulate peacetime buying' (Robinson and Staeheli 1982: 103). Even before the War, though, Waits argues that at the end of the nineteenth century high status had started to attach to certain products that could be purchased in the marketplace 'rather than to previously esteemed traits such as moral virtue, thriftiness, and productive capacity' (Waits 1993: 1–2). Ironically, it was the very fact that there was a 'perceived antiquity' around Christmas that meant it was able to sanction and legitimize this move towards a consumer culture, to the extent that as Connelly observes 'Within a very short space of time, Christmas shopping and the glories of lavishly decorated shops were perceived as Christmas customs in their own right and were thus invested with weight, propriety and meaning: they had become "traditional"' (Connelly 2012: xii).

For all the talk, therefore, that Christmas may be a 'secular' festival it is Christmas's sacred heritage that played an instrumental role in the creation of its consumerist ethos and to what Connelly refers to as 'the marking of the season in a distinct manner' (Connelly 2012: 192). Restad even construes the commercialization of Christmas as a fusion of 'the spheres of sacred and profane' (Restad 1995: 168). When Golby and Purdue thus write that 'The preparations for Christmas start even earlier, the holiday is longer and the pressures to buy an ever-widening choice of presents, food and drink are more intense'

---

[1] It is significant to this end that Schmidt writes that by the end of the nineteenth century 'Holidays, rather than being impediments to disciplined economic advancement, were seen as critical for consumption and profit' (Schmidt 1995: 37), and Forbes similarly attests that following industrialization and the rise of consumer culture merchants came to see holidays as an opportunity rather than an obstacle (Forbes 2007: 113).

and that 'For some, Christmas has become a full-time occupation' (Golby and Purdue 2000: 83), this does not sound like the antithesis of religion but a prime functionalist account of the very essence of religion.[2] Even the language is analogous to that used in more conventional religious discourse, as when Schmidt argues that 'Christmas stands out as the grand "festival of consumption," with a significant segment of American retailing living or dying on profits connected with the Yuletide season' (Schmidt 1995: 4), while Horsley is emphatic that 'In holiday retailing, economics is inseparable from religion' and that, to paraphrase Clifford Geertz, 'the consumer economy [is] inseparable from religious mood and motivation' (Horsley 2001a: 173).

PROBLEMS WITH THE RELIGION OF COMMERCIALIZATION

It is all the more significant, therefore, that consumerism is often treated in the literature as if it were a rival religious sect, organization, or value system. John Lyden makes a similar claim about popular culture when in *Film as Religion* he argues that 'Popular culture may not be as formal or as institutionally organized as "official" religions, but it functions like a religion, and may thus be viewed as a religion' (Lyden 2003: 108). Lyden's thinking here is that although historically we may have equated religion 'with formal institutions that go by that label' (Lyden 2003: 135), in reality traditional religious groups have tended to treat the 'threat' posed by aspects of 'secular' culture (for example certain films whose values are deemed to be contrary to family values) as if they constituted alternative religious sites (see Deacy and Ortiz 2008: 36). Rather than see the relationship between

---

[2] Schmidt's work thus constitutes a counterpoint to Connelly's claim that Christmas has been overlooked by theorists. According to Connelly, 'Over the last couple of decades the study of shopping and the disposal of surplus income has become a popular subject among both economic and social historians. However very few of them make the point that the great highpoint of the spending year is Christmas and the correlation between the season, the attitude of shoppers and the ploys of the retailers to sell their goods at this time has hardly been touched upon' (Connelly 2012: 189). Schmidt's detailed study of the relationship between American holidays, especially Christmas, and the culture of consumption goes some way towards addressing that deficiency which Connelly identifies in the literature.

religion and culture as taking the form of an 'either/or', 'religion' vs. 'secular' binary, Lyden insightfully suggests that popular culture could be construed to be performing a functionally comparable role to that of, say, Christianity or Islam. There is, in other words, a battle between two different kinds of religion going on rather than between religion and non-religion, and, in his words, 'By relating to it either as a demonic threat to their own religion, or a mirror image of it, religious film critics were essentially already viewing film through the categories of religion' (Lyden 2003: 132).

It is arguable that the same thing is happening in the context of the present debate, where, instead of seeing materialism as the polar opposite, even the antithesis, of religion, or as a sign that religion has been eviscerated in the modern world as consumerism has usurped or replaced Christianity, what we have in the modern consumer Christmas is a new form of *religious* expression and agency. Indeed, consumerism could be categorized in this respect as a core ritual of contemporary culture and one which is even more adept at functioning religiously than its traditional counterparts, even supplying us, in a Durkheimian sense, with the means to affirm shared values in a way that traditional religious organizations may historically (and exclusively) have done. The Durkheim connection is especially pertinent here as the sacred takes the form of the value placed on objects by social groups and entails the presence of ritual activities which bring individuals together to form a unity, as a result of which, as Giddens puts it, they are taken 'away from the concerns of profane social life into an elevated sphere, in which they feel in contact with higher forces' (Giddens 2006: 31; see also Deacy 2013: 200). To this end, there is plenty in what takes place at Christmas-time, in terms of the giving of gifts and the ritual of shopping more generally, which might go so far as to label the consumerist ethos of Christmas as a religious festival per se.

However, just as Lyden is acutely aware of the fact that the tendency among more traditional religious groups may be to discredit rather than to dignify with a higher status the new and alternative form of religion that is being presented—he gives the example of how 'early Christian explorers of the Americas were reluctant to call the practices of the "Indians" by the name of religion' (Lyden 2003: 132)—so it is not surprising that much of the literature on Christmas takes the form of an anti-consumerist (and, by definition, anti-religious) polemic. We see this, for example, in the fact that many writers in the early part of the twentieth century were inclined to draw a sharp contrast between the simplicity and purity of the Nativity story and the gross materialism that was denoted by the modern Christmas. Waits cites an author from 1909 according to whom

> Christmas represents the most important event in the history of Christianity, for on that day the greatest gift to man was made.... We may find that the real Christmas spirit exists only in the minority, and that the majority of Christmas celebrators, instead of realizing and appreciating the significance of the season, use it for playing a game of grab and graft (in Waits 1993: 183).

According to a 1907 writer, who had worked in a shop for one week, shopping customs were 'a sort of heathen revel' and that although it is ostensibly a Christian festival 'it looks something terrifyingly different when you regard it from behind a counter' (in Waits 1993: 183). Waits also cites sources from the period that describe the flurry of retail activity at Christmas as bringing 'to mind the biblical description of moneychanging in the temple before Jesus drove out the offenders' (Waits 1993: 184). According to the *Sunday School Times* in 1912, 'commercialism has come in and Christ has been crowded out ... The day has come to be for many families a burden instead of a delight. Never before was the day so widely or so expensively observed, but its deep and sacred meaning has been too greatly obscured' (in Forbes 2007: 117). Schmidt refers also to an American pastor who cautioned in 1938 that 'At Christmas time when spiritual values should be uppermost in the minds of people, the land is inundated by a tidal wave of commercial activity and materialistic self-seeking that quite obliterates the quiet, peaceful, spiritual meaning of the birth of Jesus Christ' (Schmidt 1995: 188). In more recent times, also, several Christian leaders issued a proclamation in 1992 that condemned the commercialized nature of Christmas:

> We have seen the spirit of Christmas reduced to a carnival of mass marketing. Consumption has taken on an almost religious quality; malls have become the new shrines of worship. Massive and alluring advertising crusades have waged war on the essential meaning of the spiritual life, fostering the belief that the marketplace can fulfill our highest aspirations (in Schmidt 1995: 175).

Moreover, entire books have been written which are intended to caution readers about the disparity between the divergent values attendant in its

Christmas and materialist manifestations. One of the most notable of these is Jo Robinson and Jean Coppock Staeheli's 1982 publication *Unplug the Christmas Machine: A Complete Guide to Putting Love and Warmth Back Into the Season*, where the authors take the line that over the course of the twentieth century 'Christmas has changed from a delightful folk festival and an important religious celebration to a twenty-billion-dollar-a-year commercial venture' (Robinson and Staeheli 1982: 11) and 'has become a long and elaborate preparation for an intense gift-opening ritual' (Robinson and Staeheli 1982: 13). Their objective is to enable people 'to restore the simplicity and beauty of the celebration' at a time when 'Christmas is becoming ever more commercial, expensive, hectic, pressured, impersonal, and materialistic' (Robinson and Staeheli 1982: 12) and whereby Christmas has usurped 'folk and religious traditions nurtured for centuries' (Robinson and Staeheli 1982: 13) such as festive dances and games which brought together the whole family. Accordingly, the authors attest, 'many Christians are unhappy with the fact that the spiritual message of Christ has to compete with the want-me, buy-me message of the merchants' (Robinson and Staeheli 1982: 102–3) and they note the fundamental incompatibility between celebrating the Nativity and what amounts at Christmas-time to a 'multibillion-dollar exchange of video games, popcorn poppers, designer jeans, sports equipment, and expensive adult toys' (Robinson and Staeheli 1982: 103). It is not surprising, they continue, that although 'on the surface everything looks fine' upon closer inspection many people 'realize that their celebrations lack depth and meaning' (Robinson and Staeheli 1982: 115).

Similar sentiments can be found in less overtly confessional books, as when Wiley-Blackwell published Scott C. Lowe's edited collection *Christmas—Philosophy for Everyone* in 2010, which contained a chapter by Dane Scott in which consumerism is identified as a 'problem' inasmuch as 'there is a tendency to let the products we buy define our worth as human beings, rather than traits like generosity and gratitude' (Lowe 2010: 181). As a corollary, counsels Lowe, 'this makes us nothing more than the sum of our preferences as represented by the products we buy' (Lowe 2010: 181). Schmidt similarly presents the viewpoint that for some commentators today 'Spiritual, nonmaterialistic, and eternal verities are thought to be seriously subverted in a consumer culture enthralled by abundance, self-gratification, and novelty', in which 'the transcendent claims of

Christian time, the revelatory power of the Incarnation and the Resurrection, are dwarfed by the mundane claims of merchant's time' (Schmidt 1995: 7; see also Deacy 2013: 196). Commercial endeavours, on this interpretation, can only serve to 'erode the religious significance of the holidays, disconnecting them from the transcendent and displacing their "true" meaning' (Schmidt 1995: 7).

Although there is a clear duality evidenced in much of this literature between 'the religious' and 'the material',[3] with the former presented as superior to the latter, there is no explicit identification of the consumer Christmas as being functionally religious. Rather, the opposite is the case, with religion implicitly seen as solid, wholesome, and edifying in contrast to the ersatz, insubstantial, and debilitating nature of its modern counterpart. Yet, the differences are perhaps not as substantial as the writers are prepared to countenance. Rina Arya is one of a small number of theorists prepared to draw an express link between consumerism and religion without, crucially, 'taking sides' as to whether consumerism is a deficient type of religion vis-à-vis its more traditional counterparts. For Arya, consumerism itself functions religiously in a way that corresponds to, rather than deviates from, traditional renderings of religion. As she sees it, 'many of the behaviours expressed in the cycles of compulsive buying can be described as *religious*' because they perform the same function as religion more generally: 'the sense of fulfilment striven for in the pursuit of commodity after commodity can be viewed as a desperate need to heal the self, and invariably to find salvation' (Arya 2009: 168). Consumerism is thus not the antithesis of religion but has a core salvific component, entailing as it does 'an extreme way of self-medicating . . . , as a way of rebinding the fragments [of the fractured self] through the acquisition of commodities' (Arya 2009: 168), and whereupon 'commodities become transformed into magical substances which are capable of completing the self' (Arya 2009: 172)—even if of course it is the case that as soon as one purchase is made and desire thereby satisfied another may shortly thereafter be made, thus perpetuating the cycle.

Here, then, we see the purchase of consumer goods presented not as the eclipse of religion in the modern world but as the fulfilment of

---

[3] Scott's chapter does not explicitly make the case for choosing Christianity over consumption, but his warning against materialism is certainly one which concurs with the sort of binary position advanced by Robinson and Staeheli.

needs and impulses that may be categorized as an innately and authentically religious activity. The key point is that the purchasing of material commodities 'can transform us' and, as Haire and Nelson put it, albeit disapprovingly, the said transformation 'can be achieved as easily as a trip to the department store' (Haire and Nelson 2010: 85) as by, say, attending church. Judged from a traditional religious perspective, this would be an anathema as there exists a dichotomy between the divine's sacred authority and the profanity of the earthly realm (see Haire and Nelson 2010: 85) and Paul Heelas is to that end correct when he writes that 'Religion would appear to be the very last thing that can be consumed' as 'the great religious traditions combat the temptations of human nature, including greed and self-indulgence' (Heelas 1994: 102). However, religion and consumerism do not simply lie at different ends of the spectrum, as Heelas would have it, in which consumerism is ontologically distinct from religion. Instead, they occupy an equivalent space on the spectrum. Tom Beaudoin makes the similar claim in his book *Consuming Faith* that consumerism has taken the place that was once occupied by religion, although here we have to be careful to ensure that religion is not assumed to have in any way been replaced as is suggested by Arya's claim that 'Beaudoin believes that in the secular age the brand economy provides the role that religion once occupied' (Arya 2009: 171). I would go further, here, and say that consumerism *is providing a religious role*, supplying as it does the same thing that religion has always traditionally provided, namely, in Beaudoin's words, 'the promise of conversion and new life' (Beaudoin 2003: 44).

In a Durkheimian sense this is demonstrably a religious practice rather than a surrogate for, or pale imitation of, religion. Indeed, as Arya says of Beaudoin's interpretation of the brand economy, 'Just as a religion binds believers, through a collective set of beliefs, symbols and practices, into a community that is based on the idea of the sacred, the brand binds people through an understanding of its beliefs (the corporate message), its symbols (logos and insignias) and practices (the mission statement of the company)' (Arya 2009: 171). On this basis, the argument should not be about whether materialism or shopping at Christmas-time is a poor substitute for celebrating the Nativity and the polar opposite of that which is truly or authentically religious. Beaudoin is spot on in this respect when, as Arya says of his position, 'consumption is not simply about the acquisition of material goods but arguably has a more important function—that of providing

trust, fulfilment and a sense of community' (Arya 2009: 171–2). We
see this also in Christy M. Newton's analysis of the theological
dimensions of the Wal-Mart brand in the US in which 'Wal-Mart is
a "way of life." It supplies all one's needs. No one can live without it. It
offers "salvation." It is redemptive, omniscient, omnipotent, omni-
present' (Newton 2009: 43).

The relationship between the economic and religious spheres is
thus inseparable on such a reading as here a retail outlet that supplies
'the values it wants people to access and consume' (Newton 2009: 43)
is functioning religiously by the way that 'regardless of class, it is
irresistibly appealing, because it is a throbbing, consumer hub, offering consumer delights like sacraments, and guilt-free disposability
like ritual ordinances', thereby comprising 'the beliefs and behaviors
that regulate Wal-Mart consumers' lives' (Newton 2009: 44). Using
explicitly theological language, Newton even writes that 'There is no
seeming end to the rivers of "grace" flowing forth from the doors
of the Wal-Mart store' (Newton 2009: 44), conscripting as it does
'the power, the life-force, in a person's or a community's identity'
(Newton 2009: 45). Accordingly, the ritual of shopping is no less
religiously fecund than a traditional religious ritual, even if it is far less
rooted in the social or collective sphere than was Durkheim's understanding of the 'collective effervescence' of the sacred. This is not of
course to say that shopping is not without its problems. Arya is quite
right to this end when she writes that 'The belief that desire can be
fulfilled by the acquisition of commodities is the myth that compulsive buyers fall prey to' (Arya 2009: 174). But, even if gross materialism and consumerism can lead to behaviour that is 'non-rational,
compulsive and uncontrollable' (Arya 2009: 174), this does not make
it any less authentically *religious*.

The effort that traditional religious groups put into denigrating
the modern Christmas, as with such injunctions over the years to
'Keep Christ in Christmas' or 'Jesus Is the Reason for the Season' (see
Schmidt 1995: 5 and Forbes 2007: 32), only, then, serves to draw
attention to, rather than to diminish the power of, modern consumer
culture. As Schmidt contends, indeed, what is striking about such
campaigns 'was not its protest of Christmas commercialism, but its
consecration of it' (Schmidt 1995: 189). The fact, moreover, that such
campaigns were less about returning to a hallowed past, free from the
profanity of the modern commercialized festival, than about reclaim-
ing Christmas' traditional Christian 'meanings within, rather than

apart from, the modern consumer culture' (Schmidt 1995: 189) demonstrates just how entrenched the religion of consumerism has now become, and how its traditional counterparts are now on the defensive, having even to resort to issuing advertising slogans for their voices to be heard.[4]

In the same way that it was argued in chapter 2 that Santa and Jesus inhabit separate religious realms which for the most part have nothing to do with each other and where it is normal practice for Christians to believe in the existence of both Jesus and Santa without conflict or contradiction as they exist in their own designated spaces, so we can see here that it is not tenable for traditional Christian organizations to call for a return to a prelapsarian, pre-commercialized 'golden age' of Christmas. Aside from the question of whether such a period ever actually existed, as evinced by Tracy's contention that 'The fact is that the Christmas festival has never—since its inception—been particularly spiritual' (Tracy 2001a: 2), it would be a misnomer to assert that Christians today live lives where they are not contaminated by the 'pollution' that is modern consumer capitalism. Christians do not live in a separate economy-free sphere from 'everyone else', and they indulge in retail therapy no differently from their 'secular' counterparts. Instead of prizing out or usurping traditional forms of religion, Mundy is right when he argues that 'Christmas is a global festival dedicated largely to expenditure on, and consumption of, commodities, whatever religious, cultural and spiritual allegiances are ostensibly in operation' (Mundy 2008: 170). Just as Christians can and do celebrate both Jesus *and* Santa, so there need be no fundamental incompatibility between Christianity and the modern commercial Christmas festival, which is in its own right 'the religious expression of consumer capitalism' (Tracy 2001a: 2).[5]

Tracy is right when he says that 'it is certainly not the case that the marketplace has co-opted a Christian celebration to increase sales'

[4] This position is documented well by Jennifer Rycenga who refers to how in a manner similar to when 'secular authorities have used the "higher" mandates of religion as a justificatory device for secular policies, advertising for religious products can invoke a religious aura to insinuate that they are above the base aspects of commercialism' (Rycenga 2011: 143).

[5] Horsley makes the similar claim in the same volume that 'it is difficult to avoid the conclusion that Christmas has become the great religious festival of consumer capitalism' (Horsley 2001a: 185).

(Tracy 2001a: 2) as that would suggest that there was a co-dependency between them. That said, there are some notable exceptions, as when Schmidt refers to how 'The Christmas emporium itself was not necessarily secular, and there emerged in the late nineteenth and early twentieth centuries an increasingly close fit, however incongruous and paradoxical, between Christmas shopping and Christian symbols' (Schmidt 1995: 159). He refers, for example, to 'the Christmas cathedrals of the department stores' (Schmidt 1995: 159) and observes that American 'department stores regularly turned to Christianity for many of their grandest effects. With pipe organs, choirs, religious paintings and banners, statues of saints and angels, stained glass, floral emblems of anchors and crosses, miniature churches, and Nativity scenes, the stores often brimmed with Christian figures and symbols' (Schmidt 1995: 161). Indeed, he continues, 'Religious symbols hallowed and mystified Christmas gift giving; such displays bathed both the stores and holiday shopping in the reflected glory of Christianity' (Schmidt 1995: 161).

For all of these functional analogies, however, it does not follow that Christmas has become more commercialized at the expense of the Nativity as, ultimately, these displays do not inhabit the same terrain as their Christian counterparts. They are simply appropriating Christian symbols as merchandising icons and evoking 'religious referents in order to point to gifts and goods' (Schmidt 1991: 896) and to sell commercial products. This conflation of commerce and Christianity has ultimately had the same negative impact as those endeavours, as outlined in chapter 2, to insert Santa into the recreation of the Nativity scene in department store windows. There are exceptions, of course, as when Schmidt refers to the case of a woman who wrote on the back of a Christmas card to the Wanamaker department store in Philadelphia in 1950: 'I certainly want to congratulate you on your Christmas Decorations. It made me feel that Christ my Lord and Savior was in the midst of it all' (in Schmidt 1995: 166). But today, in Schmidt's own words, 'religious symbols have been increasingly removed from the marketplace' (Schmidt 1995: 168). It is not the case that people have deserted the Church in order to queue up 'before the sacrificial altar of the cash register' (deChant 2002: 114) in department stores, shopping malls or, increasingly, online. Rather, what has happened is that what Tracy calls 'that multiheaded hydra that has become America's cultural hegemon—namely, consumer capitalism' (Tracy 2001a: 2) is itself an autonomous site of religious activity where 'Hidden in the mystery and magic of all the lights, glitter, gifts, and glorious performances of the season, is the god that the great festival serves' (Horsley 2001a: 186). There may of course be more to Christmas than the economy—as Simonds puts it, 'The language of commerce is not the exclusive source of our sense of meaning, community, and identity'—but, crucially, 'it is the most important one' (Simonds 2001: 103–4), and in giving 'fulsome expression to the spirit of giving, we bless and validate the spirit of consuming' (Simonds 2001: 104).

Familiar though it may therefore be to find in the literature about Christmas references to how, for example, the festival amounts to 'the commercialization of the sacred' (Braybrooke 1999: 30), it would be more accurate to categorize the commercialized Christmas as the sacred personified. Jennifer Rycenga refers to how 'Christmas has a commercial density, calendric certainty, and religious patina that no other holiday can match' (Rycenga 2011: 147), whereby 'When the market says it is time to buy, the Christmas rush begins, basking in a hallowed glow' (Rycenga 2011: 151), and although she does not go so far as to see capitalism as itself a religion but merely that capitalism and religion are different entities which functionally work together,[6] there is plenty of evidence to suggest that capitalism should be understood in just these terms.

We see the apotheosis of this position in the work of Dell deChant for whom economic and material success and affluence is what he calls 'the great meta-myth of postmodern culture' (deChant 2002: 37). According to deChant, when we engage in the ritual of consumption many of us go about it 'with a seriousness that in earlier times was restricted to religious activity' (deChant 2002: 40). But, for deChant, the key factor is that such activity should still be categorized as religious, even if it lacks the transcendental dimension that characterizes traditional religious agency. Whether we know it or not, deChant's premise is that we are beholden to, and indeed serve, the economy, and if we do so properly and seriously then we will prosper: 'We are not mindful of the cultural imperative to consume, we simply do so' (deChant 2002: 71). It is the very naturalness about the drive to

---

[6] Indeed, Rycenga refers at one point to 'The subservient role of religion within capitalism', and she proceeds to argue that there are 'manifold parallels between religious practices and structures of the marketplace' (Rycenga 2011: 145; see also Deacy 2013: 196).

purchase products that makes the religious aspect of the enterprise so pertinent, as, indeed, such behaviour is 'in harmony with the sacred order and process of the economy' (deChant 2002: 40; see also Deacy 2013: 201). This is not religion as distinct from everything we do but is integral to how we live, move, and have our being.

Whereas, as Bultmann and Cupitt saw it, there is a disjuncture between the religious sphere and everything else we do when religion is defined in terms of a mythological, miraculous, and supernatural world-view involving seeing heaven and hell in spatial terms and where angels and demons are believed in as literal forces and agencies, so for deChant a different type of religion is entailed here. deChant's model is one which precedes the transcendental understanding of religion that we categorize as normative today and is closer to primordial approaches to religion where the ground of the sacred was nature and 'everything depended on the cycles of nature and fertility' (deChant 2002: 30; see also Deacy 2013: 201). What deChant has done is to appropriate this model whereupon the economy now performs the role that in the ancient world was performed by nature, with there being an analogy between the ritualistic practices that took place in the ancient world in temples and shrines and the ritualistic practices of acquisition and consumption that take place in our modern retail culture. If we are prepared to see religion in non-transcendental terms then, according to deChant, it would not be possible to argue that Christmas has lost its religious significance. Rather, as the quintessence of the ritual of consumerism, Christmas is, for deChant, the prime example of religiosity in postmodern culture, in which, in a Durkheimian sense, 'we collectively re-establish our community's right relationship with the economy' by shopping, and 'confirm the legitimacy of our place and often our family's place in the social order' (deChant 2002: 113; see also Deacy 2013: 203).

To this end, Horsley is not incorrect when he writes that, at Christmas, 'there is no longer any separation between religion and retailing, between the spirit and consumption' (Horsley 2001a: 174). But, in keeping with deChant's thesis, it would be more accurate to take the line that at Christmas retailing *is* religion and that consumption is the 'sacred spirit' of postmodern culture. Our very values and identity, both individual and communal, are inextricably bound up with the sacred order of the economy, which is why Forbes is able to make the claim that 'Commerce had more influence than Christianity in making Christmas the culturally dominant holiday it is in the

United States today' (Forbes 2007: 114). Whether one likes it or not, Horsley rightly concedes that 'The Force that now determines our lives is capital', and Christmas in particular constitutes 'the religious festival of historically unprecedented scope in which we serve that Force with the value of our labor in fantastic rituals of abundance and consumption' (Horsley 2001a: 184). Inevitably, there will be detractors from this position who feel that capitalist and consumerist activity militates against a religious interpretation, as when Jeffrey Scholes refers to the difficulty in conceiving of Coca-Cola as 'a long-lasting sacred object' due to the fact that it has been created by 'a corporation that only wants to make money off of consumers' (Scholes 2012: 152). In Scholes' words, it 'will always have trouble doing the kind of religious work that corresponds to the sacred because it can never escape the fact that its fetishized product was and is created by a group of human beings motivated by very human things' (Scholes 2012: 152). Yet, if deChant is right in his premise that the economy *is* the sacred in the postmodern world then there is no barrier in seeing a material product of human derivation as being quintessentially religious in scope.

deChant's *The Sacred Santa* is not solely about Christmas, but as Christmas is the apotheosis of the ritual of acquisition and consumption then it warrants particular attention, and, as he argues, this is a time of the year when 'Every desired object stands before us, and every desire can be ritually satisfied during this month-long stretch of numinous days' (deChant 2002: 161), which begins in the US straight after Thanksgiving on so-called Pilgrimage Friday and lasts around a month.[7] Whereas the Christian celebration of Christmas is marked by the onset of the first Sunday in Advent—ironically a penitential period in the Church's liturgical calendar—Connelly writes, with specific reference to England at the end of the nineteenth century, that this was 'overridden by a new determinant, that of mass consumerism' (Connelly 2012: 191). Likewise, as deChant attests with respect to the turn of the twenty-first century, the average American spends nearly $800 per annum on Christmas gifts (see deChant 2002:

---

[7] deChant writes that the top ten shopping days of the year all occur during the Christmas festival (see deChant 2002: 165) and Christmas cards account for more than sixty per cent of total card sales during the whole year, with Valentine's Day way behind at twenty-five per cent (see deChant 2002: 170). Many industries rely on Christmas sales to keep them afloat throughout the rest of the year (see Restad 1995: 167).

183). Rather than being restricted, however, to the end of the calendar year, Simonds makes the crucial point that 'Christmas spending . . . is the climax of annual consumption patterns but it is not an exception to them' (Simonds 2001: 100), and 'The spirit of Christmas, the spirit of giving, the *spirit of buying* lives on through the entire twelve-month cycle' (Simonds 2001: 101). Accordingly, in addition to celebrating consumerism, Christmas is responsible for nurturing 'the attitudes and assumptions that keep desire for commodities strong well after the Christmas season has come to an end' (Simonds 2001: 102).

FINDING THE SPIRITUAL IN THE MIDST OF THE MATERIAL: THE PARADOX OF CHRISTMAS FILMS

On one level, such a perspective could be taken to suggest that Christmas loses some of its sacrality if its essence is diffused across the year. As we discussed in chapter 1, Durkheim understood holidays as important for the way in which they punctuated the rhythm of the year and provided clearly demarcated boundaries between sacred and profane time. If the calendrical boundaries within which Christmas is situated are displaced then Christmas may not be the period of 'sacred time' that has hitherto been suggested. Yet, as previous chapters have highlighted, Christmas radio programmes and movies are not readily transferable to any other period in the calendar. The festival-specific music and supernatural content, respectively, are set apart from what is on offer at other times in the year, concomitantly giving Christmas a heightened experience of *communitas*. In the same way that Christmas films tantalizingly comprise sites where the supernatural and transcendental appear in an *oeuvre* that would otherwise be construed as quintessentially secular, so here I would venture that there is a paradox in the case of the representation of unalloyed materialism in Christmas movies. Even if the backdrop of such pictures tends to be a materialist or consumerist teleology, what comes to the fore in Christmas movies is a surprisingly subversive challenge to the dictates of the market and of consumption in a way that counters deChant's uncritical assumption that the economy is 'late capitalism's ultimate concern' (deChant 2002: 5; see also Deacy 2013: 202).

To deChant's credit he is not seeking in his book to extol the virtues of consumerism or to critique those more conservative voices which proclaim that Christianity has been threatened or usurped by the commercialization of the Nativity celebration. His aim is not to take sides but to simply construe the economy for what it is—the dominant site of religious activity in the world today and thus 'to present a neutral and straightforward analysis of the religious dimension of Christmas' (deChant 2002: 106). He is emphatic that he is seeking objectivity: 'My aim is not to move Christians to action or even to suggest that the eclipse of Christianity by postmodern cosmological religion is undesirable' (deChant 2002: 198). Yet, how accurate is deChant's thesis and might there be alternative models at work, even in a body of films that appear to celebrate consumerism, that qualify and precipitate a revisiting of the way in which we tend to construe the relationship between the spiritual and the material in the twenty-first century?

Certainly, at face value, Christmas movies would not seem to be especially adept at supplying a critique of the very rituals of consumption that, as we discussed in chapter 5, are one of their most conspicuous characteristics. Indeed, Restad takes the line that such films are something of a disappointment in the way that they have 'tended to leave unquestioned...the perceived tension between material and spiritual' (Restad 1995: 177), and Myers insightfully notes that films such as *It's a Wonderful Life, Miracle on 34th Street,* and *Holiday Inn* have in common 'a view that what is of ultimate importance is independent of the Christian narrative and wholly in conformity with consumer capitalism' (Myers 2001a: 54). As Myers states, when all the community of Bedford Falls gather around George at the end of *It's a Wonderful Life,* at his hour of need,

> both the need and the help are presented in the form of money. This is a true capitalist community built on a cash-nexus. In fact, George's accountant underlines this by setting up his cash register to receive and record the contributions of the town's folk in front of the Christmas tree in George's living room, almost as an altar on which the towns-people all leave their votive offerings. The subtext is plain: real need is lack of cash, real help is giving cash, and cash is the appropriate gift at Christmas (Myers 2001a: 54).

In a way that counters readings of the film that draw attention to the sanctity and sacrality of family and community—as when Richard A. Blake emphasizes the fact that George Bailey's 'strength comes from the community' and that 'In his dependence on family and friends, he has something far more potent than the material wealth of Mr. Potter', to the point that 'The citizens of Bedford Falls become better people because of their devotion to George Bailey' (Blake 2000: 123)—Myers is more cynical in his assertion that 'we are entitled to ask whether it is money after all instead of authentic human relationships that makes life wonderful, just as its absence earlier made life miserable' (Myers 2001a: 54). There is a certain irony, here, that, for Myers, if there is any discernible 'community' in Bedford Falls it is predicated on 'the exchange of cash that brings people together out of their private worlds' (Myers 2001a: 54). Human relationships are, simply, inseparable from economic and capitalistic considerations, in a manner that fits deChant's thesis. In *The Santa Clause*, also, Connelly astutely observes that 'The sense of a society used to consuming big is obvious by the shot of the street: all the houses are beautifully lit for Christmas and are filled with affluent families' (Connelly 2000b: 127). Haire and Nelson go even further and attest, with specific reference to *A Christmas Story*, that 'consumerism mimics the role religion plays and has played in the lives of most Americans', and that, moreover, 'Consumerism has become the new American religion' (Haire and Nelson 2010: 80).

Yet, just as chapter 5 outlined how the focus on shopping, consumerism, and material acquisition in those pictures is offset by the delineation of a supernatural and magical world which challenges any notions that the secular has supplanted the traditionally religious, so here I want to counter the thesis that the economy comprises the ground of our being and is a source of meaning and purpose in the way that for deChant is a straightforward and indisputable hallmark of the world today. While conceding that films are made for profit— no Hollywood studio is going to invest capital in a film that has little chance of returning a viable income—it is also a staple of the genre that Christmas films exhibit a certain ambivalence about the role that money plays in the pursuit of Christmas happiness. We see this typified in the 1947 version of *Miracle on 34th Street*, in which Kris Kringle (Edmund Gwenn) declaims that

> for the past fifty years or more I've been getting more and more worried about Christmas. It seems to me that we're all too busy trying to beat the other fellow and making things go faster and look sharper. Christmas and I are sort of getting lost in the shuffle.

In the novella from the same year, written by Valentine Davies who also scripted the movie, Kringle even decries at one point 'Is this what Christmas has degenerated into? . . . It's pure commercialism! Is there no true Christmas spirit left in the world?' (Davies 1947: 4). Such sentiments comprise the premise of the mid-1980s epic *Santa Claus: The Movie* where emphasis is laid on the fact that the toys made at the North Pole should be completed with the attention to detail of a true craftsman, such that the ruthless toy manufacturer, played by John Lithgow, is demonized as he is interested not in quality but in profit, even when there is evidence that the toys concerned may be injurious to a child's health as they do not meet basic health and safety regulations. As Connelly points out, the message is that 'modernity and profit-making go hand-in-hand and can be taken too far' (Connelly 2000b: 123).

It would be naïve to suggest that this is the only plausible reading of these films. In actuality, *Santa Claus* is a movie littered with product placement, thus somewhat qualifying the idea that what we see in the film is 'antipathy toward mass produced toys from factories and a removal of any association of Santa's gifts with market-place transactions' (Belk 2001: 81). Leslie Felperin's review of *How the Grinch Stole Christmas* in the January 2001 edition of *Sight and Sound* is similarly aware of the double standards here in the assertion that the narrative's 'critique of consumerism reeks of bad faith considering how heavily merchandised the film has been in the US' (Felperin 2001: 50). Even *Miracle on 34th Street* is not immune from the charge of hypocrisy, as when Myers discerns in the opening sequence of the film the fact that 'we are thrust unquestioningly into the world of the commercial American Christmas with all its assumptions of proper images and values intact' (Myers 2001a: 46). What is more, although Kris Kringle bemoans the fact that Christmas has become increasingly commercialized, this needs to be seen in context since, as Schmidt observes, he also 'displays considerable faith in the modern Christmas as it is staged in America's great department stores' (Schmidt 1995: 172). We see this exhibited, principally, by his scheme of sending parents of children looking for presents in Macy's, where he has been employed as the department store Santa, to different toy stores around New York City where the prices are cheaper, which, though undoubtedly undertaken on philanthropic grounds, ends up becoming the store's new merchandising strategy. In Schmidt's words, 'The very values of giving, charity, reciprocity, and public service are made part of the commercial Christmas, and goodwill becomes an indispensable technique of merchandising, a stunt, a trick of the trade' (Schmidt 1995: 173).

The film thus seems to be having its cake and eating it, too, insofar as it both laments and then celebrates the forces of the capitalist economy, culminating at the end of the film with the material reward for Susan Walker (Natalie Wood)—the little girl who comes to believe in Santa despite the best efforts of her mother, Doris (Maureen O'Hara), to ensure that she should give up her childish beliefs since, to quote from the film, 'We should be realistic and completely truthful with our children and not have them growing up believing in a lot of legends and myths like Santa Claus'—of 'a new house on Long Island, complete with a backyard swing' (Schmidt 1995: 174). Belk offers the similar reflection that 'despite the apparent incompatibility between the values of Santa Claus and the values of the department store, there is really no conflict; Santa's compassionate caring and Macy's profit-motivated business practices can flourish together after all' (Belk 2001: 92). At the end of the day, Kringle is employed by Macy's in order to increase Christmas sales, and in his *Sight and Sound* review of the 1994 remake Philip Strick goes so far as to see plenty of evidence that 'rampant materialism' (Strick 1995: 50) lies at the core of the story. To this end, Connelly is not wide of the mark in his assessment that in such films 'The spiritual world is very firmly connected to that of the secular and acquisitive' and that it is 'noticeable that Santa Claus only becomes a significant figure in the movies once America truly became an acquisitive and mass-consumerist nation' (Connelly 2000a: 6) after the Second World War.

Significantly, therefore, what we have in Christmas films is an attempt to hold together two potentially disparate and competing dynamics, in keeping with Niebuhr's 'Christ and Culture in Paradox' model, as outlined in chapter 2, according to which Christians are constantly having to negotiate between two sets of conflicting demands—between Christian injunctions on the one hand and those of secular authority on the other. Such a model is predicated on the need to compromise by way of tolerating the norms of a secular culture which falls short of ideal Christian teachings and values. The fact that such films offer a critique of consumerism while at the same time operating within an environment where capitalism and material acquisition and consumption is normative is analogous in this respect to Niebuhr's premise that 'man is seen as subject to two moralities' (Niebuhr 1952: 56). Here, the duality may not be predicated quite so explicitly between Christianity and capitalism, but it is firmly rooted in the same way between competing spiritual and material values. As Schmidt says in relation to *Miracle on 34th Street*, 'The movie hinges on the possibility of recovering myth, fantasy, faith, imagination, and sentimentality within a world of economic self-interest and enlightened rationality' (Schmidt 1995: 173).

It does not, in other words, have to be a case of one or the other in terms, for example, of Niebuhr's 'Christ against Culture' model according to which Christians must make 'an "either-or" decision' between 'the customs of the society' (Niebuhr 1952: 54) in which they dwell and that of Christ who 'has words of eternal life' (Niebuhr 1952: 61). Christmas films tend to offer a 'both/and' model whereby, as typified by *Miracle*, faith (in Santa and all that he represents) 'will be rewarded with prosperity and security, and the American Christmas is the vehicle of that promise' (Schmidt 1995: 174). After all, it is perhaps *because of* rather than *in spite of* 'the disenchanting forces of the Enlightenment and a market economy' (Schmidt 1995: 173) that at the end of the film true happiness and, indeed, 'magic', is attained, construed in unmitigated material terms as the perfect Long Island home. For all of the criticism that the film offers of a commercialized Christmas and what Schmidt calls 'the smoke and mirrors of market calculation' and 'the superficial shine and whirling speed of modernity' (Schmidt 1995: 175), it does not seek, *à la* Niebuhr's 'Christ against Culture' model, to turn back the clock to a utopian era of pre-consumerist purity or faith but, rather, it underscores, promulgates, and sanctifies 'the gospel of abundance and the enchantments of the consumer culture' (Schmidt 1995: 175; see also Deacy 2013: 196).

This sort of 'trade-off' between commerce and simplicity, the material and the spiritual, is not exclusive to the genre of Christmas movies. In the Victorian era, Tara Moore notes, for example, that 'Christmas book writers occasionally had cause to be defensive about commodifying Christmas good cheer', citing in this regard a reviewer in *The Times* who 'accused Christmas book authors of hiding monetary motivations behind the writing of books for the holiday' (Moore 2009: 24). This is no different from the way in which Christmas movies will be made for commercial purposes but will customarily deal with the theme (familiar from Dickens) of giving to the poor and needy and will be torn between competing narratives of philanthropic giving on the one hand and naked acquisitiveness and capitalist greed on the other. Of course, this is not to say that filmmakers always get the balance right. In his review of the 1994 remake of *Miracle on 34th Street* for the *Evening Standard*, Alexander Walker dismissed the picture as cynical free publicity for New York department stores, like the one depicted in the movie (see Connelly 2000b: 123), while the review in the *Financial Times* dismissed the film as 'a tie-in puffumentary for Christmas; an on-location hype spree in snowiest Manhattan, filled with a glutinous glow' (in Connelly 2000b: 123). In *The Guardian* also disquiet was expressed concerning the fact that this 'is a film which tries to make as much money as possible out of Christmas while abjuring the rest of us to do no such thing' (in Connelly 2000b: 123). Similarly, when *Santa Claus: The Movie* was released in UK cinemas, Kim Newman's review in the December 1985 edition of the *Monthly Film Bulletin* made the now familiar charge that the film 'contrives to strike every false note in the register, to whine about the commercialisation of Christmas while indulging in it on a monumental scale' (Newman 1985: 388).

But, Christmas films are by and large keen to compromise, to strike a balance between competing value systems, as when Marling cites the 1965 TV special *A Charlie Brown Christmas*, in which the eponymous protagonist hears a recitation from Luke's Gospel and vows that 'I won't let all this commercialism spoil my Christmas', as evidence that 'secular' and 'sacred' interpretations of Christmas can be reconciled. In Marling's words, 'With its innocent appeal to the Gospels, *A Charlie Brown Christmas* manages to give the material trappings of Christmas a thin veneer of religious significance' (Marling 2000: 337). Marling is referring here to traditional religious (and in this case specifically Christian) dimensions of Christmas, rather than seeing consumerism itself as being potentially amenable to categorization through the lens of 'religion', but the balance she evidences here is symptomatic of the genre of Christmas movies as a whole. None of this ameliorates or excuses the worst excesses of capitalism—and Connelly is correct to this end when he writes that 'The flip side of the debate over faith and innocence in these movies is the nature of American society as a capitalist, consumerist, acquisitive organism' (Connelly 2000b: 122)—but not every Christmas film is beholden to what Marling calls 'the terrible, empty materialism of

Christmas' even if she thinks that this is what *Jingle All The Way* (which she labels 'a thoroughly unpleasant film in which the desperate father bullies and attacks the retail world relentlessly for eighty-five minutes in his effort to get the last "Turbo Man" action figure') 'ultimately endorses' (Marling 2000: 347).

In the case, for example, of *Santa Claus: The Movie*, it is worth noting that following a dismissive review in *Sight and Sound*, one of the members of the crew working on the film, Jim Smith, sent a letter to the publisher calling for a 'balanced appraisal' (Smith 1985/6: 70) in the way the film was treated by critics. According to Smith, 'Admittedly, the film like all films is a capitalistic enterprise aiming to make money and on which a great deal of money (too much) has been spent, but its aim is also genuinely to delight very young children' (Smith 1985/6: 70). While conceding that 'It can hardly be claimed that the film industry in general is alive to these responsibilities, preferring on the whole to chase the fast buck of corruption' (Smith 1985/6: 70), Smith was evidently keen to emphasize that the film, for all of its flaws, was conceived with good intentions which were not solely profit-orientated. This very much gets to the heart of what it is that Christmas films do, in the respect that they characteristically walk a delicate tightrope between extolling the virtues of authenticity while also being consumerist and money-making products. We see this reflected more generally in Rycenga's claim that 'The ritualization of the Christmas shopping season . . . plays on deep-seated desires for authentic human relations and friendships; but it uses these impulses to jump-start a (profitable) buying frenzy' (Rycenga 2011: 146). Christmas films lie at the very apex of this bewildering and contradictory landscape, as encapsulated by Mazur and McCarthy's identification of the inherent paradox that 'Because popular culture sites are very often commercial sites, their role in religious meaning-making is always ambiguous' (Mazur and McCarthy 2011c: 18).

Yet, once religion is not seen to lie in a category apart from the site of the secular—and deChant's thesis that the economy is the supreme manifestation of religion in the postmodern world goes a significant way towards breaking down these traditional boundaries between the sacred and the profane—then it becomes less problematic that two seemingly disparate polarities are being affirmed simultaneously. As Robert J. Thompson sees it, indeed, 'Christianity has a long history of being an effective lubricant of the American economic machine', as epitomized by the Protestant work ethic[8]—so much so, in fact, that 'The tradition goes so deep that few recognize the contradiction' (Thompson 2005: 51). When 'popular Christmas stories encourage the purchasing of gifts at the same time they preach of how unimportant material things are' (Thompson 2005: 51), this appears not so much as a contradiction as the sort of practical, expedient compromise entailed in Niebuhr's 'Christ and Culture in Paradox' model with all of the attendant disunity and differentiation that such a 'dualist' model necessarily entails. Rather than attempt to reconcile or overcome this sort of dichotomy, Niebuhr's model is effective at showing that living with this tension is part and parcel of what it is to be a Christian in a world that does not always uphold or prioritize Christian ethical values. The model is quite emphatic that, imperfect though it may be (a necessary evil, even), we cannot abstain from worldly impurity—rather, we belong to our culture and cannot disaggregate ourselves from it (see Deacy and Ortiz 2008: 49).

Dissimilarity and paradox is thus to be expected, and, in keeping with Niebuhr's understanding that secular laws can act as a corrective against even greater sin and injustice, so Christmas films tend to be adept at demonstrating that, as Connelly puts it, 'The way in which the distasteful elements of this modern, spending-fest Christmas are assuaged is via the analgesic of a caring consumerism' (Connelly 2000b: 124). This comes to the fore in *Miracle on 34th Street* where Kris Kringle is genuinely concerned for the children who come to him and he recommends the parents go to other stores where the prices of the toys are cheaper. Capitalism does not disappear, but it is through this softer, more philanthropic form of capitalist enterprise that a different set of values is promoted. Through consumerism we may be helping big businesses to make profits, but we are also transforming

---

[8] Restad articulates this well when she writes in chapter 5 of *Christmas in America* that 'As middle-class American Protestants began to establish a new Christmas during the first half of the [nineteenth] century, the notion that money and commerce might taint the holiday was significantly absent. This was in part because Protestantism itself used financial success as an indicator of faith . . . In a time that could see God's reward for virtue, Christmas gift-giving became an exercise in religious training' (Restad 1995: 72). She proceeds to write in chapter 9 that 'Mixing traditional Protestant and American doctrines of individualism with the newer vision of Social Darwinism, many in the Christian community felt that American prosperity was proof and extension of God-ordained success, a link confirmed by lavish Christmas giving' (Restad 1995: 138). She adds that ministers even preached commercial gain from the pulpits, with virtue and success seen as congruous (Restad 1995: 138).

the lives (it is hoped) of our family and friends, something facilitated by the notion, which especially comes to the fore in *Santa Claus: the Movie*, that 'Santa enables us to pretend that the gifts are not mass-produced for profit by industrial firms but handmade by elves or the kindly avuncular Santa himself and personally delivered on Christmas Eve' (Horsley 2001a: 184).[9]

CONCLUSION: MOVING BEYOND THE MATERIAL

What thus comes to the fore in Christmas movies is a deceptively subversive and surprisingly complex array of ideological and thematic dispositions, beliefs, and values. Despite seeming, at first sight, to comprise the apotheosis of Christmas materialism and greed, they function within a context of familial, social, and interpersonal connection and, even, transformation. Grounded though Christmas movies may be in the consecration of consumption and capitalism, they concomitantly sanctify charity, magic, and wish-fulfilment and, above all, it is the sacrality of relationships that underpins even the most crass Christmas fare, as typified by *Jingle All The Way* and *Surviving Christmas*. Whereas the 'real' economy is predicated on one's financial means—in the respect that provided one has the money then there is no limit to the number of commodities that can be transacted—the economy that is constructed in celluloid Christmas fantasies is one whereby *need, giving, philanthropy,* and *generosity,* which are difficult to measure in terms of monetary value, are the overarching determinants, in a manner that is closer in essence to what Kuper calls 'the Christian economy' (Kuper 2001: 168; see also Deacy 2013: 196) than to the machinations of the 'real' economy. To this end, Christmas movies represent the antithesis of deChant's attestation that the capitalist economy is normative. Important though the economy may be at Christmas, a better qualification of deChant's position would be to see the economy as a

---

[9] Sands makes the astute point here that when it comes to Christmas present-giving 'market forces are made to appear not as market forces at all but rather as the free expression of personal desire and choice' (Sands 2001: 79). Horsley similarly attests that when it comes to Christmas 'the concrete economic service of capital is veiled' (Horsley 2001a: 184).

means to an end—namely, that of facilitating and giving concrete, material expression to the way we conduct and prioritize our familial and personal relationships. A.P. Simonds may be right that 'The discontent of those who are troubled by the commercialization of Christmas is well-founded' (Simonds 2001: 105), but criticisms of Christmas consumerism and materialism are only really sustainable when that consumerism and materialism constitutes an end in itself rather than a means towards a more wholesome, edifying, and spiritual end.

In like manner, while the objective of Bill McKibben's Methodist church-based book, *Hundred Dollar Holiday: The Case for a More Joyful Christmas*, is to offer 'some suggestions on how to rethink Christmastime, so that our current obsession with present-buying becomes less important than the dozens of other possible traditions and celebrations' (from the inside cover flap of McKibben 1998), the problem with McKibben's argument is that it does not allow for any shades of grey. Estimable though it may be to attack 'those relentless commercial forces who have spent more than a century trying to convince us that Christmas does come from a store, or a catalogue, or a virtual mall on the Internet' (McKibben 1998: 11), what is missing is an understanding of *why* people (feel the need to) buy presents in the first place. Ironically, McKibben attests that the motivation behind the writing of his book was that many people, Christian and otherwise, 'felt that too much of the chance for family togetherness was being robbed by the pressures of Christmas busyness and the tensions of gift-giving' (McKibben 1998: 12). Yet, I would venture that, while an over-indulgence on spending and consumption along the lines that McKibben is suggesting is indeed something worth resisting, his plea for 'more music, more companionship, more contemplation, more time outdoors, more love' at Christmas is not necessarily obviated by the profusion of 'so many gifts' (McKibben 1998: 13) in the way that he is bemoaning.

McKibben thinks that we should change Christmas in order to 'help us get at some of the underlying discontent in our lives' (McKibben 1998: 47), but it is a moot point as to whether this can best be achieved by spending less, as per his suggestion that families should limit the amount of money that they spend each Christmas to $100. Golby and Purdue, for example, respond to claims that 'commerce now directs the festival' by arguing that 'the wrapping of gifts symbolically personalizes them and rescues them from their commodity status, while part of the moral economy of Christmas is a vast seasonal increase in charitable donations' (Golby and Purdue 2000: 140). As depicted in films such as *Miracle on 34th Street*, Marling may be correct that 'Christmas is all about stores and shopping', but, she adds, 'the things we buy in our annual Christmas frenzy represent more than material trappings' (Marling 2000: 356). For Marling, 'A Christmas present is love in a box—giving something to bring pleasure and comfort to others' (Marling 2000: 356). We see this in a number of Christmas films, as when, writing about *All I Want For Christmas* (1991), John Mundy discerns that 'Though the film's mise-en-scène exudes material abundance', as typified by 'the expensive costumes worn by most of the characters', thematically at any rate 'commodities and material possessions are deemed . . . to be of less value than a loving, united family' (Mundy 2008: 171) in a film that, as he sees it, manages to 'reaffirm the importance of family in an increasingly commodified, impersonal world' (Mundy 2008: 173). Admittedly, not all interpretations of the film are quite this positive, as typified by Lucy O'Brien's *Sight and Sound* review in February 1992 which dismisses the picture as 'a Pepsi advert with *angst*' and for comprising 'sugary Christmas fare' (O'Brien 1992: 38), while the publication's video review of the film the following December denounced *All I Want For Christmas* as a 'Horrible, saccharine-sweet movie about two kids who conspire to fix their parents' bad marriage' (Anon. 1992b: 58). But, even if the film is deemed unsuccessful at achieving what it sets out to do, the bottom line is that it endeavours, ostensibly at any rate, to accentuate and prioritize the importance of family over commerce per se.

Even *Jingle All The Way*, which was slated by critics for its unconvincing attempt at critiquing Christmas consumerism while ultimately endorsing it, is also recognized by some writers as having some integrity in the way that it endorses and sanctifies the importance of familial relationships. While conceding that it 'may appear to be ideologically confused' (Mundy 2008: 176), Mundy notes, for example, that the film 'offers an intriguing commentary on parental pressures during the Christmas season, as grown men fight to fulfil anticipated expectations' (Mundy 2008: 175), and that, at the end of the film, 'What matters is not a plastic, material simulation of an action hero, but the reality of a loving, caring father who is able to demonstrate familial love and responsibility' (Mundy 2008: 176). In an inversion of the Scrooge narrative, where a man with wealth chooses not to spend any money on Christmas gifts, the protagonist,

Howard Langston (Arnold Schwarzenegger), 'is swept up in the compulsion to articulate love for his child through the act of shopping, to transform a commodity item into a gift that betokens emotional attachment and engagement' (Mundy 2008: 176). Mundy's argument underscores the paradox at the heart of Christmas in a manner that deChant's concentration on the unmitigated significance of the economy per se is not able to engender. Even in a film as two-dimensional as *Jingle All The Way* (or, perhaps, precisely *because* the film is so lacking in depth), Mundy's thesis is that the greater the emphasis on rampant materialism and impersonal consumerism, the more likely it is that a counter-thesis will emerge that foregrounds love and personal relationships. deChant may be correct that the economy is central to what Christmas (and indeed postmodern culture as a whole) is about, but his thesis is only half the story. Whereas for deChant the economy is indubitably key, Christmas films are often adept at showing us that consumerism falls short when a conflict, perceived or real, arises between what Mundy calls 'an impersonal world of work and commodities' (Mundy 2008: 176) and the sacrality of family ties and bonds. It is thus love which quells and ameliorates the excesses of consumerism and materialism and which ultimately has the last word.

This is very much reminiscent of the thesis advanced by Daniel Miller in *A Theory of Shopping*, based on fieldwork carried out in a North London street in 1994, where it is proposed that 'Shopping may be a vicarious entry into social relations' (Miller 1998: 4) and in which 'commodities are used to constitute the complexity of contemporary social relations' (Miller 1998: 8). Miller's ethnographical research has suggested that in purchasing goods the act is almost always other- rather than self-directed, for example expressing 'a relationship between the shopper and a particular other individual such as a child or partner', and ultimately says something about 'the values to which people wish to dedicate themselves' (Miller 1998: 12) instead of about how acquisitive or individualistic we may be. Rather than taken, moreover, as short-term goals or priorities, Miller discerns in retail the presence of 'values that are long lasting and opposed to the contingency of everyday life' (Miller 1998: 20). It is *love* which, according to Miller, 'remains as a powerful taken-for-granted foundation for acts of shopping' (Miller 1998: 20)—something which is missing from, say, deChant's analysis of how the economy is the foundation of our postmodern cares and concerns.

While 'selfishness' and 'hedonism' (Miller 1998: 22) may lie at the heart of some people's shopping predilections, Miller is clear that 'love is not only normative but easily dominant as the context and motivation for the bulk of actual shopping practice' (Miller 1998: 23), and he gives the example of how 'A mother who is concerned that her child always has the latest thing so that he or she will not be looked down upon in the playground is expressing her love for and anxiety about the child just as much as when she buys Heinz tomato soup' (Miller 1998: 142). Material culture is thus able to give expression to rather than to detract from the relationships that we foster to the point that, as Miller attests, 'The purpose of shopping is not so much to buy the things people want, but to strive to be in a relationship with subjects that want these things' (Miller 1998: 148). Accordingly, he proposes that 'Shopping, so far from being, as it is inevitably portrayed, the essence of ungodliness, becomes as a ritual the vestigial search for a relationship with God' (Miller 1998: 150).

We see similar sentiments in the anthropological literature on gift-giving, as denoted in *The Gift*, Marcel Mauss' treatise on the potlatch, first published in 1954, in which the exchanges of gifts in ancient societies is shown to be paramount to the ordering and cohesion of those societies, even to the extent that 'To refuse to give . . . , just as to refuse to accept, is tantamount to declaring war' (Mauss 1990: 13). Building on Mauss' theory of the gift as constitutive of human solidarity, David Cheal has written about the role of Christmas gift-giving in capitalist societies as the antithesis of the notion of excessive commercialization on the grounds that 'Within contemporary western moral economies it is above all conventional sentiments of friendship, love, and gratitude that are thought to inspire giving' (Cheal 1988: 18). In tandem with Miller, Cheal's thesis is that 'showing love to others by giving gifts to them is a highly valued ritual in intimate ties' (Cheal 1988: 18), with the giving of gifts an integral and indispensable part of helping tie a family together (see Cheal 1988: 77). For Jacques T. Godbout, similarly, 'nothing can be initiated or undertaken, can thrive or function, if it is not nourished by the gift' (Godbout 1998: 11), whereupon 'families would disintegrate instantly if, disavowing the demands of gift and counter-gift, they came to constitute no more than a commercial venture or a battlefield' (Godbout 1998: 12). This foregrounding of personal relationships is not an addendum or a by-product of what Christmas is essentially about since, as Cheal construes it, at Christmas 'the central value of the occasion is the physical availability of significant others to each other as individuals who are co-present in space and time' (Cheal 1988: 96). Accordingly, compassion and love are the pre-requisites for Christmas expenditure, in which the nature and extent of the relationship between family members is expressed or symbolized by the giving of presents, which accounts for why, as Cheal attests, 'Gifts are not given to just anybody' but are, rather, presented 'to individuals with whom the donor has personal ties, or who occupy social positions within a community to which the donor also belongs' (Cheal 1988: 173).

When it comes to Christmas, therefore, we can see that, based on Miller's and Cheal's theses, there is more to the festival than the manifestation of sheer capitalism. For all the criticism meted out to Christmas films, Mundy is right that 'commercial mainstream family entertainment Hollywood movies continue to reflect the paradoxes enshrined in our experiences of contemporary Christmas, centred as they are on our need to negotiate complex relationships that exist between family, wider society and materialism' (Mundy 2008: 167). Outside of movies, also, Robert J. Thompson has conducted a study of the role of television at Christmas in which the argument is adduced that 'While filled with commands to buy, network television is also filled, for an entire month every winter, with stories and songs that ask us to be nice, not naughty' (Thompson 2005: 53). Shopping and consumption may continue unabated in a world where competition, material prosperity, and acquisition are normative, but Christmas is as much about the transcendence of impersonal material and market forces as it is about the blind and naked subservience to them. We see this reflected in how, in many Christmas movies, the festive season inspires action, engagement, and community—'other-centred' activities, in other words, which militate against the notion that the only thing that matters is making money. At the end of *Miracle on 34th Street* 'a new family unit has been formed', while in *Elf* (2003) not only are an estranged father and son reconciled but the emphasis at the end of the picture is on 'a community united in the Christmas spirit' (Garrett 2007: 160) as seasonal cheer spreads among the crowds gathered in New York's Central Park.

The films themselves may be made for profit, but their narratives are bound up with the importance of generosity, wonder, miracles, joy, belief, fellowship, giving, celebration, community, love, and even redemption because of, rather than in spite of, rampant acquisitiveness and consumption. For Garrett, moreover, Christmas movies are not incompatible with more traditionally spiritual and theological questions relating to the centrality of belief, devotion, and fellowship (Garrett 2007: 156). As he attests, 'even bad Hollywood Christmas movies show how important our culture finds some of the core components of faith and belief, and we can draw valuable lessons from them' (Garrett 2007: 156). For Connelly, also, Christmas for many people will be about 'the sense of community and family that we have seemingly lost in our atomised world' and where 'solidity, clear relationships, harmony and happiness' (Connelly 2012: xiv) are ideals to strive for (whether or not actually achieved). Christmas is thus a notoriously contested and inscrutable festival—riven by paradox, where competing and antithetical principles and ideologies come to the fore, but also one where a radio programme made by the BBC ostensibly for entertainment or a crass Christmas movie sneered at by the critics for being infantile and lightweight can actually engender some of the more profound and sophisticated insights about the 'real' meaning behind the festive season. Whether or not one is dreaming of a white Christmas or roasting chestnuts on an open fire, Christmas may amount to one of the most unexpected and fecund manifestations of religion in the world today.

Bibliography

Agajanian, Rowana, 2000. '"Peace on Earth, Goodwill to All Men": The Depiction of Christmas in Modern Hollywood Films'. In *Christmas at the Movies: Images of Christmas in American, British and European Cinema*, edited by Mark Connelly, London and New York: I.B. Tauris, 143–64

Aiken, Scott F., 2010. 'Armed for the War on Christmas'. In *Christmas— Philosophy for Everyone: Better than a Lump of Coal*, edited by Scott C. Lowe, Oxford: Wiley-Blackwell, 49–58

Alexander, Cecil Frances, 1852. *Hymns for Little Children*, London: Joseph Masters

Anon., 1944. Review of *Christmas Holiday*. *Monthly Film Bulletin* 11/129 (30 September): 101

Anon., 1945(a). Review of *The Cheaters*. *Monthly Film Bulletin* 12/140 (31 August): 96

Anon., 1945(b). Review of *I'll Be Seeing You*. *Monthly Film Bulletin* 12/143 (30 November): 135

Anon., 1959. Review of *It Happened to Jane*. *Monthly Film Bulletin* 26/304 (May): 55–6

Anon., 1960. Review of *La Grande Speranza* (aka *Torpedo Zone*). *Monthly Film Bulletin* 27/321 (October): 142

Anon., 1992(a). 'Away in a Manger'. In *Christmas Carols: Complete Verses*, edited by Shane Weller, Mineola NY: Dover Publications, 3

Anon., 1992(b). Video review of *All I Want for Christmas*. *Sight and Sound* 2/8 (December): 58

Anon., 1997. Video review of *White Christmas*. *Sight and Sound* 7/12 (December): 62

Anon., 1998. 'The deal'. *Sight and Sound* 8/4 (April) 1998: 4

Anon., 2002. DVD review of *The Grinch*. *Sight and Sound* 12/2 (February): 71

Anon., 2006. DVD review of *Bad Santa*. *Sight and Sound* 16/1 (January): 86

Arya, Rina, 2009. 'The Religious Dimensions of Compulsive Buying'. *Implicit Religion* 12/2: 165–85

Augustine, St., 1998. *The City of God against the Pagans*, edited and translated by R.W. Dyson, New York: Airmont

Badertscher, John, 2001. 'Introduction'. *Implicit Religion* 4/2: 69–72

Badertscher, John, 2010. 'On Creation Myths'. *Implicit Religion* 13/2: 195–209

Badham, Paul and Linda Badham, 1984. *Immortality or Extinction?*, London: SPCK

Bailey, Edward, 1998(a). *Implicit Religion: An Introduction*, London: Middlesex University Press

Bailey, Edward, 1998(b). '"Implicit Religion": What Might That Be?' *Implicit Religion* 1: 9–22

Bailey, Edward. 2006. *Implicit Religion in Contemporary Society*, Leuven, Paris, and Dudley MA: Peeters

Bailey, Edward, 2012. '"Implicit Religion": What Might That Be?' *Implicit Religion* 15/2: 195–207

Barth, Karl, 1968. *The Epistle to the Romans*, Oxford: Oxford University Press

BBC Media Centre, 2013. 'A celebration of religious programming on the BBC this Christmas'. 25 November: www.bbc.co.uk/mediacentre/latestnews/2013/religious-programmes-christmas.html

BBC News, 2004. 'Britain is best at Christmas, says Cook'. 17 December: http://news.bbc.co.uk/1/hi/uk_politics/4104745.stm

BBC News, 2007. 'Dawkins: I'm a cultural Christian'. 10 December: http://news.bbc.co.uk/1/hi/uk_politics/7136682.stm

BBC News, 2013. 'John Lewis's Christmas ad: 10 interpretations'. 11 November: www.bbc.co.uk/news/magazine-24901114

Beaudoin, Tom, 2003. *Consuming Faith: Integrating Who We Are With What We Buy*, Lanham MD: Sheed and Ward

Beaudoin, Tom, 2009. 'The Ethics of Research in Faith and Culture: Scholarship as Fandom?' In *Exploring Religion and the Sacred in a Media Age*, edited by Christopher Deacy and Elisabeth Arweck, Farnham and Burlington VT: Ashgate, 23–41

Belk, Russell W., 2001. 'Materialism and the Making of the Modern American Christmas'. In *Unwrapping Christmas*, edited by Daniel Miller, Oxford: Clarendon Press, 75–104

Bennett, William J., 2009. *The True Saint Nicholas: Why He Matters to Christmas*, New York, Nashville, London, Toronto, Sydney: Howard Books

Blackburn, Tony, 2007. *Poptastic: My Life in Radio*, London: Cassell

Blake, Richard A., 2000. *AfterImage: The Indelible Catholic Imagination of Six American Filmmakers*, Chicago: Loyola Press

Blizek, William L., 2009. 'Using Religion to Interpret Movies'. In *The Continuum Companion to Religion and Film*, edited by William L. Blizek, London and New York: Continuum, 29–38

Bowen, Desmond, 1968. *The Idea of the Victorian Church*, Montreal: McGill

Brabazon, Tara, 2008. 'Christmas in the Media'. In *Christmas, Ideology and Popular Culture*, edited by Sheila Whiteley, Edinburgh: Edinburgh University Press, 149–63

Brant, Jonathan, 2012. *Paul Tillich and the Possibility of Revelation through Film: A Theoretical Account Grounded by Empirical Research into the Experiences of Filmgoers*, Oxford: Oxford University Press

Braybrooke, Marcus, 1999. 'Response to David Craig'. *Implicit Religion* 2/1 1999: 30–1

Brooks, Xan, 2005. Review of *Bad Santa*. *Sight and Sound* 15/1 (January): 42–3

Bruce, Steve, 2011. *Secularization: In Defence of an Unfashionable Theory*, Oxford: Oxford University Press

Bultmann, Rudolf, 1964. *Jesus Christ and Mythology*, London: SCM

Bultmann, Rudolf, 1972. 'New Testament and Mythology'. In *Kerygma and Myth: A Theological Debate*, edited by Hans-Werner Bartsch, London: SPCK

Campbell, Heidi, 2010. *When Religion Meets New Media*, Abingdon: Routledge

Campbell, Robert A., 2001. 'When Implicit Religion Becomes Explicit: The Case of the Boy Scouts in Canada'. *Implicit Religion* 4/1: 15–25

Carrier, James G., 2001. 'The Rituals of Christmas Giving'. In *Unwrapping Christmas*, edited by Daniel Miller, Oxford: Clarendon Press, 55–74

Cathode, Ray, 1998. 'Ginger Spices BskyB'. *Sight and Sound* 8/2 (February): 34

Cavalcanti, Alberto, 1938. 'A Pioneer'. *Sight and Sound* 7/26 (Summer): 55–6

Chapman, James, 2000. 'God Bless Us, Every One: Movie Adaptations of *A Christmas Carol*'. In *Christmas at the Movies: Images of Christmas in American, British and European Cinema*, edited by Mark Connelly, London and New York: I.B. Tauris, 9–37

Charity, Tom, 1993. Review of *Home Alone 2: Lost in New York*. *Sight and Sound* 3/1 (January): 47

Cheal, David, 1988. *The Gift Economy*, London and New York: Routledge

Church of England Doctrine Commission, 1995. *The Mystery of Salvation*, London: Church House Publishing

Cipriani, Robert, 2012. 'Sport as (Spi)rituality. *Implicit Religion* 15/2: 139–51

Clark, Terry Ray, 2012. 'Introduction: What is religion? What is popular culture? How are they related?' In *Understanding Religion and Popular Culture*, edited by Terry Ray Clark and Dan W. Clanton, Jr, Abingdon: Routledge, 1–12.

Coffin, Tristram P., 1973. *The Book of Christmas Folklore*, New York: Seabury Press

Collins, Philip, 1993. 'The Reception and Status of the Carol'. *The Dickensian* 431/89, Part 3 (Winter): 170–6

Connelly Mark, 2000(a). 'Introduction'. In *Christmas at the Movies: Images of Christmas in American, British and European Cinema*, edited by Mark Connelly, London and New York: I.B. Tauris, 1–8

Connelly, Mark, 2000(b). 'Santa Claus: The Movie'. In *Christmas at the Movies: Images of Christmas in American, British and European Cinema*, edited by Mark Connelly, London and New York: I.B. Tauris, 115–34

Connelly, Mark, 2012. *Christmas: A History*, London: I.B. Tauris

Count, Earl W. and Alice Lawson Count, 1997. *4000 Years of Christmas: A Gift from the Ages*, Berkeley, California: Ulysses Press

Cupitt, Don, 1995. 'After Liberalism'. In *Readings in Modern Theology: Britain and America*, edited by Robin Gill, London: SPCK

Cupitt, Don, 2003. *The Sea of Faith*, London: SCM

Davies, Douglas J., 1999. 'Implicit Religion and Inter-faith Dialogue in Human Perspective'. *Implicit Religion* 2/1: 17–24

Davies, Valentine, 1947. *Miracle on 34th Street*, San Diego, New York and London: Harcourt

Dawkins, Richard, 2006. *The God Delusion*, London: Transworld

Day, Abby, 2012. 'Nominal Christian Adherence: Ethnic, Natal, Aspirational'. *Implicit Religion* 15/4: 439–56

Deacy, Christopher, 1999. 'Screen Christologies: An evaluation of the role of Christ-figures in film'. *Journal of Contemporary Religion* 14/3: 325–37

Deacy, Christopher. 2001. *Screen Christologies: Redemption and the Medium of Film*, Cardiff: University of Wales Press

Deacy, Christopher, 2005. *Faith in Film: Religious Themes in Contemporary Cinema*, Aldershot: Ashgate

Deacy, Christopher, 2007. 'From Bultmann to Burton, Demythologizing the Big Fish: The Contribution of Modern Christian Theologians to the Theology-Film Conversation'. In *Reframing Theology and Film: New Focus for an Emerging Discipline*, edited by Robert Johnston, Grand Rapids MI: Baker Academic, 238–58

Deacy, Christopher, 2008. '"Escaping" from the world through film: Theological perspectives on the "real" and the "reel"'. In *Recent Releases: The Bible in Contemporary Cinema*, edited by Geert Hallbäck and Annika Hvithamar, Sheffield: Sheffield Phoenix Press, 12–29

Deacy, Christopher, 2009. 'Introduction: Why Study Religion and Popular Culture?' In *Exploring Religion and the Sacred in a Media Age*, edited by Christopher Deacy and Elisabeth Arweck, Farnham and Burlington VT: Ashgate, 1–22

Deacy, Christopher, 2011. 'Applying redemption through film: Challenging the sacred-secular divide'. In *Escape Routes: Contemporary Perspectives on Life After Punishment*, edited by Stephen Farrall et al., London: Routledge, 22–42

Deacy, Christopher, 2012(a). *Screening the Afterlife: Theology, Eschatology and Film*, Abingdon: Routledge

Deacy, Christopher, 2012(b). 'Apocalypse Now? Towards a Cinematic Realized Eschatology'. In *Seeing Beyond Death: Images of the Afterlife in Theology and Film*, edited by Ulrike Vollmer and Christopher Deacy, Marburg: Schüren Verlag

Deacy, Christopher, 2013. 'The "religion" of Christmas'. *Journal of Scandinavian Cinema* 3/3: 195–207

Deacy, Christopher and Gaye Ortiz, 2008. *Theology and Film: Challenging the Sacred/Secular Divide*, Oxford: Wiley-Blackwell

deChant, Dell, 2002. *The Sacred Santa: Religious Dimensions of Consumer Culture*, Cleveland: The Pilgrim Press

deChant, Dell, 2012. 'Religion and ecology in popular culture'. In *Understanding Religion and Popular Culture*, edited by Terry Ray Clark and Dan W. Clanton, Jr, Abingdon: Routledge, 28–40

de Groot, Kees, 2012. 'Playing with Religion in Contemporary Theatre'. *Implicit Religion* 15/4: 457–75

Dickens, Charles, 1987 (first pub. 1843). *A Christmas Carol*, Harmondsworth: Puffin

Diski, Jenny, 1992. 'Curious tears'. *Sight and Sound* 2/4 (August): 39

Dodd, Charles H., 1944. *The Apostolic Preaching and its Developments*, London: Hodder and Stoughton

Dupré, William, 2007. 'Why (and When) Should We Speak of Implicit Religion?' *Implicit Religion* 10/2: 132–50

Durkheim, Émile, 2001. *The Elementary Forms of Religious Life* (trans. Carol Cosman), Oxford: Oxford University Press

Dutton, Edward, 2010. 'Cultural Uniqueness and Implicit Religion'. *Implicit Religion* 13/2: 173–94

Ebert, Roger, 2004. Review of *Christmas with the Kranks*. *Chicago Sun-Times* (23 November): www.rogerebert.com/reviews/christmas-with-the-kranks-2004

Ebon, Martin, 1975. *Saint Nicholas: Life and Legend*, New York, Evanston, San Francisco, London: Harper and Row

Elmes, Simon, 2012. *Hello Again . . . Nine Decades of Radio Voices*, London: Random House (Kindle edition)

Evans, Peter William, 2000. 'Satirizing the Spanish Christmas: *Plácido* (Luis García Berlanga 1961)'. In *Christmas at the Movies: Images of Christmas in American, British and European Cinema*, edited by Mark Connelly, London and New York: I.B. Tauris, 211–21

Fahy, Patrick, 2006. DVD review of *Christmas with the Kranks*. *Sight and Sound* 16/1 (January): 87

Fahy, Patrick, 2007. Review of *Deck the Halls*. *Sight and Sound* 17/2 (February): 50, 52

Felperin, Leslie. 2001. Review of *The Grinch*. *Sight and Sound* 11/1 (January) 2001: 49–50

Fiddes, Paul S., 2000. *The Promised End: Eschatology in Theology and Literature*, Oxford: Blackwell

Floyd, Nigel. 1991. Review of *Home Alone*. *Monthly Film Bulletin* 58/684 (January): 19–20

Flynn, Tom. 1993. *The Trouble with Christmas*, Buffalo, NY: Prometheus

Forbes, Bruce David, 1997. 'Batman Crucified: Religion and modern superheroes'. *Media Development* 44/4: 10–12

Forbes, Bruce David, 2007, *Christmas. A Candid History*, Berkeley and London: University of California Press

Garrett, Greg, 2007. *The Gospel According to Hollywood*, Louisville and London: Westminster John Knox

Gauthier, François, 2005. 'Orpheus and the Underground: Raves and Implicit Religion—From Interpretation to Critique'. *Implicit Religion* 8/3: 217–65

Giddens, Anthony, 2006. *Sociology*, Cambridge and Malden: Polity Press

Gilbey, Ryan, 2004. *Groundhog Day*, London: British Film Institute

Glancy, H. Mark, 2000. 'Dreaming of Christmas: Hollywood and the Second World War'. In *Christmas at the Movies: Images of Christmas in American, British and European Cinema*, edited by Mark Connelly, London and New York: I.B. Tauris, 59–76

Godbout, Jacques T., 1998. *The World of the Gift*, Montreal and Kingston, London and Ithica: McGill-Queen's University Press

Golby, J.M. and A.W. Purdue, 2000. *The Making of the Modern Christmas*, Stroud: Sutton Publishing Limited

Gollnick, James, 2002. 'Implicit Religion in the Psychology of Religion'. *Implicit Religion* 5/2: 81–92

Graham, Elaine, 2007. 'What We Make of the World: The Turn to "Culture" in Theology and the Study of Religion'. In *Between Sacred and Profane: Researching Religion and Popular Culture*, edited by Gordon Lynch, London and New York: I.B. Tauris, 63–81

Grainger, Roger, 1999. Review of Edward Bailey's *Implicit Religion: An Introduction*. *Implicit Religion* 2/1: 51–2

Grainger, Roger, 2003. 'Believing and Belonging: A Psychological Comment on a Paper Given by E.I. Bailey at Windsor, 1990'. *Implicit Religion* 6/1: 53–7

Haire, Erin and Dustin Nelson, 2010. 'Crummy Commercials and BB Guns: Son-of-a-bitch Consumerism in a Christmas Classic'. In *Christmas— Philosophy for Everyone: Better than a Lump of Coal*, edited by Scott C. Lowe, Oxford: Wiley-Blackwell, 80–90

Hales, Steven D., 2010. 'Putting Claus Back into Christmas'. In *Christmas— Philosophy for Everyone: Better than a Lump of Coal*, edited by Scott C. Lowe, Oxford: Wiley-Blackwell, 161–71

Hamilton, Malcolm, 2001. 'Implicit Religion and Related Concepts: Seeking Precision'. *Implicit Religion* 4/1: 5–13

Harrison, Michael, 1951. *The Story of Christmas: Its Growth and Development from the Earliest Times*, London: Odhams Press

Hasted, Nick, 1995. Review of *Trapped in Paradise*. *Sight and Sound* 5/4 (April): 52–3

Hawkes, Steve, 2013. 'John Lewis launches nationwide contest to find new voice for its Christmas ad'. *Daily Telegraph* (20 November): www. telegraph.co.uk/finance/newsbysector/retailandconsumer/10460348/bear-

and-hare-best-Christmas-ads-Lily-Allen-John-Lewis-Christmas-adverts-Xmas-ads-Steve-Hawkes.html

Heelas, Paul, 1994. 'The limits of consumption and the post-modern "religion" of the New Age'. In *The Authority of the Consumer*, edited by Russell Keat et al., London: Routledge, 102–15

Heelas, Paul, 2012. 'Theorizing the Sacred: The Role of the Implicit in Yearning "Away"'. *Implicit Religion* 15/4: 477–521

Hey, John, 2012. 'Believing Beyond Religion: Secular Transcendence and the Primacy of Believing'. *Implicit Religion* 15/1: 81–95

Hick, John, 1976. *Death and Eternal Life*, London: Collins

Hills, Peter and Michael Argyle, 2002. 'A Psychological Dimension to Implicit Religion'. *Implicit Religion* 5/2: 69–80

Hoover, Stewart M., 2005. 'The Cross at Willow Creek: Seeker Religion and the Contemporary Marketplace'. In *Religion and Popular Culture in America*, edited by Bruce David Forbes and Jeffrey H. Mahan, London: University of California Press, 139–53

Horsfield, Peter, 2008. 'Media'. In *Key Words in Religion, Media and Culture*, edited by David Morgan, Abingdon and New York: Routledge, 111–22

Horsley, Richard, 2001(a). 'Christmas: The Religion of Consumer Capitalism'. In *Christmas Unwrapped: Consumerism, Christ, and Culture*, edited by Richard Horsley and James Tracy, Harrisburg PA: Trinity Press International, 165–87

Horsley, Richard, 2001(b). 'Epilogue'. In *Christmas Unwrapped: Consumerism, Christ, and Culture*, edited by Richard Horsley and James Tracy, Harrisburg PA: Trinity Press International, 219–24

Horsley, Richard and James Tracy, 2001. *Christmas Unwrapped: Consumerism, Christ, and Culture*, Harrisburg PA: Trinity Press International

Ivan, Sophie, 2010. Review of *Christmas in Wonderland*. *Sight and Sound* 20/2 (February): 59

Jafaar, Ali, 2005. Review of *Christmas with the Kranks*. *Sight and Sound* 15/2 (February): 44–5

Jamieson, Alastair, 2009. 'St Winifred's choir reunites for charity version of "There's No-one Quite Like Grandma"'. *Daily Telegraph* (22 November): www.telegraph.co.uk/culture/culturenews/6622821/St-Winifreds-choir-reunites-for-charity-version-of-Theres-No-one-Quite-Like-Grandma.html

Jarman-Ivens, Freya, 2008. 'The Musical Underbelly of Christmas'. In *Christmas, Ideology and Popular Culture*, edited by Sheila Whiteley, Edinburgh: Edinburgh University Press, 113–34

Jenkins, Timothy, 2005. 'Sacred Persons in Contemporary Culture'. *Implicit Religion* 8/2: 133–46

Jespers, Frans et al., 2012. 'Qualifying Secular Sacralizations'. *Implicit Religion* 15/4: 533–51

Jobling, J'annine, 2010. *Fantastic Spiritualities: Monsters, Heroes, and the Contemporary Religious Imagination*, London and New York: T&T Clark

Kelly, J.N.D., 1968. *Early Christian Doctrines*, London: Adam and Charles Black

Kelly, Joseph F., 2004. *The Origins of Christmas*, Collegeville, Minnesota: Liturgical Press

Kemp, Daren, 2001. 'Christaquarianism: A New Socio-Religious Movement of Postmodern Society'. *Implicit Religion* 4/1: 27–40

Kemp, Philip, 1998. Review of *Ulee's Gold*. *Sight and Sound* 8/4 (April): 56

Kuper, Adam, 2001. 'The English Christmas and the Family: Time Out and Alternative Realities'. In *Unwrapping Christmas*, edited by Daniel Miller, Oxford: Clarendon Press, 157–75

Lamacraft, Jane, 2008. Review of *Fred Claus*. *Sight and Sound* 18/2 (February): 62–4

Lawrenson, Edward, 2003. Review of *The Santa Clause 2*. *Sight and Sound* 13/1 (January): 50, 52

Lawther, Sarah, 2009. 'What is "*on*": An Exploration of Iconographical Representation of Traditional Religious Organizations on the Homepages of their Websites'. In *Exploring Religion and the Sacred in a Media Age*, edited by Christopher Deacy and Elisabeth Arweck, Farnham and Burlington VT: Ashgate, 219–35

Lévi-Strauss, Claude, 2001. 'Father Christmas Executed'. In *Unwrapping Christmas*, edited by Daniel Miller, Oxford: Clarendon Press, 38–51

Lipman, Amanda, 1999. Review of *Jack Frost*. *Sight and Sound* 9/3 (March): 44

Lord, Karen, 2006. 'Implicit Religion: Definition and Application'. *Implicit Religion* 9/2: 205–19

Loughlin, Gerard, 2007. 'Alien Sex: The Body and Desire in Cinema and Theology'. In *The Religion and Film Reader*, edited by Jolyon Mitchell and S. Brent Plate, Routledge: Abingdon, 337–42

Lowe, Scott C., 2010. 'Introduction'. In *Christmas—Philosophy for Everyone: Better than a Lump of Coal*, edited by Scott C. Lowe, Oxford: Wiley-Blackwell, 1–8

Lyden, John C., 2003. *Film as Religion: Myths, Morals and Rituals*, New York: New York University Press

Lynch, Gordon, 2007(a). 'What is this "Religion" in the Study of Religion and Popular Culture?' In *Between Sacred and Profane: Researching Religion and Popular Culture*, edited by Gordon Lynch, London and New York: I.B. Tauris, 125–42

Lynch, Gordon, 2007(b). 'Some Concluding Reflections'. In *Between Sacred and Profane: Researching Religion and Popular Culture*, edited by Gordon Lynch, London and New York: I.B. Tauris, 157–63

Lynch, Gordon, 2012. *The Sacred in the Modern World: A Cultural Sociological Approach*, Oxford: Oxford University Press

Lynch, Gordon et al., 2012. 'Introduction'. In *Religion, Media and Culture: A Reader*, edited by Gordon Lynch et al., Abingdon: Routledge, 1–6

Macnab, Geoffrey, 2001. Review of *The Family Man. Sight and Sound* 11/2 (February): 41–2

Mahan, Jeffrey H., 2007. 'Reflections on the Past and Future of the Study of Religion and Popular Culture', in *Between Sacred and Profane: Researching Religion and Popular Culture*, edited by Gordon Lynch, London and New York: I.B. Tauris, 47–62

Mamet, David, 2002. 'Christmas in happyland'. *Sight and Sound* 12/1 (January): 22–3

Marling, Karal Ann, 2000. *Merry Christmas! Celebrating America's Greatest Holiday*, Cambridge MA and London: Harvard University Press

Marsh, Clive, 2007. *Theology Goes to the Movies: An Introduction to Critical Christian Thinking*, London and New York: Routledge

Mauss, Marcel, 1990. *The Gift: The Form and Reason for Exchange in Archaic Societies*, translated by W.D. Halls, London: Routledge

Mazur, Eric Michael and Kate McCarthy, 2011(a). 'Preface'. In *God in the Details: American Religion in Popular Culture*, edited by Eric Michael Mazur and Kate McCarthy, Abingdon: Routledge, xvi–xviii

Mazur, Eric Michael and Kate McCarthy, 2011(b). 'Introduction: Finding Religion in American Popular Culture'. In *God in the Details: American Religion in Popular Culture*, edited by Eric Michael Mazur and Kate McCarthy, Abingdon: Routledge, 1–14

Mazur, Eric Michael and Kate McCarthy, 2011(c). 'Part I, Popular myth and symbol'. In *God in the Details: American Religion in Popular Culture*, edited by Eric Michael Mazur and Kate McCarthy, Abingdon: Routledge, 15–19

Mazur, Eric Michael and Kate McCarthy, 2011(d). 'Part II, Popular ritual'. In *God in the Details: American Religion in Popular Culture*, edited by Eric Michael Mazur and Kate McCarthy, Abingdon: Routledge, 103–7

Mazur, Eric Michael and Tara K. Koda, 2011. 'The Happiest Place on Earth: Disney's America and the Commodification of Religion'. In *God in the Details: American Religion in Popular Culture*, edited by Eric Michael Mazur and Kate McCarthy, Abingdon: Routledge, 307–21

McCarthy, Kate, 2011. 'Deliver Me from Nowhere: Bruce Springsteen and the Myth of the American Promised Land'. In *God in the Details: American Religion in Popular Culture*, edited by Eric Michael Mazur and Kate McCarthy, Abingdon: Routledge, 20–40

McCracken-Flesher, Caroline, 1996. 'The Incorporation of *A Christmas Carol*: A Tale of Seasonal Screening'. *Dickens Studies Annual* 24: 93–118

McDannell, Colleen, 2012. 'Scrambling the sacred and the profane'. In *Religion, Media and Culture: A Reader*, edited by Gordon Lynch et al., Abingdon: Routledge, 135–46

McGrath, Alister, 2003. *A Brief History of Heaven*, Oxford: Blackwell

McKibben, Bill, 1998. *Hundred Dollar Holiday: The Case for a More Joyful Christmas*, New York: Simon and Schuster

Ménard, Guy, 2001. 'Religion, Implicit or Post-Modern?' *Implicit Religion* 4/2: 87–95

Ménard, Guy, 2004. 'The Moods of Marianne: Of Hijabs, Nikes, Implicit Religion and Post-Modernity'. *Implicit Religion* 7/3: 246–55

Mercer, Mark, 2010. 'The Significance of Christmas for Liberal Multiculturalism'. In *Christmas—Philosophy for Everyone: Better than a Lump of Coal*, edited by Scott C. Lowe, Oxford: Wiley-Blackwell, 70–9

Miles, Clement A., 1912. *Christmas in Ritual and Tradition, Christian and Pagan*, London: T. Fisher Unwin

Miller, Daniel, 1998. *A Theory of Shopping*, Oxford: Polity

Miller, Daniel, 2001. 'A Theory of Christmas', in *Unwrapping Christmas*, edited by Daniel Miller, Oxford: Clarendon Press, 3–37

Miller, J. Hillis, 1993. 'The Genres of *A Christmas Carol*'. *The Dickensian* 431/89, Part 3 (Winter): 193–206

Miller, Patrick D., 2000. 'Judgment and Joy'. In *The End of the World and the Ends of God: Science and Theology on Eschatology*, Harrisbury PA: Trinity Press International, 155–70

Moore, Clement Clarke, 1912. *Twas the Night Before Christmas: A Visit from St. Nicholas*, Boston: Houghton Mifflin Company

Moore, Tara, 2009. *Victorian Christmas in Print*, New York: Palgrave MacMillan

Morgan, David, 2008. 'Preface'. In *Key Words in Religion, Media and Culture*, edited by David Morgan, Abingdon and New York: Routledge, xi–xv

Munby, Jonathan, 2000. 'A Hollywood Carol's Wonderful Life'. In *Christmas at the Movies: Images of Christmas in American, British and European Cinema*, edited by Mark Connelly, London and New York: I.B. Tauris, 39–57

Mundy, John, 2008. 'Christmas and the Movies: Frames of Mind'. In *Christmas, Ideology and Popular Culture*, edited by Sheila Whiteley, Edinburgh: Edinburgh University Press, 164–76

Myers, Max A., 2001(a). 'Christmas on Celluloid: Hollywood Helps Construct the American Christmas'. In *Christmas Unwrapped: Consumerism, Christ, and Culture*, edited by Richard Horsley and James Tracy, Harrisburg PA: Trinity Press International, 39–54

Myers, Max A., 2001(b). 'Santa Claus as an Icon of Grace'. In *Christmas Unwrapped: Consumerism, Christ, and Culture*, edited by Richard Horsley and James Tracy, Harrisburg PA: Trinity Press International, 188–98

Nathan, Ian, 1995. Review of *Trapped in Paradise*. *Empire* (March): www.empireonline.com/reviews/reviewcomplete.asp?FID=3442

Newman, Kim, 1985. Review of *Santa Claus: The Movie*. *Monthly Film Bulletin* 52/623 (December): 387–8

Newman, Kim, 2000. 'You Better Watch Out: Christmas in the Horror Film'. In *Christmas at the Movies: Images of Christmas in American, British and European Cinema*, edited by Mark Connelly, London and New York: I.B. Tauris, 135–42

Newton, Christy M., 2009. 'The "Sin" of Wal-Mart Architecture: A Visual Theology Reflecting Economic Realities'. *Implicit Religion* 12/1: 21–50

Niebuhr, H. Richard, 1952. *Christ and Culture*, London: Faber and Faber

Nissenbaum, Stephen, 1996. *The Battle for Christmas*, New York: Vintage (Kindle edition)

Nissenbaum, Stephen, 2010. 'Foreword: Joining the Manger to the Sleigh?' In *Christmas—Philosophy for Everyone: Better than a Lump of Coal*, edited by Scott C. Lowe, Oxford: Wiley-Blackwell, x–xii

O'Brien, Lucy, 1992. Review of *All I Want for Christmas*. *Sight and Sound* 1/10 (February): 38

Office for National Statistics, 2013. 'Top 100 baby names in England and Wales in 2012'. 12 August: www.ons.gov.uk/ons/rel/vsob1/baby-names-england-and-wales/2012/stb-baby-names-2012.html#tab-Top-100-baby-names-in-England-and-Wales-in-2012

Ostwalt, Conrad, 2003. *Secular Steeples: Popular Culture and the Religious Imagination*, Harrisburg PA: Trinity International

Otto, Rudolf, 1959. *The Idea of the Holy*, Penguin: Harmondsworth

Pals, Daniel L., 2006. *Eight Theories of Religion*, Oxford: Oxford University Press

Parker, David, 2005. *Christmas and Charles Dickens*, New York: AMS Press

Pärna, Karen, 2004. 'Why Study Implicit Religion? An Account of the 27th Denton Conference on Implicit Religion, 7–9 May 2004'. *Implicit Religion* 7/2: 101–7

Pärna, Karen, 2006. 'Believe 'in the Net: The Construction of the Sacred in Utopian Tales of the Internet'. *Implicit Religion* 9/2: 180–204

Pärna, Karen, 2012. '"Spiritual Labour": Working on the Spiritual Marketplace and Producing Spirituality'. *Implicit Religion* 15/4: 395–405

Pope Pius XI, 2007. 'Encyclical Letter *Vigilanti Cura*'. In *The Religion and Film Reader*, edited by Jolyon Mitchell and S. Brent Plate, New York and Abingdon: Routledge, 35–42

Pope, Robert, 2007. *Salvation in Celluloid: Theology, Imagination and Film*, London: T&T Clark

Porter, Jennifer, 2009. 'Implicit Religion in Popular Culture: The Religious Dimensions of Fan Communities'. *Implicit Religion* 12/3: 271–80

Price, Joseph L., 2005. 'An American Apotheosis: Sports as Popular Religion'. In *Religion and Popular Culture in America*, edited by Bruce David Forbes and Jeffrey H. Mahan, London: University of California Press, 195–212

Pym, John, 1988. Review of *Scrooged*. *Monthly Film Bulletin* 55/659 (December): 369–71

Reinhartz, Adele, 2003. *Scripture on the Silver Screen*, Louisville KY: Westminster John Knox

Reinhartz, Adele, 2009. 'Jesus and Christ-Figures'. In *The Routledge Companion to Religion and Film*, edited by John Lyden, London and New York: Routledge, 420–39

Restad, Penne L., 1995. *Christmas in America: A History*, Oxford and New York: Oxford University Press

Riis, Ole, 2012. 'The Emergence of Post-dogmatic Religion'. *Implicit Religion* 15/4: 423–38

Robinson, John A.T., 1963. *Honest to God*, London: SCM

Robinson, Jo and Jean Coppock Staeheli, 1982. *Unplug the Christmas Machine: A Complete Guide to Putting Love and Warmth Back Into the Season*, New York: Quill-William Morrow

Ruffles, Tom, 2004. *Ghost Images: Cinema of the Afterlife*, Jefferson NC and London: McFarland

Rycenga, Jennifer, 2011. 'Dropping in for the Holidays: Christmas as Commercial Ritual at the Precious Moments Chapel'. In *God in the Details: American Religion in Popular Culture*, edited by Eric Michael Mazur and Kate McCarthy, Abingdon: Routledge, 140–53

Said, S.F., 2003. 'Zero Gravity'. *Sight and Sound* 13/1 (January): 16–18

Sands, Kathleen M., 2001. 'Still Dreaming: War, Memory, and Nostalgia in the American Christmas'. In *Christmas Unwrapped: Consumerism, Christ, and Culture*, edited by Richard Horsley and James Tracy, Harrisburg PA: Trinity Press International, 55–83

Schmidt, Leigh Eric, 1991. 'The Commercialization of the Calendar: American Holidays and the Culture of Consumption, 1870–1930'. *The Journal of American History* 78/3 (December): 887–916

Schmidt, Leigh Eric, 1995. *Consumer Rites: The Buying and Selling of American Holidays*, Princeton NJ: Princeton University Press

Schnell, Tatjana, 2000. 'I Believe in Love'. *Implicit Religion* 3/2: 111–22

Scholes, Jeffrey, 2012. 'The Coca-Cola brand and religion'. In *Understanding Religion and Popular Culture*, edited by Terry Ray Clark and Dan W. Clanton, Jr, Abingdon: Routledge, 139–56

Scott, Dane, 2010. 'Scrooge Learns It All In One Night: Happiness and the Virtues of Christmas'. In *Christmas—Philosophy for Everyone: Better than a Lump of Coal*, edited by Scott C. Lowe, Oxford: Wiley-Blackwell, 172–82

Segal, Robert A., 1999. *Theorizing about Myth*, University of Massachusetts Press: Amherst

Simonds, A.P., 2001. 'The Holy Days and the Wholly Dazed: Christmas and the "Spirit of Giving"'. In *Christmas Unwrapped: Consumerism, Christ, and Culture*, edited by Richard Horsley and James Tracy, Harrisburg PA: Trinity Press International, 84–109

Smart, Ninian, 1998(a). *The World's Religions*, Cambridge: Cambridge University Press

Smart, Ninian, 1998(b). 'Implicit religion across culture'. *Implicit Religion* 1: 23–6

Smith, Jim, 1985/6. 'Elf No 24', Letters. *Sight and Sound* 55/1 (Winter): 70

Smith, Jonathan Z., 1982. *Imagining Religion: From Babylon to Jonestown*, Chicago and London: University of Chicago Press

Smith, Wilfred Cantwell, 1997. *Modern Culture from a Comparative Perspective*, Albany: State University of New York Press

Spencer, Liese, 1997. Review of *The Preacher's Wife*. *Sight and Sound* 7/3 (March): 61

Stables, Kate, 2009. Review of *Four Christmases*. *Sight and Sound* 19/2 (February): 59

Stahl, William A., 2002. 'Technology and Myth: Implicit religion in technological narratives'. *Implicit Religion* 5/2: 93–103

Stewart, Ed, 2005. *Out of the Stewpot: My Autobiography*, London: John Blake Publishing

Storey, John, 2008. 'The Invention of the English Christmas'. In *Christmas, Ideology and Popular Culture*, edited by Sheila Whiteley, Edinburgh: Edinburgh University Press, 17–31

Strachan, Robert H., 1920. *The Fourth Gospel: Its Significance and Environment*, London: SCM

Strick, Philip, 1995. Review of *Miracle on 34th Street*. *Sight and Sound* 5/1 (January): 49–50

Swatos Jr, William H., 1999. 'Revisiting the Sacred'. *Implicit Religion* 2/1: 33–8

Swatos Jr, William H., 2001. 'Meaning and Contradiction'. *Implicit Religion* 4/2: 97–106

Sweet, Matthew, 2012. 'Charlie's Ghost'. *Sight and Sound* 22/2 (February): 48–51

Sweetman, Will, 2002. 'Hinduism: An implicit or explicit religion?'. *Implicit Religion* 5/1: 11–16

Tallman, Ruth, 2010. 'Holly Jolly Atheists: A Naturalistic Justification for Christmas'. In *Christmas—Philosophy for Everyone: Better than a Lump of Coal*, edited by Scott C. Lowe, Oxford: Wiley-Blackwell, 185–96

Taubin, Amy, 2000. *Taxi Driver*, London: British Film Institute

Ter Borg, Meerten B., 2004. 'Some Ideas on Wild Religion'. *Implicit Religion* 7/2: 108–19

Ter Borg, Meerten B., 2008. 'Transcendence and Religion'. *Implicit Religion* 11/3: 229–38

Thompson, Ben, 1995. Review of *Nobody's Fool*. *Sight and Sound* 5/4 (April): 49–50

Thompson, Robert J., 2005. 'Consecrating Consumer Culture: Christmas Television Specials'. In *Religion and Popular Culture in America*, edited by Bruce David Forbes and Jeffrey H. Mahan, London: University of California Press, 44–55

Till, Rupert, 2009. 'Possession Trance Ritual in Electronic Dance Music Culture: A Popular Ritual Technology for Reenchantment, Addressing the Crisis of the Homeless Self, and Reinserting the Individual into the Community'. In *Exploring Religion and the Sacred in a Media Age*, edited by Christopher Deacy and Elisabeth Arweck, Farnham and Burlington VT: Ashgate, 169–87

Tillich, Paul, 1964. *Systematic Theology, Vol. 1*, Welwyn, Herts.: James Nisbet and Company

Todd, Liz, 2008. 'Why I celebrate Christmas, by the world's most famous atheist'. *Daily Mail* (23 December): www.dailymail.co.uk/debate/article-1100842/Why-I-celebrate-Christmas-worlds-famous-atheist.html

Tracy, James, 2001(a). 'Introduction'. In *Christmas Unwrapped: Consumerism, Christ, and Culture*, edited by Richard Horsley and James Tracy, Harrisburg PA: Trinity Press International, 1–6

Tracy, James, 2001(b). 'The Armistice over Christmas: Consuming in the Twentieth Century'. In *Christmas Unwrapped: Consumerism, Christ, and Culture*, edited by Richard Horsley and James Tracy, Harrisburg PA: Trinity Press International, 9–18

Turner, Victor W., 1969. *The Ritual Process: Structure and Anti-Structure*, Chicago: Aldine Publishing Company

Vaux, Sara Anson, 2012. *The Ethical Vision of Clint Eastwood*, Grand Rapids and Cambridge: Eerdmans

Vidler, Alec, 1988. *The Church in an Age of Revolution*, London: Penguin

Wagner, Rachel, 2012(a). *Godwired: Religion, Ritual and Virtual Reality*, Abingdon: Routledge

Wagner, Rachel, 2012(b). 'Religion and video games: Shooting aliens in cathedrals'. In *Understanding Religion and Popular Culture*, edited by Terry Ray Clark and Dan W. Clanton, Jr, Abingdon: Routledge, 118–38

Waits, William B., 1993. *The Modern Christmas in America: A Cultural History of Gift Giving*, New York and London: New York University Press

Walsh, John, 2003. *Are You Talking to Me?: A Life Through the Movies*, London: Harper Collins

Walsh, Joseph J., 2001. *Were They Wise Men or Kings? The Book of Christmas Questions*, Louisville: Westminster John Knox Press

Wender, Andrew M., 2007. 'State Power as a Vehicle for the Expression and Propagation of Implicit Religion: The Case Study of the "War on Terrorism"'. *Implicit Religion* 10/3: 244–61

Wender, Andrew M., 2009. 'Helping Students See What Ordinarily Remains Hidden: How Implicit Religion Can Enrich Teaching'. *Implicit Religion* 12/3: 281–94

Whiteley, Sheila, 2008. 'Christmas Songs—Sentiments and Subjectivities'. In *Christmas, Ideology and Popular Culture*, edited by Sheila Whiteley, Edinburgh: Edinburgh University Press, 98–112

Williams, Harry, 1972. *True Resurrection*, London: Mitchell Beazley

Wright, Melanie J., 2007. *Religion and Film: An Introduction*, London: I.B. Tauris

Index